T0086168

Other Books by W. Patrick Lang

Strike the Tent Trilogy:

  The Butcher's Cleaver
  Death Piled Hard
  Down the Sky

Tattoo: A Memoir of Becoming

The Human Factor: The Phenomenon of Espionage

THE PORTABLE PAT LANG

ESSENTIAL WRITINGS ON HISTORY, WAR, RELIGION, AND STRATEGY

W. PATRICK LANG

THE PORTABLE PAT LANG
ESSENTIAL WRITINGS ON HISTORY, WAR, RELIGION, AND STRATEGY

Copyright © 2022 W. Patrick Lang.

All rights reserved. No part of this book may be used or reproduced by any means, graphic, electronic, or mechanical, including photocopying, recording, taping or by any information storage retrieval system without the written permission of the author except in the case of brief quotations embodied in critical articles and reviews.

iUniverse books may be ordered through booksellers or by contacting:

iUniverse
1663 Liberty Drive
Bloomington, IN 47403
www.iuniverse.com
844-349-9409

Because of the dynamic nature of the Internet, any web addresses or links contained in this book may have changed since publication and may no longer be valid. The views expressed in this work are solely those of the author and do not necessarily reflect the views of the publisher, and the publisher hereby disclaims any responsibility for them.

Any people depicted in stock imagery provided by Getty Images are models, and such images are being used for illustrative purposes only. Certain stock imagery © Getty Images.

ISBN: 978-1-6632-4842-8 (sc)
ISBN: 978-1-6632-4844-2 (hc)
ISBN: 978-1-6632-4843-5 (e)

Library of Congress Control Number: 2022922384

Print information available on the last page.

iUniverse rev. date: 12/12/2022

Contents

Introduction

A Lifetime Of Experiences Presented Here

After decades of dedicated service to his country as a Colonel in the United States Army, as a Military Attaché in the Middle East, as founder, along with his wife Marguerite, of the Arab language and Arabic studies program at West Point, as head of the Defense Intelligence Agency's global humint (human intelligence) service, and as the Defense Intelligence Officer for the Middle East, W. Patrick Lang embarked on new careers in the private sector. He did international business consulting, was a regular analyst on major news networks, was an expert witness in several trials related to the Espionage Act and served on the board of a major philanthropic foundation.

In the aftermath of the 2003 invasion of Iraq, he created his own blog which to this day still serves as a committee of correspondence for a large network of former military and intelligence officers, diplomats, and scholars of international affairs.

Since its launch in 2005, Col. Lang's Turcopolier website has had over 40 million unique visits.

He is one of America's most prolific analysts of current affairs.

Since leaving the government, he has also authored five books, including a Civil War espionage trilogy, a memoir of his years in government service, and a primer on human intelligence.

This present volume—his sixth book—is an anthology of some of his most important writings. The book is organized into eight sections, grouping his writings by topics. The material is not organized chronologically in all instances. There are three sections of historical fiction.

The content speaks for itself. So have at it.

HARPER
November 3, 2022

PART I

The Intelligence Process

This section is focused on the process of intelligence gathering and analysis, as told by an author with three decades-plus of active-duty experience. Some of the essays provide an overview of the structure and responsibilities of the intelligence organizations (there are 16 separate agencies that make up the U.S. Intelligence Community), while others focus on the intelligence failures that led up to the March 2003 invasion of Iraq.

A National Intelligence Fantasy
(October 2002)

It is one of the most important responsibilities of the Director of Central Intelligence (DCI) to supervise the writing of National Intelligence Estimates (NIEs) An NIE is a considered judgment by the major agencies of the national intelligence community with regard to some particular issue of national importance. Once approved, an NIE becomes the "ground truth" of the United States Government. It is the document always cited in deliberations leading to the most serious and dangerous decisions made by the government. The judgments given in a fully coordinated NIE are usually determinative in establishing the basis of presidential decisions. NIEs are usually, but not always drafted by the Central Intelligence Agency (CIA), negotiated as to the judgments and evidence in it with the major agencies, and then voted on by the heads of the major agencies in a meeting of the National Foreign Intelligence Board (NFIB) with the DCI himself in the chair and voting. In spite of this apparatus of consultation and consensus, there is no doubt in the mind of anyone in the intelligence community that an NIE is the DCI's document. No one else in the community has the authority to initiate an NIE. His own agency (CIA) almost always drafts it and only he can approve it before it goes to the president and other senior authorities.

These facts make the NIE published in October 2002 on Iraq's WMD programs uniquely the property of George Tenet, the Director of Central Intelligence. As a retired official of the intelligence community, I often participated in the writing, editing, and approval process of NIEs. After watching George Tenet's spirited defense of his conduct of his office at Georgetown University, I was moved to re-examine the publicly available portions of the WMD NIE because the Bush Administration has heavily relied upon that document as a justification for the decision to go to war in Iraq.

The NIE in question is the worst constructed, most illogical and indeed dishonest document of its kind that I have ever seen. The NIE makes assertions concerning the existence of Iraqi weapons stocks and active programs that are unqualified on their face. "Baghdad has weapons of mass destruction..." "We assess that Baghdad has begun renewed production of mustard, sarin, GP (cyclosarin), and VX," would be examples. At the same time the document states, "We lack specific information on many key aspects of Iraq's WMD programs." One may fairly ask how it could be that the DCI, George Tenet, thought himself justified in making judgments to be given to the president of the United States which might lead to war on the basis of his expressed belief that he "lacked…information…on key aspects" of the programs in question.

This NIE is "riddled" with statements of "evidence" conditioned by words and phrases like "could make" (nuclear weapons), "chances are even that…" (smallpox as a part of Iraq's BW holdings), "Probably has developed…" (genetically engineered BW germs) or most spectacularly, "although we have little specific evidence.…. we assess that Saddam probably has at least 100 Metric Tons and possible as much as 500 Metric Tons of CW (chemical weapons) agents.…"

When offered the chance to vote at the NFIB for an NIE with which they have "problems" the heads of the intelligence agencies have a "way out." They can say that they will vote for this NIE if they are allowed to place footnotes or alternative text in the document which give their dissenting views. This enables them to vote for the DCI's document without actually agreeing with it, a nicely done piece of politics. Not surprisingly, there was dissent concerning this NIE. As an example, the USAF said it "does not agree…" that Iraq's unmanned aircraft program are "primarily intended" for WMD delivery. Instead, the USAF said that the evidence "suggests a primary role of reconnaissance…" The State Department's Bureau of Intelligence and Research (INR) wrote alternative text which said clearly that "although Saddam continues to want nuclear weapons" "the activities we have detected do not, however, add up to a compelling case that Iraq is currently pursing… an integrated and comprehensive approach to acquire nuclear weapons…INR considers the available evidence inadequate to support such a judgment…" (of the existence of an effective Iraqi nuclear weapons program in October, 2002).

Taking into consideration the exaggerated statements of certainty in the NIE which are based on what the document itself says are highly ambiguous bits of information and INR's dissent from the key judgment, this NIE should not have been approved by the DCI.

There were other arguments made for war with Iraq, but the WMD argument was certainly central to the case made to the American people that war was both necessary and inevitable. This NIE carries the burden of having been the "best judgment" of the intelligence community on this subject. The vice president still shows the unclassified parts of this NIE to visitors as justification for the war. The president still says that much of what was in the NIE must be correct.

George Tenet's responsibility for this document and its effect on history is direct and personal. It is his document. He cannot avoid that responsibility. This document makes his speech at Georgetown ring hollow.

Humint: Against the Islamic Zealots
(2002)

The Enemy: The United States government has fallen into the habit of referring to the enemy that we are fighting around the world as "Terrorism." This title has come to denote and connote both the specifically Islamic Sunni and Shia Jihadi movements as well as all other movements and groups that resort to political violence to achieve their ends through intimidation. The impression has been created that these groups are allied to each other, share common goals and all present roughly equal threat levels against our country. This is a useless and deluded view of the level of threat posed by such violent groups around the world. The Islamic sectarian groups are willing to cooperate from time to time on specific issues against the West but will never form permanent alliances since they hate each other almost as much as they do us. The non-Islamic terrorist groups at times may supply weapons or other assistance in return for payment but are unlikely to become part of the real concentration of Islamic terror against us.

The real enemy is now Jihadi Islamic terrorism and not the various national terrorist movements such as ETA, the IRA, etc. Why is this? Simply put, the national terrorist resistance groups do not see themselves as enemies of the West and particularly not of the United States. They are typically tightly focused on specific "positive" goals related to national identity or some ideological cause.

In contrast, the Jihadis are obsessed with the idea of reversing the course of the history of the last few centuries and restoring to its former glory and power the trans-national empire of Islam, variously called the Caliphate, the "Umma" or "Dar Al-Islam." The Jihadis are not an organization. They are a movement, an influence, and a faith. They are many organizations, many individuals and there are people of wealth, skill and faith who are the members and supporters of that faith at one level or another all over the world.

No Capability: To penetrate that "gathering" of groups within the movement is possible but not a task likely to be accomplished by the bureaucratically hidebound group of organizations that the intelligence agencies have become. The Jihadi groups can be penetrated through the use of Muslim owned businesses and not for profit groups as "cover platforms." There are many Muslims who would be willing to make their facilities available for a joint struggle against the Jihadis. In fact, the intelligence agencies have been offered such facilities over the last ten years and were unable to overcome the internal resistance of lawyers, comptrollers, and risk-averse managers to take advantage of these opportunities.

<u>A New Capability Is Needed:</u> The consensus of the "wise men" of the intelligence business now in retirement, (and by this I mean, "real intelligence officers," as opposed to the bureaucratic politicians who now burden the leadership of the "community") is that a new beginning should be made, and that while the existing structures of intelligence will work just fine for combat intelligence, targeting of air strikes and similar "mechanical" and technical aspects of intelligence work, they are no longer capable of running espionage operations against really difficult targets or delivering analysis that may convey opinions that the political administration of the day may dislike. There will always have to be large organizations that perform the more routinized business of collecting the general run of information needed for policy support, but a new organization is needed to do the essential work in HUMINT collection against the Jihadi target outside the United States.

Intelligence collection and investigation within the US should be left to the FBI, and the Homeland Security Department in the interest of the preservation of our civil liberties. These are essentially police organizations and can and should be bound by the strictures of US constitutional limits on the power of government while clandestine espionage units operating outside the US cannot be so restricted if they are to have any chance of success.

What is needed is the creation under law of a new clandestine collection unit outside the present intelligence agencies. This unit should be small, composed of people of high education and talent, recruited from across the spectrum of US society and located away from the bureaucratic maze of Washington politics, turf wars and budget struggles. This group should have no business except the conduct of sophisticated espionage against important and difficult targets in the Jihadi world with a special emphasis on long-term introduction of "moles" into the heart of the wilderness of Jihadi organizations and groups. The idea would be to isolate this group behind a wall of cover effectively presented by the present intelligence agencies, to isolate it from contact with the other intelligence groups and to have it work independently on the difficult mission described above. The main reason for the level of isolation recommended here is not to protect it from the enemy but rather to protect it from the rivalries and risk-averse mentality of the existing agencies.

There will have to be a few clandestine intelligence people brought over from the existing groups to transfer their wisdom and skills to the new people, but they should be carefully chosen to make sure that the fearful bureaucrats mind set is not imported with them.

This clandestine intelligence unit should not be a covert action arm as well. Decisions to act against identified personalities or groups should be given to other parts of the government for execution. The reason for this is clear. Involvement in covert action missions is a major distraction from the work of espionage and tends to divert important assets to jobs necessary to information collection. Additionally, involvement in the execution of policy driven covert action inherently tends to cloud judgment by making the intelligence unit "invested" in the policy underlying the covert action. Information produced by this operation should be released on a strict need to know basis to decision makers, operational forces, and congressional oversight.

<u>Chain of Command, Legal Basis and Oversight:</u> A unit like this must be a truly national asset. I would recommend control of this unit by a three-person committee made up of the DCI, SecDef and SecState. I would recommend that the budget be separately funded by law outside the intelligence community budget program to keep the existing bureaucracies from gaining control of it in this way. A truly select committee of Congress meeting in secret should exercise oversight of this new group. This committee should be made up of leaders of the Congress from both parties and houses and it should have minimal staff who should be located outside Washington and forbidden to communicate with staff and members of other bodies within the Congress.

Speaking Truth to Power
(America Magazine July 30, 2003)

What is truth?" John the Evangelist attributes this question to Pilate in his examination of Jesus. Pilate was expressing his frustration over the unpleasant reality that the man before him was probably innocent of the charge of treason to the Roman state, but that it would nevertheless be necessary, for reasons of imperial policy, to kill him. Ultimately Pilate ignored the truth, which too often also is a temptation for government officials who are making decisions about national security.

In order to protect themselves from such temptations, many governments have developed safeguards to insure that policy decisions are not made on the basis of the fixed opinions of individuals or small groups. Among the most important of such safeguards are intelligence analysts, who are generally career specialists in analytic thinking who have acquired encyclopedic knowledge of a particular subject. Policy staffs and decision makers are supposed to rely on intelligence analysts for data and expert judgments about significant issues of fact on which policy decisions should be made.

To make sure that the judgments are truly independent, elaborate safeguards are established. Intelligence organizations are generally positioned within the government in such a way that they are not directly subordinated to the policy makers whom they support. These organizations may support the national government as a whole, as the C.I.A. does, and have as its only superior the President of the United States. Or they may be within a department of government, as are the Defense Intelligence Agency or the Bureau of Intelligence and Research in the State Department.

In the case of these two groups, their only boss is the secretary of the department. In this way, it is possible for the analysts to work with and support the policy formulating staffs with a certain degree of independence in their judgments. They can present hard data unfettered by fear of retaliation that could affect career advancement or budgets.

The Israelis carry this process of insulation to an extreme by maintaining within their Directorate of Military Intelligence a section named The Devil's Advocate, which has the mission of presenting analyses that directly oppose those of the rest of the D.M.I. and indeed of the government itself. A senior intelligence officer is selected for this duty who understands that this normally will be his last tour of duty. A few men who have held this point have moved on to other ministries, but most have gone from this job into a retirement covered with honors.

In the world of foreign policy formulation there are two main groups of players. On the one hand are the intelligence analysts and their managerial supervisors, who are usually career professionals who have spent many years acquiring the skills and ethos of their craft. Their function in the process of foreign policy formulation is to describe reality as best they can. On the other hand, are the policy formulation team of ministerial staff and politically selected seniors, who are responsible for proposing useful policy options and making decisions.

Their purpose is to shape reality. Between these two groups there is constant tension, which is probably inevitable.

From time to time, new people in a new administration try out the intelligence analysts to see how firmly they resist producing intelligence tailored to advance the agenda of the administration. In nearly all cases, a firm display of friendly distance is all that is required to set an appropriate tone for relations.

As a result, the government normally receives estimates, which are carefully vetted to allow for the vagaries of source reliability and the probable truth of individual pieces of information. Such estimates are made on the basis of the probabilities that develop from reliable sources and information that is believed by the intelligence community to be credible. To make sure that finished intelligence is not the "brainstorm" of one person or some small group, estimates are submitted to various agencies to see whether they hold water. Intelligence estimates should never be policy prescriptive. For the intelligence people to support a unique course of action through their work product would pervert their function. If they were to do that, they would become just one more element in the policy-making apparatus rather than the guardians of truth that they should be. "Facts, nothing but the facts" should be their motto.

In the Bush administration, this carefully constructed system of checks and balances appears to have been distorted. It is now well known that some appointees in the Defense Department, the Vice President's Office, the National Security Council and even the State Department entered office with a rigid and very ambitious set of geo-strategic goals for the future of the United States and indeed the world. As a result, the measured judgments of the intelligence community concerning such issues as the continuing presence of weapons of mass destruction and the degree of connection between Al Qaeda and the former government of Iraq were considered unsatisfactory by these people and insufficiently committed to the task of uncovering the "truth" of Iraqi culpability.

Unhappiness with what the intelligence community was producing grew to be so great after the first year of the Bush administration that the Defense Department created a small "cell" of civilians within the office of the secretary of defense dedicated to the task of critiquing the work of the intelligence community and re-examining the raw data from the vast stream of information available to the government. Its job was to find "tidbits" of information that had been overlooked by the professional analysts and that made the case for military action against Iraq. Not surprisingly, this group was able to apply the yardstick of its previous convictions to the available raw information (which included the self-interested statements of Iraqi émigrés) to find a pattern of information that could be packaged for the management of opinion at home and abroad.

Did they lie? No, the men involved would surely not lie. They can point to individual bits of information that were the basis of their arguments. It was certainly dishonest, however, to depict the strategic information warfare campaign that they were conducting as equivalent to the responsible work of American intelligence.

The next time a president of the United States appeals to his people or other nations to trust his words, there will be a noticeable coolness in the reception given to him. The very system for measured deliberations in deciding United States policy has been undermined by men obsessed with their own cleverness and dismissive of the cumulative wisdom of those who went before them in government. A retired senior C.I.A. officer recently remarked that he had never thought that the United States would, in the end, invade Iraq, but that now he understood what had happened. "The normal work of government was ignored," he said. "Now they can do anything; anything can be justified in this way."

Americans, their Congress, and the President should ask themselves if they want to see this distortion of their foreign policy apparatus continue. Pilate was the representative of a mighty and unforgiving empire. There were no checks and balances in the structure of the Roman government. Our great republic has sought to carry out its business in the world on the basis of rational and careful judgments. Are those days behind us?

"Bureaucrats Versus Artists..."

(2004)

"Were we right or were we wrong?" This was Director of Central Intelligence (DCI) George Tenet's central question in his 2004 talk to the faculty and students of his alma mater, Georgetown University. What he was talking about, of course, was the critical political issue of whether or not the Intelligence Community (IC) of which he was the titular head "got it right" in telling the American people and their government that Iraq was a clear danger to the United States, as opposed to being a threat to regional states, and if that danger was substantial enough to serve as a justifiable basis for war, invasion and occupation.

In Tenet's address there was much of self-protection and an implicit warning that neither he nor the Central Intelligence Agency (CIA) would accept to be "scapegoated" in a search for the roots of misadventure in Iraq. His words establish a claim to blamelessness for the CIA and the larger Intelligence Community in the decisions leading up to the Iraq campaign and a related claim to have done as well as could fairly have been expected. In other words, he wished to be thought innocent in this matter. Is that reasonable? Is it fair to expect American citizens and officials to believe that the Intelligence Community did its work well in helping the government of the United States to make sound decisions about Iraq? This is an important question, because if they did not, then why were their judgments so flawed, in spite of the incredible amounts of taxpayer money lavished on the agencies of the IC? Why should so much money have been lavished on these agencies if they could do no better?

In spite of the importance of this question, impatience with the performance of the intelligence people ought to be somewhat dependent on the outcome of a national debate as to what should be expected of the process labeled "intelligence." Reporters sometimes ask rhetorically if decisions should really be made on the basis of intelligence. At first hearing, questions like this seem to be both naïve and nonsensical since it is obvious that information is the stuff that decisions must be founded on. Nevertheless, decipherment of these statements leads to an understanding that those who say things like this think that "intelligence" is a form of thinking both esoteric and obscure, a dark art, separate and distinct from the normal way of knowing things and subject to acceptance or rejection by special rules of perception. In other words, they think that it is something like astrology, to be judged by its own "rules."

In fact, "Intelligence" is simply another word for "information" and in ages gone by the term was used in that way by authorities like Clausewitz or Jomini. There is nothing mystical or mysterious about the process by which information or "intelligence" is collected, collated, analyzed, and disseminated. "Intelligence" is scholarship conducted in the service of the state. The great bulk of the information used as data in this scholarship comes out of the huge archival files of the major agencies supplemented by daily "feedings" of diplomatic chit-chat, aerial and satellite reconnaissance, intercepts of communications, and hopefully the products of espionage (clandestine HUMINT). Like any labor of scholarship involving the study of human beings by human beings, the work is nearly always conducted with incomplete and ambiguous information as a basis for the analysis. This natural phenomenon is aggravated by the desire of the studied group to hide something, usually, that which is under study.

When George Tenet said before his Georgetown audience that "We never get things altogether right in the Intelligence business, nor altogether wrong," he was correct; but his statement was irrelevant to a discussion of the utility of the intelligence process since the quality of the analytic product depends on many variables, among them: good information and the quality of the minds brought to bear on the imperfect information. It is both trite and a truism that "intelligence is an art and not a science." What this means is that human beings may succeed, or they may fail in making judgments based on less than complete data and that the skill, intelligence, and experience of those involved is the most important factor in determining the outcome.

To say that "Intelligence" is a flawed process is simply meaningless in a discussion of the effectiveness of the state in making decisions. If the "Intelligence Community" as it now exists were abolished, some other group would have to assume the burden of performing the same functions for the benefit of the state. What would they be called? Perhaps it might be, "The Agency for Special Planning?" The issue of the effectiveness and efficiency of the existing Intelligence Community is a separate but linked question from that of knowing whether or not the elected or appointed officials of the Bush Administration may have intruded themselves inappropriately into the deliberations of the Intelligence Community in a way that led to distortions in the estimates of Iraq's significance that were presented to the president and the Congress. It is widely believed now that this occurred but that is not the subject of this essay.

The question under examination here is simple. Premise: "The Intelligence Community produced poor quality intelligence on Iraq." Therefore, one asks - Are there imbedded structural defects in the present United States Intelligence Community that contributed either directly or indirectly to the production of estimates that were unsound, and which failed the nation? And, moreover, are there characteristics in the present intelligence community of the United States which now prevent and will prevent it from "reforming" itself?

It is clear the inability of the Intelligence Community to forecast or estimate Iraq's true condition was a major failure. Why did this happen, and how can the defects in the "community" be repaired? What "limits" are there in the psychology and structure of the government that may prevent "repair" of the system?

The author's conclusion after a working lifetime of studying the flaws in the system from within the community and from the evidence of continuing contacts with old colleagues and new friends in the intelligence agencies is that there are a multitude of problems in the intelligence forces of the United states and that most of them have grown up over a very long time, are now "built into" the system and are unlikely to be resolved without outside intervention by the Congress of the United States. It is impossible to consider them all, but a few of the most important are so intractable as to be worth discussing here:

-Leadership. There is a natural tendency in the general public to believe that the upper levels of the Intelligence Community are filled with learned, avuncular and sensitive people somehow reminiscent of "George Smiley," the wonderful British spy and spymaster whose presence fills the earlier novels of John Le Carre. The character, "Smiley" is wise, sadly pessimistic, a profound student of mankind and devoted to his "people." He has a deeply empathic nature, is widely read, speaks several languages, and is so dedicated to his craft and its ethic that he fears nothing and will take any risk either to protect his own "people" or to "launch" operations that, if they fail may destroy him. What a marvelous conception this man is! There are people like that in the leadership of US Intelligence. There are a few, but there once were many more and they are fewer all the time. In fact, the "system" works in such a way that people like "Smiley" are feared and distrusted by the bureaucratic politicians who really run the intelligence agencies. What are really to be found in the upper echelons of the "community" are either people who early in their government service became specialized in the generalized management of organizations (often after early substantive analytic work) or others who were "staff" of some kind, (budgetary planners, lawyers. liaison staff, etc.)

The Directors of the various agencies are naturally attracted to such people because they are focused on the administrative functions of the agencies and the protection of their ultimate superior, the Director. This makes them a kind of "insurance policy" for the directors of the agencies. The old veterans of the intelligence trade often make a distinction between "real intelligence officers" and "managers." "Real intelligence officers" are those who are known to be qualified and capable of the difficult work of analysis and field collection of information and who are known to have the moral character required to stand up to the pressure that is present in every political administration to make the "reality" presented by the "Intelligence Community" conform to the "reality" envisioned by the policy of the administration in power. The "managers" are essentially courtiers grouped about the throne of whichever baron of the Intelligence Community they may serve. The "managers" functions center on liaison with the other barons, lobbying the Congress for money and "protection" of the boss (the Director of their agency). Such people as the "managers" are easily recognized by the directors of the agencies as very valuable to their career survival in the stylized "dance" conducted around Washington by the various parts of the United States Government but they are not well suited to leading "real intelligence officers" to feats of brilliant analysis or imaginative collection operations because they are always in a "defensive crouch" fearing that the "real intelligence officers" will cause trouble for them or "the boss" through disagreement with the "picture" desired by the administration of the day or in Human Intelligence (HUMINT) operations (espionage) gone bad which result in publicity that could be damaging to the "managers'" careers.

Incredibly, these are the people who tend to be promoted to "line" command "at the top" in the collection, and analytic functions of the agencies over the heads of the "real intelligence officers." This pattern of rule by the "managerial" class is now so well established in the intelligence agencies that it is simply expected that senior jobs which control large parts of the agencies in the analytic and HUMINT collection fields will be held by "managers" as opposed to "real intelligence officers." This tendency is so firmly rooted now that the author has often heard very senior "real intelligence officers" described as "just an analyst," or "just an operator" in the context of a selection board picking someone for a high-level leadership job in the very field in which the "real intelligence officer" is an authority respected throughout the government. This tendency is perpetuated and reinforced by a process of "mirror-imaging" in personnel selections in which the ever-growing number of "managers" who are in senior leadership position simply select others like them in the next generation for the top jobs.

This results in a leadership cadre in the Intelligence Community which is more and more hostile to the risks demanded as the price of real success in collection and analysis and more and more favorable to the self-indulgence of a focus on the "turf battles and budget wars" endemic to Washington and at the same time less and less driven by the desire to do good intelligence work. The personnel management disaster described above is ultimately the responsibility of the directors of the agencies that make up the Intelligence Community. If they wanted to have a different focus in their agencies, there would be a different focus. There have been many fine and devoted heads of the various American intelligence agencies, but all too often the directors themselves are members of the "managerial class" within the Intelligence Community or simply politically selected party functionaries. All too often directors see themselves as "travelers" on a journey to yet further heights within the government and therefore not "decisively committed" to the work of their people. For many directors, the "managerial class" within their agencies is a natural ally in controlling the "wilder impulses" of the "real intelligence officers" in the organization.

-Risk Aversion. One of the most trite and tedious of the many things said in the national media and in the U.S. Congress about the failures of the Intelligence Community in Iraq and with regard to so many issues is that "HUMINT (espionage in this context) must be improved!" Repetition of this thought has become obligatory in any "serious" discussion of security issues but in fact, no one has done much to improve US espionage capabilities. This would be amusing in its inanity if the underlying phenomenon were not so serious.

In fact, the media and the Congress are largely responsible for creating the operating environment in which the wreck of once formidable American espionage capabilities became inevitable. In the aftermath of the Vietnam War, the public and its representatives convinced themselves that the intelligence services were somehow the enemies of the American people. The FBI COINTELPRO program aimed at Director Hoover's personal list of enemies and the Nixon Administration's meditations (the Houston Plan) on the possibility of effectively combining all U.S. counterintelligence groups into one force contributed to that idea.

The Houston Plan was never approved or implemented but the concept itself was enough to "trigger" demand for congressional investigations into the "misdeeds" of U.S. counterintelligence groups. Rather inevitably the "witch hunt" spread to include U.S. clandestine intelligence. The "Church Committee" in the US Senate resulted. Up until that time it was generally believed in the population of the United States that the intelligence services were filled with honorable people trying to protect the country, but the spirit of that age disagreed, and a barrage of "literature" and films spread the idea that career intelligence officers were amoral opportunists animated by a kind of nihilistic sadism. "The Three Days of the Condor," "The Bourne Identity," and similar rubbish which portrayed a universe unfamiliar to anyone who had ever worked in intelligence filled people's heads with the idea that the clandestine services were to be tolerated but only just barely tolerated and that they must be closely watched and restricted.

American espionage capabilities began to decline from that time and the process has not yet been reversed. A mass of regulations was enacted in those and following years which tied the hands of the clandestine services so effectively that they have never recovered. Several categories of people were placed "off limits" as possibilities for recruitment as foreign agents (for example, reporters, professors, employees of American companies) without regard for the fact that these very people have inherent access to people and information often needed to carry out effective intelligence work. The rationale seemed to be that some kinds of people needed to be "protected" from the "dirty" business of espionage.

The same kind of "thinking" has caused the clandestine services to rely far too much on "liaison" relationships with foreign intelligence services as a substitute for conducting American run espionage against difficult targets. The reason? Disclosure of foreign operations does not entail the career risk for the "managers" that the failure of an American operation would bring. The creation of this kind of operating environment served as a powerful "enabling" mechanism for the not so gradual assumption of power in the intelligence agencies by the "managerial class." In an atmosphere dominated by fear of violation of legislated restrictions on behavior and the use of clandestine funds, it was only natural that the directors of the agencies would look to those who had little interest in driving forward the limits of accomplishment and every interest in "limiting the damage" and "preventing surprises" for themselves and "the boss."

This has resulted in a degree of control over operations by lawyers and financial officers that is suffocating to the ability of skilled operatives to mount the kind of potentially rewarding but risky operations that would be needed, for example, to penetrate "Al-Qa'ida."

Clandestine operations are inherently dangerous. It follows that if they are evaluated by people who "know the cost of everything but the value of nothing," they will inevitably be disapproved before execution if the risks are considerable. Those in Congress who wrote the rules used as excuses to disapprove these operations will then "bleat" pitifully about the need for "better HUMINT" the next time a disaster occurs.

-Analysis by Committee. Much the same phenomena exist on the analytic "side" of the intelligence business. Brilliant people from the best schools "sign up" for a career in intelligence work from a sense of patriotism, intellectual curiosity, and a desire to "make a difference" in the world. What typically happens to them after that is that they are "eaten alive" by bureaucracies utterly controlled by the "managerial" mentality. Young analysts are called on to write papers that demand a fresh look, hard work and an undying devotion to the truth. The draft papers they write are not their property and these papers should not be subject to the vanities of "pride of authorship" so common in other works of scholarship, but neither should they be treated with a lack of respect for the views of the analysts and the creativity that the authors bring to the task.

Too often, the "editing by committee" system that prevails results in papers that are not only irrelevant to the security needs of the nation but are actually misleading because of their lack of intellectual honesty. In the "managerial" world, nothing matters so much as "staying in step" with the consensus in the various agencies of the intelligence world as well as making sure that analysis does not deny the political leadership of the country an intellectual "platform" from which they can proclaim their vision of the future. The "mere" belief of the analysts counts for little in the judgment of the "managers" when weighed against the career destroying effect of disapproval or disfavor from on high. As a result, analysis is "ironed out" in a "layer cake" system of committees at ever-higher layers of bureaucracy. These committees are made up of supervisors at the appropriate layer and they "take care" to insure that the interests of the various parties within an agency are protected in the text that goes forward to the next higher layer and that untoward results are avoided.

When this process is ended, what is typically produced is a stereotypical example of the "lowest common denominator," not something on which the country should "hang its hat" in making decisions affecting the national fate, and certainly. Such papers are inevitably reflective of the kind of "group think" that grows up in any highly integrated and hierarchical bureaucracy that controls the career long expectations of its inhabitants. In other words, an individual analyst has no chance whatever of having his or her views expressed at the national level unless a large and self-serving group of careerists approve them and find them not to be threatening to their collective view of what serves the group's perceived best interest in terms of its relations with the rest of the intelligence community and the sitting government.

The rule of the "managerial class" in the intelligence community ensures the permanence of this "system." The ruling group will reproduce itself through "mirror imaging" ad infinitum and will be maintained in position through the perceived self-interest of the kind of people who typically become directors of the major intelligence agencies. This is not to say that there have not been brave, courageous, and creative directors of the major intelligence agencies. The author has had the honor of serving under several. It was a pleasure, and they know who they are, but the sad truth, known to all who have served for extended periods in intelligence is that most directors are part of the problem.

The truth is that intelligence is an art best practiced by gifted eccentrics, people widely and deeply educated, favored by nature and training with intuition beyond the average and who care more for the truth than anything else. Such people consistently will follow their "nose" and their instincts on a trail of information like bloodhounds until they arrive at a truth that matters to the people of the United States. In the espionage field of endeavor, the function of managers is to be "enablers," to make workable the environment in which gifted case officers can break through the manifold barriers that will enable the penetration of groups that threaten the lives of our people. What must be avoided is the selection of managers who instinctively feel that their function is to "hold back" the operators and analysts in order to preserve "peace" within the bureaucracy.

-Domination of the Intelligence Function by the Executive Branch: All the intelligence agencies are parts of the Executive Branch. The CIA is a separate organization within the Executive Branch and directly subordinated to the president. The Defense Intelligence Agency is part of the Defense Department as is the National Security Agency. The State Department Bureau of Intelligence and Research (INR) is obviously part of that department.

All these groups are deeply imbedded within these "ministries" of government in a constitutional system which ensures that the authority of the political party that controls the white House will control the intelligence agencies as well. This means that the temptation that will always be presented to politicians to attempt to "shape" both information collection and the analysis of that information to their taste is likely to be overwhelming. In most American administrations, the most senior authorities (generally elected) are wise enough to know that without sound and objective judgments from the intelligence agencies, the information upon which they base decisions is worthless.

The reason one creates separate information gathering and analysis systems under the rubric of "intelligence" is that there is an inherent "conflict of interest" in any system that allows policy decision makers to be the same people who judge what the reality is upon which such decisions are based. Decision makers can always choose to decide policy questions based on their own view of the world, but it is intuitively obvious that this is not the best way to insure good decisions. For this reason, the most senior authorities generally restrain their subordinates on the policy side of government and prevent excessive interference with the process of judging information. The danger is that the wisdom of that attitude is not universally appreciated and in some government past, present or future, policy officials may choose to drive the intelligence people supporting their deliberations towards judgments unsupported by convincing and dependable evidence.

If one doubts the seriousness of the possible consequences of such a "cattle drive" one need only consider such historical examples of misadventure as the US strategic obsession with the likelihood of a Japanese first strike on the Philippines in 1941. This led the US Government to focus attention of its analytic force in that direction so firmly that Japanese preparations for an attack in Hawaii were completely missed. Another example would be the obsession with the "inevitability" of victory that influenced intelligence to "miss" completely enemy preparations for the Tet Offensive of 1968, in spite of the mass of information available that indicated something really "big" on the way. In both cases the results of policy or strategic thinking having been allowed to "intrude" on analysis were simply catastrophic.

Strong leadership by "real intelligence officers" can help to prevent such disasters. The "dissent" taken by the State Department in the October 2002 NIE on Iraq may well have been an example of the survival of such leadership. How can this be prevented? This problem exists across the world in every country where serious foreign policy and military issues must be considered and decisions on policy and strategy made on the basis of a systematic consideration of available data.

In every country there is the problem of trying to insure that the judgments of the information or intelligence people are untainted by external pressures. There have been various methods and structures adopted to deal with this danger to the national security. In some places external "think tanks" are used to "test" the result of internal analysis. In other countries, reliance is placed on the competitive analysis of two or more intelligence agencies, often one military and the other civilian. In Israel, within the Directorate of Military Intelligence there exists something called the "Devil's Advocate" a name borrowed from the process of canonization within the Catholic Church in which a cleric is appointed to oppose the sainthood of one who has been presented for consideration for that honor. In the Israeli "Devil's Advocate" section, the officers so employed have the job of opposing the analysis accepted by the government and of preventing the acceptance of institutional "group think" as the basis for decisions. For the senior Israeli officers who serve in the "Devil's Advocate" section it is understood that opposition to the judgments of the rest of the intelligence community will have a career price and that the officers who do this work should look forward to a fruitful life in retirement from the army soon after their service in this job. Nevertheless, they perform a vital; perhaps "priceless" is not too strong a word, service for their country.

None of these devices seem altogether suitable for the United States as a "safeguard" against overwhelming pressure to bring their analysis into conformity with policy. The sheer scale of the institutions involved in American life dictate modification of the methods used in smaller governments. Some approach that combines the better features of these institutional "fixes" would probably be appropriate. Can the "Intelligence Community" change itself to eliminate the problems discussed above? No. It cannot. The United States "Intelligence Community" is a "mature bureaucracy," a group of institutions that have reached a stable equilibrium in their internal politics and in their relationships with the other parts of the government. The leaders of these intelligence agencies are bureaucrats and politicians identical in character and mentality to those of all the other departments and agencies of the U.S. government. Typically, they are focused on group and individual survival and advancement, not on the quality of the informational product so desperately needed by their country.

For the majority of these senior leaders, the most important work-related event in their lives is the annual justification of the agency budget to the Congress rather than the opportunity to lead "their people" to new heights of achievement in the "art" of intelligence. There are few "virtuoso performers" among the senior leaders (military or civilian) of the "artists" who must be relied on to protect the United States in the unending intelligence wars that never end around the world.

If the Congress really wants better intelligence to avoid future disasters, it will have to "grasp the nettle" itself and dictate re-organization and a new beginning which seeks to protect the artists from the bureaucrats. If this does not happen, then superficial changes may occur but nothing of significance will be produced from within "the community," and we will all just wait for "the next time."

"Civic Virtue Took a Holiday"
(2003)

In a recent statement Senator Carl Levin, Ranking member of the Senate Select Committee on Intelligence told us that Undersecretary of Defense Douglas Feith tried to persuade the Pentagon's own espionage unit, the Defense Intelligence Agency, to change its conclusion that there was no alliance between Iraq and Al Qaeda and when the Defense Intelligence Agency rebuffed this blatant interference, Mr. Feith's own non-intelligence team wrote its own report asserting that this relationship was solid.

In this election season, partisans will simply dismiss the senator's "report" to America.

That will be a terrible mistake.

The fact is that our country went to war in Iraq on the basis of a lie. That lie was that Iraq was a "nexus" of the worldwide Islamic Jihadi terrorist conspiracy and that because it had been established that Iraq possessed weapons of mass destruction it was likely that Iraq would provide them to the Jihadis to use in attacking us here in America.

We have now searched Iraq thoroughly and know without a doubt that they had no special weapons in March 1993 and no prospects for having any in the foreseeable future. They had given up on their special weapons programs after the First Gulf War under pressure from the US intelligence backed UN inspections and the crippling economic sanctions laid upon the country throughout the '90s. We also know that the "evidence" of a "relationship" between Iraq and the Jihadis is really only a record of the kind of contacts any Arab government maintains with dangerous actors in order to keep track of what they are doing.

We know from this senate report that the two intelligence agencies tried to tell the policy people in the Bush administration that to say the Iraqis were a "gathering threat" to the US would be a lie and that they were then scorned and bypassed so that the lie could be told to the world.

What happened then? Did the Directors of the two agencies demand that truth should be told to the American people? Did the two Directors resign in protest rather than participate by their silence in the lie?

No. They did not. Instead, they acted as "enablers" in this moral crime against the American people. They had sworn to protect the Republic, its Constitution and its Citizens, and they did not. Instead, they encouraged the conspirators in the lie by their silence, and indeed by their intimidation of their subordinates.

Where was the "civic virtue" in this? Where was the "Pietas," the reverence for all that we hold most dear? Where was the willingness to fight and die for our integrity as a people?

It was absent from these men. Who will answer for this? Who?

"Stranger passing by, go and tell the Spartans that here obedient to their law we lie."

That is the inscription at Thermopylae.

The men who failed our country miserably in the leadership of our intelligence agencies did not meet that standard. Our soldiers are now dying because of their cowardice and self-serving sycophancy.

They must pay.

Clandestine HUMINT in Counterinsurgency— The Vietnam Example
(2005)

In Vietnam the theater army component intelligence collection architecture matured by the Spring of 1968. There was a brigade level collection group for SIGINT and a battalion level reconnaissance photo exploitation unit. The theater level army clandestine HUMINT task was centrally managed by the 525th Military Intelligence Group (525 MIG). HUMINT implies purposeful employment of human sources of information to learn things. Having a conversation with a source who is not under friendly control is not HUMINT. It is a chat. In addition to the theater army clandestine HUMINT operation, combat arms divisions and separate brigades conducted force protection operations employing sources who were largely unvetted and untested. These activities were often conducted by the combat arms unit's counter-intelligence (CI) detachments.

US Army counter-intelligence personnel in these detachments were not trained to conduct such operations and the results were of uniformly low quality and reliability. SOF activities such as the 5th Special Forces Group and "United States Military Assistance Command Vietnam Studies and Observations Group" (USMACVSOG) also operated a variety of intelligence projects of varying quality. Often, the quality was directly proportional to the availability of well-qualified personnel to run them. The major responsibility for clandestine HUMINT support to the US Army in Vietnam rested squarely on the 525th MIG. The group employed four 2 numbered battalions to do clandestine HUMINT collection work on both unilateral and bi-lateral bases in the Areas of Responsibility (AOR) of the Vietnamese Corps Tactical Zones (CTZ) which were numbered One to Four from North to South. There was a fifth battalion in 525th MIG responsible for countrywide and out of country operations. The 525th MIG had other, non-HUMINT responsibilities in the area of "housekeeping" for staff personnel attached to major headquarters, etc. The 3rd Combat Battalion (Provisional), 525 MIG (3rd Bn.) was responsible for an AOR which reached from the northeastern reaches of the Mekong Delta southwest of Saigon to a line about 50 miles east of Saigon and from the South China Sea to the Cambodian border inland.

In reality the AOR extended into Cambodia because many of the targets addressed by the battalion's border detachments extended into Cambodia. The in-country AOR was exactly the same as that of the Vietnamese (ARVN) 3rd Corps Tactical Zone. Someone had decided to match the 525 MIG AORs to the responsibilities of the ARVN rather than to that of "United States Military Assistance Command Vietnam" (USMACV). US maneuver forces were commanded by I Field Force and II Field Force. These were army corps level headquarters. The US maneuver forces moved around a good bit throughout the country in ways not conducive to sound clandestine HUMINT practice.

Effective clandestine HUMINT operations depend on stability of personnel and operating areas for success, and this may have been a major factor in this decision as the ARVN CTZs never changed. In addition, the 525th MIG was responsible for advising the ARVN countrywide clandestine HUMINT activity and co-extensive boundaries of AORs was undoubtedly helpful in that task. 3 The 3rd Bn was organized with headquarters in Bien Hoa (near Saigon). The headquarters performed normal C2 functions and was co-located with an attached CI detachment for area support throughout 3rd CTZ.

An operations section controlled the activities of subordinate detachments in the areas of source control, planning, and funding of operations.

The 3rd Bn had an attached element from the 525th MIG's Aviation Detachment. This element operated half a dozen helicopters in support of the 3rd Bn's activities and was a great convenience. The "guts" of the 3rd Bn's activities were carried out by four clandestine HUMINT Detachments each of which had an AOR consisting of one or more South Vietnamese Government (SVN) provinces. Each detachment was commanded by a captain or major who was a clandestine HUMINT qualified and often experienced officer and was manned by military case officers (COs) of various ranks junior to the commander, as well as enlisted intelligence operations clerks whose function was to support case officer activities in report writing, file keeping and other administrative and sometimes tactical duties in defense of position.

The case officers were a mixed lot. Some were long service MI personnel who had done this work in Germany and Japan for many years. Some were bright young men selected out of the basic training pool for this work. They were subsequently trained at the Army Intelligence School at Ft. Holabird and language school before deployment, and some were CIA "Career Trainees" (CTs) who were doing their military duty. 4 Each of the four Detachments was deployed in several team locations throughout its AOR. The four detachments were tasked from 525th MIG and 3rd Bn against a variety of targets. Some were general in nature, (report of all enemy activity in AOR), and some quite specific (report on the activities of enemy Line of Communications (LOC) between coordinate #### and coordinate ####). The main function of such tasking was to serve as an authorization for the expenditure of operational funds.

Headquarters far away in Saigon and Bien Hoa were ill equipped to have the detailed knowledge of the situation necessary to direct operational activities at the detachment level and they had the good sense to realize that and leave detailed operational planning to detachment commanders. Successful detachment commanders understood that US Army and US Air Force activities within their AORs were their real customers. As a result, detachment commanders made close and continuous liaison with both static activities (MACV Advisory Teams and USAF Forward Air Controller Teams (FAC)) and Combat Arms units temporarily located within the detachment's AOR. Tasking was sought and accepted from these directly supported activities and reports were rendered directly to them on a timely basis, normally by hand delivery.

The same material was then subsequently reported electronically to higher headquarters where it contributed to the detachment's "box score" and eventually ended up at MACV J-2, PACOM and the JCS. Evaluations of the reports were sent by supported units and activities to 525th MIG in Saigon. Detachment A, 3rd Bn 525th MIG (the Det.) was typical in its structure and operations. The Det. had teams of two to four men in six surrounded and defended Vietnamese towns in Binh Long and Phuoc Long Provinces on the 5 Cambodian border directly north of Saigon. The Detachment headquarters was located in Song Be, the provincial capital of Phuoc Long Province (some times known as the Siberia of SVN).

No detachment personnel were co-located with US combat arms units because such units lived in their own defended positions (Landing Zones and Fire Bases) outside the Vietnamese towns where there was no substantial access to indigenous inhabitants. The ability to recruit and then handle agents in this or any other situation is entirely dependent on extended access to a large group of people from whom to choose prospective sources and a continuing ability to associate with them within the protection of plausible cover. None of that existed in the "world" of the Big Army units.

Consequently, it was decided to "cover" Army COs as military or civilian members of the Civil Operations Revolutionary Development Support (CORDS) apparatus located at province and district (county) levels of the SVN government. This organization was all pervasive throughout SVN after 1967 and had many positions for advisory personnel in military training, agriculture, government operations, medical affairs, education, etc. throughout the country. The positions for American civilian personnel were particularly difficult to fill in the very parts of the country in which enemy presence and subsequent danger were high. These were the parts of the country that the US Army was most interested in from the point of view of the need to support combat operations and therefore there was a natural symbiosis between the needs of CORDS and the needs of 525th MIG.

As a result, CORDS, especially in 3rd CTZ where John Vann was in charge, was quite willing to provide cover positions for 525th MIG personnel so long as they did the cover work better than the "real" civilian and military CORDS people did. Vann remarked on many occasions that the COs under cover were the best workers that he had. The way this system worked all the 6 525th MIG people were under CORDS cover in

Det A's operation including the detachment commander. The enemy never successfully penetrated this cover arrangement in the three years of the existence of Det A, 3rd Bn 525th MIG.

Since all Americans in these surrounded border towns were targets for assassination or elimination there was no significant increase in the risk for non-MI personnel. The operating locations were all very dangerous places, subject to intermittent but frequent attacks by fire and weekly ground "probes." In 1968-69, there were major ground assaults on all the Det A locations. All were defeated, but in the case of Song Be, the detachment headquarters location the VC held 2/3rds of the town for seven days before the 1st Cavalry Division drove them out with heavy casualties. Det A's sources and COs in the Song Be area continued to function and report throughout this episode.

All US personnel of necessity took a lot of chances, but this was war and higher headquarters understood this fact. Most of the Det A operations involved Vietnamese and Montagnard agents. The Montagnards often had to be taught the concepts of; time, distance and number before they were useful. The detachment had some Chinese and European agents. These were rubber plantation managers. The French consulate and its "Service de Documentation et Contre-Espionage" (SDECE) office in Saigon turned over to their control a rubber company apparatus of informants which had been maintained by the French Government for thirty years. It was useful. The detachment's operations were fully documented with; operations plans, recruiting plans and contact 7 reports in addition to the product Intelligence Information Reports (IIR).

Sources were frequently tested. Singleton sources were tested directly in safe houses in situ or in the coastal cities. Many operations had to be run as principal agent networks because of the inaccessibility of primary sources deep in enemy controlled territory outside the detachment's operating locations. In these cases the principal agents were directly tested and the primary sources were usually judged on the basis of the direct combat result of the employment of their information. When fully developed the detachment had four commissioned officers, five warrant officers and about twenty enlisted people. The detachment ran around a hundred agents at any given time. Det A's operation earned high marks for productivity and accuracy. Anecdotal evidence of the performance of the 525th MIG throughout the country indicates that not all operations were as productive. The difference in performance seems to have been largely a function of leadership.

Counterinsurgency – a much failed strategy?
(November 12, 2009)

Bernard Fall was one of the most significant theoreticians and practitioner of Counterinsurgency (COIN) in the 20th Century. He was the expert most listened to at the Special Warfare Center at Ft. Bragg when LTG William Yarborough commanded the school there in the Kennedy and Johnson eras.

Fall defined COIN clearly. He said that: Counterinsurgency = political reform + economic development + counter guerrilla operations

This theory of warfare was developed by the colonial powers as a "cure" for the wave of "wars of national liberation" that swept through their overseas possessions after World War Two. Because of these revolts against authority most of the European powers found themselves faced with colonized populations engaged in extended attempts to obtain independence from the metropole. Such rebellions were usually based on ethnic and racial differences with the colonizers and were often led by vanguard Left parties with communist connections. That connection caused an eventual American policy commitment to the COIN struggle. That commitment sometimes occurred as a partner of the colonial power (Vietnam in the late '40s and '50s) and sometimes as a successor to the colonial power after at least partial independence had bee achieved. (Vietnam after the French)

COIN theory was seen by both the former colonial officers who taught it at Bragg and their American disciples of the time as the opposite of the methods of the anti-colonial insurgents who were thought to practice something called "revolutionary warfare." (RW)

Revolutionary Warfare + Political subversion (including propaganda) + economic transformation (usually socialist) + guerilla warfare (to include terrorism)

The central idea behind COIN was seen as competitive reformed government and economic development for the population that was at least potentially supported the insurgents RW movement. It was believed that if this population was "protected" from the RW efforts of the insurgent movement, then the population would choose to side with the counterinsurgents whether the counterinsurgents were the local post-colonial government or an occupying power.

This doctrine was widely applied across the world in the middle and late 20th Century. There were successes and there were failures.

Successes:

The British suppression of the "Malayan Emergency" was probably the greatest success of the counterinsurgents. In Malaya the British colonial authorities faced a clearly communist guerrilla movement that consisted altogether of overseas Chinese living in the midst of a majority Malay and Muslim population. The area of operations was a peninsula nearly completely surrounded by ocean areas dominated by the British Navy. The British forces suffered from cross department coordination issues early in the campaign, but once those were solved and the "Communist Terrorists" (CTs) isolated in the jungles and rubber plantations all that was needed to defeat them was persistence in small unit patrolling until the CTs were exterminated. There were never more than a few hundred of them. The British succeeded in suppressing this revolt but what did this successful effort cost them. It was enormously expensive, and success was followed by British withdrawal from Malaya and the creation of an independent Malaysia completely dominated by the Malay ethnic adversaries of the overseas Chinese.

Kenya and Cyprus were both gripped by revolts by the Kikuyu and Greek populations respectively. In both cases, RW campaigns based on terrorism were fought to a standstill by the British only to be followed by political decisions on the part of the British government to abandon these countries and allow the ascent to power of the former leaders of the insurgencies, Kenyatta and Makarios respectively.

In Latin America, where I participated in several COIN efforts, the Kennedy created "Alliance for Progress" sought to defeat local insurgencies inspired and led by cadres from Castro's Cuba. These countries were particularly good targets for communist inspired RW because the political and economic structures of the Central American and Andean states were so clearly unfair and un-democratic that local populations of underfed Indians and peasants could be easily proselytized in the process of RW. In many cases in Latin America the low-level economic development efforts of the civil and military arms of the US Government met with considerable success. Villagers were protected from the insurgents, local (village economies) were improved. Medical treatment was provided to those who had never known it. Nevertheless, the "Alliance for Progress" cannot be considered a strategic success. Why? The local elites in all these countries quickly perceived the COIN campaign as a threat to their political privilege and wealth in land and simply refused to institute the reforms sponsored by the alliance. Much the same thing happened in various parts of Africa and Southwest Asia where it was attempted.

Failures

The American war in Vietnam is a typical example of failure of the COIN theory. The massive communist led Viet Minh independence movement was a classic example of RW in all its components taken to its ultimate development in the creation of a regular army for the insurgent movement under the sponsorship of its Chinese communist ally. The United States participated in the French COIN effort against the Viet Minh and then became the sponsor of the post-colonial government left behind by the French on their departure. Contrary to popular legend (I served there for two years) the initial approach of the United States to the situation in South Vietnam was pure COIN right out of the Ft. Bragg School. Populations of villagers were protected, the South Vietnamese armed forces were developed, village militias were created for self- defense, good government was preached to the Diem government in Saigon. Economic development was fostered. It was only when the government of North Vietnam decided that these methods were a serious bar to their eventual success in RW in the South and brought its regular army into South Vietnam in 1964 that US forces escalated their own deployment to the conventional war level. This was a necessary step if the eradication of the South Vietnamese government and the US COIN effort was to be avoided. There followed three years of conventional warfare between US and North Vietnamese forces. This warfare was largely conducted outside populated areas. COIN efforts continued during this period but took second place to the need to defeat or at least seriously weaken North Vietnam's army. In 1967 it was judged that this had been accomplished and COIN was once again made the centerpiece of American efforts in Vietnam. To accomplish this, a fully integrated civil/military COIN structure was created under the combined military command in Vietnam. This was called "Civil Operations, Revolutionary Development Support" (CORDS). I worked in this program for a year. (1968-1969) This effort had virtually unlimited money, ten thousand advisers in every aspect of Vietnamese civil society, business and government function and a massive coalition and south Vietnamese conventional force standing by to protect the population and the counterinsurgents of CORDS while they did their work. This COIN program was largely successful. A handover to the South Vietnamese forces was devised in the form of the "Vietnamization Program" and US forces were withdrawn in "trenches" (slices) over a couple of years. Following the Christmas, 1972 renewed bombing effort over North Vietnam (caused by North Vietnamese intransigence in Geneva) a ceasefire was reached and for two years there was quiet in South Vietnam with the South Vietnamese government holding much of the country. It was only after some minor incident on the world stage caused a revulsion in the American press and public against any further involvement in Vietnam that the US Congress passed a law forbidding any further aid to South Vietnam that the North Vietnamese decided to use their fine army to over run the country in a conventional war. Lesson: You can win the COIN war and still be defeated conventionally or politically at home.

The French war in Algeria is another example of COIN success followed by political defeat and withdrawal. After a prolonged struggle, the French security force had largely defeated the Algerian native guerrillas of the *Front National de Liberation* (FLN). This struggle had been waged with all the aspects of classic COIN doctrine. The revolt had started in 1955. By 1960 the French Army, police and their Algerian allies had largely won the fight. As in Vietnam, two years then passed in relative quiet. In 1962 De Gaulle was elected president of France with a political vision that required independence for Algeria. That negated all the struggle and success of the CIIN war. Failure once again at the strategic level.

Our war in Iraq is now cited as an example of the success of the COIN theory and its methods. In fact, nothing of the sort occurred in Iraq. Remember – COIN = political reform + economic development + counter-guerilla operations. We have not brought on political reform in Iraq. What we have done is re-arrange the "players" in such a way that the formerly downtrodden Shia Arabs are now the masters. This has in no way reduced the potential for inter-communal armed struggle. We did not defeat the insurgents in counter guerrilla operations. What we did was bring more troops into the Baghdad area to enforce the separation of the ethno-sectarian communities while at the same time using traditional methods of "divide and conquer" to split off enough insurgents to form an effective force to use against Al-Qa'ida in Iraq and others whom we disapproved of. This is not counterinsurgency!!!

Conclusion

COIN is a badly flawed instrument of statecraft: Why?

- The locals ultimately own the country being fought over. If they do not want the "reforms" you desire, they will resist you as we have been resisted in Iraq and Afghanistan. McChrystal's strategy paper severely criticized Karzai's government. Will that disapproval harden into a decision to act to find a better government or will we simply undercut Afghan central government and become the actual government?

- Such COIN wars are expensive, long drawn-out affairs that are deeply debilitating for the foreign counterinsurgent power. Reserves of money, soldiers and national will are not endless. Ultimately, the body politic of the counterinsurgent foreign power turns against the war and then all that has occurred has been a waste.

- COIN theory is predicated on the ability of the counterinsurgents to change the mentality of the "protected" (read controlled) population. The sad truth is that most people do not want to be deprived of their ancestral ways and will fight to protect them. "Hearts and Minds" is an empty propagandist's phrase.

- In the end the foreign counterinsurgent is embarked on a war that is not his own war. For him, the COIN war will always be a limited war, fought for a limited time with limited resources. For the insurgent, the war is total war. They have no where to escape to after a tour of duty. The psychological difference is massive.

- For the counterinsurgent the commitment of forces must necessarily be much larger than for the insurgents. The counterinsurgent seeks to protect massive areas, hundreds of built-up areas and millions of people. The insurgent can pick his targets. The difference in force requirements is crippling to the counterinsurgents.

What should we do?

- Hold the cities as bases to prevent a recognized Taliban government until some satisfactory (to us) deal is made among the Afghans.
- Participate in international economic development projects for Afghanistan.
- Conduct effective clandestine HUMINT out of the city bases against international jihadi elements.
- Turn the tribes against the jihadi elements.
- Continue to hunt and kill/capture dangerous jihadis,

How long might you have to follow this program? It might be a long time but that would be sustainable. A full-blown COIN campaign in Afghanistan is not politically sustainable.

Human Terrain Teams

(2010)

The US military is sometimes accused of inflexibility and a lack of willingness to adapt to changing circumstances. The old saw about "preparing for the last war" is still widely accepted but there is now a good example of the military's desire to learn from hard experience. This example has to do with what is now called "Human Terrain Mapping" and the creation of "Human Terrain Teams."

The United States intervened in Iraq in 2003 believing that the population of Iraq was more-or-less one "people," who were very secular in their orientation and that this population would welcome American intervention to rid them of the tyrant Saddam Hussein. The Bush Administration also thought that a new government representing the majority interests of the Shia Arab people of south Iraq would easily gain acceptance from all the other groups. The Bush Administration believed that to be true because they had been told that the Iraqi people were so westernized that they would agree to any government that was created in a fair election conducted on the basis of "one person, one vote."

Much of this set of ideas proved to be incorrect. The Iraqis proved not be one people, but several. The truth was that only a minority of the population of the country had adopted European ways of life. The rest were still firmly attached to traditions that had evolved over millennia. These mores "codified" a social "system of systems" in which competition among ethnic, kinship, sectarian and regional groups was the governing truth. In fact, the police power of the state and a nascent over-arching nationalism embodied in the personnel of the army and civil service were all that had held the country together. Our invasion of the country was welcomed by the previously down-trodden Shia Arabs and Kurds but firmly rejected by the Sunni Arabs, a minority who had ruled Mesopotamia for fourteen hundred years.

Our destruction of the government and army led to initial chaos followed by prolonged and seemingly ever-growing irregular resistance on the part of the Sunni Arabs and secular Shia Arabs, both of whom saw themselves as displaced by American fiat from their rightful place as the leaders of a modernizing country.

By late 2005, the war situation had degenerated to such an extent that American defeat and withdrawal from the country seemed all but inevitable. Arrayed against the occupation force of UN chartered troops (mostly

American) were a variety of resistance groups. The international terrorists inspired by Osama bin Laden (takfiri jihadis) were few in numbers but distinguished by their willingness to die in their cause and relentless desire to dominate, control and re-shape Iraqi life in a pattern of puritanical Islam new to the country among both Sunni and Shia. By far the largest grouping of insurgents was a "galaxy" of loosely related forces made up of Iraqi nationalists (mostly ex-army), Baath Party cadres and their hired gunmen, local religious enthusiasts, and tribal variations of all of those types.

Ambushes by fire, kidnappings for ransom or execution (especially among the *takfiri* jihadis), were much used tactical devices, but the favorite was ambush using a roadside bomb. These were often remotely controlled and sometimes covered by fire as well. Such devices had been encountered in many of America's other wars but in Iraq their employment reached a level of development unseen before. The strong Iraqi national educational program had produced many people capable of building and continuously "improving" what quickly became called "improvised explosive demolitions" (IED). Former Iraqi Army soldiers played a major role in building such devices. Coalition forces casualties rose higher and higher even as political resistance to the prolonged and unexpectedly bloody and expensive war grew steadily. At the same time the obvious success of the insurgent forces in creating a stalemate against occupying forces led to a growing support for the insurgents among an Iraqi populous uneasy with the continuing presence of foreign forces on their soil.

In response to such a predicament, the US armed forces tried to deal with the challenges it met in Iraq through the application of advanced technology both in countermeasures directly applied against the roadside bomb planters and in trying to use sophisticated electronic sensors to find the bombs and bomb makers. As of now, over three billion dollars have been spent in the search for the perfect "gadget" that would neutralize the ever changing and developing IEDs. In this race, the Iraqi insurgents seem to be always in "the lead." Many creative and ingenious countermeasures have been developed in the hunt for a solution, but the guerrillas have always "kept up." At the same time, US Military Intelligence had little success against the elusive terrorists and guerillas. Their problems were largely a product of a highly developed reliance on technical, electronic means of information collection. This reliance developed following the end of the Vietnam War and perhaps in reaction to that war. At that time there was a thorough examination of Vietnam problems and the US armed forces largely discarded many of the "people based" systems of information collection that it had previously relied on. In particular the controlled use of native human assets (spies) to collect information was abandoned in favor of technical means of information collection. An insurgent enemy is a human target system. It has few "signatures" that are accessible to aerial photography or signals intelligence. As a result, the ability of Army and Marine intelligence to find the bomb makers and other parts of the insurgent organizations was severely limited.

Such a story would seem destined for a bad ending, but although the end has not been reached, it is now possible to say that a "happy" ending is a distinct possibility. The lives and limbs of the sacrificed dead and wounded can never be restored, but a future in which there is a relatively peaceful Iraq and also a graceful exit from Iraq for the United States now seems possible if not sure.

This radical change in prospects from the situation in 2005 can be attributed largely to a serendipitous set of events that began in mid-2006 and which continue into the present.

The first and most important of these events was a growing and spreading revolt of rural and initially tribal Iraqis against the tyranny of the *takfiri jihadis* associated with Al-Qa'ida. These were mostly foreign Muslim fanatics who came to Iraq to fight the western occupation but also to impose their peculiar vision of a very puritanical way of life on Iraqi Muslims already content with traditional life. The *takfiris* were so tyrannical, brutal and murderous in their attempts to control the population that by early 2006 the people (especially the tribes) were ready to fight them for their freedom. They then began to do so and approached US forces for help in so doing.

The second event (or perhaps development would be a better word) was the growing influence of culturally attuned foreign counterinsurgency specialists on the policy of the coalition armed forces command in Iraq. A small group of soldiers and scholars (many of whom had very wide experience in the Arab World and in counterinsurgency) had insisted from the beginning of the intervention in Iraq that wide-spread insurgency would be the result of the profoundly unsettling political changes made in the first years of the occupation and that the insurgents were mainly people who did not share a common cause other than a detestation of what they saw as a renewal of colonialism, The expert group had insisted throughout that the various insurgent groups were not one force, but, rather, many and that they could be split apart by a skilful use of incentives and then used against the *takfiris*. The rapidly worsening situation in 2005 and the arrival on the scene of a commander of similar views (Petraeus) made the American armed forces in Iraq more receptive to the advice of the counterinsurgency experts. As a consequence, the requests for help from Sunni Arabs were increasingly welcomed with cooperation in operations, intelligence and supply. The results were "revolutionary" in causing massive damage to the *takfiri* forces first in Anbar Province and then increasingly across central Iraq. The presence of more American conventional troops during the "surge" only amplified the effect.

To institutionalize this approach to counterinsurgency in Iraq and in Afghanistan, the US Army began in the autumn of 2006 to train and deploy to the war zones what it calls Human Terrain Teams (HTT). These are tailored five-person mixed military and civilian teams designed to advise brigade commanders of the combat arms on the business of counterinsurgency in the context of the culture, politics, religion, ethnology, and economy of the specific region in which the advised brigade is operating. The emphasis is on acceptance of the realities of existing ways of life and deep understanding of the internal dynamics of the society in which the counterinsurgents must work and fight for the loyalty or control of the people. The teams are typically made up of a commander, an anthropologist or other social scientist, a master linguist, a communications person, and an intelligence analyst. The military people usually have extensive combat experience and are usually reservists who have volunteered to be called for active duty for this mission. Teams stay on site at least a year and may be extended if they agree. People who volunteer for this kind of work are dedicated to seeing the wars through to success.

The teams are trained and educated for the task to which they are being sent for about four months. The curriculum includes a lot of instruction in counterinsurgency based on the new Army field manual on that subject. The team members also receive a thorough grounding in the academic subjects mentioned above from leading academics in these fields from around the world. The training is centered on Fort Leavenworth, Kansas where the Army has many of its senior schools. These are mixed gender teams. Thus far, teams have been deployed to both Iraq and Afghanistan and reports from the field indicate a high degree of success in both countries. It is likely that the success of this program and a general resurgence of belief in counterinsurgency methods will lead to further successes in the field.

"Peter Rabbit"

(2011)

This is a true story. It is a kind of "war story.' "Basilisk' asked me to tell you this story. We were out wandering around the Virginia countryside in the rain. "Harper" joined us for lunch at a country inn. We have those.

In the middle of the Vietnam War, I was in an Army school for captains and majors. It was a long course, nine months long. There were about 100 officers in the class. Nearly all had already served one 12 month "tour" in the war. They were all intelligence officers but as lieutenants or captains they had served with infantry or other combat arms battalions, or in SF or so far out in the "boondocks' that what branch one belonged to did not matter much.

They were all going back to the war as soon as they graduated and were not very tolerant of people they thought of as "REMFs." (rear-echelon mother-fuckers). They had seen a lot of death, had inflicted a lot of death, and were going to do it again. There were not a lot of West Point grads in the group.

They were difficult students. I have a couple of examples:

We all had very high security clearances because of the material being taught. To make it easier for the MPs to screen us for admittance into the classroom in which the whole class sat, we wore photo badges that had a green strip down one side. After a few months of listening to the mainly REMF faculty lecture us on things they only dimly understood, the class decided to give an "asshole" of the week award to some worthy soul who had tried to teach something beyond his reach. The award was presented on Mondays after weekend consultation in some saloon. The honored person was presented the "elements' of the award by a committee of officers, usually in his office but occasionally on stage in our classroom. I remember one poor soul begging to be forgiven rather than be honored. The award was one of those Thai or Filipino wooden statue of a nude man bent over forward so far that his head had disappeared in his anus. A vertical green strip encircled his body. This was, of course called the "HUYA" award. We were repeatedly lectured about this by the school commandant, a full colonel. The response was to give him the HUYA Award at the end of one of these speeches. He took it.

On another occasion, the Chemical Corps REMFs came in to give their preening lecture and demo about what they did to try to justify their existence. There were three of them in white lab coats with jungle uniform pants and boots sticking out underneath. There was the usual boring catalog of their "accomplishments." In the middle of the stage was a large wire and wood cage containing a white rabbit that sat looking at the strange crowd and at times looking up at his REMF "friends." In other courses we students had all seen the chemical Corps demonstration of the lethality of VX, a nerve gas that kills mammals within a minute if as little is absorbed as a single droplet. The chemical REMFs loved to kill rabbits this way for the wonderment of a captive audience. They finally got to that point in their "dog and pony show." The chemical instructor approached the cage with his vial of murder. He was wearing long black, rubber gloves and a gas mask. The rabbit looked at him.

One of the guys in the class was a white captain from Alabama, whose affectionate nickname was "H. Rap Smith." He stood up and said, "Colonel we have all seen this demonstration and know that VX will kill the rabbit, or any of us... Please don't kill the rabbit." He stood there waiting for a response...

The colonel ordered him to sit down and reached for the door in the top of the cage.

The class stood as one and a kind of animal sound ran around this room full of killers. The Chemical corps colonel took a step back and made a few weakly threatening statements.

When he finished and stood on the stage, confused as to what to do, another "student' said that his children would want the rabbit. He walked up onto the stage, took the rabbit out of the cage and returned to his place among us, holding the animal in his arms. We were all still standing.

The chemical people left and we all went to lunch. The rabbit went home to the children.

We were lectured again and threatened with punishment. Someone in the back of the room replied that the school would have to punish us all.

Nothing more was said about this incident.

We graduated and went back to our war where some died, some were mutilated but all could nurture in their hearts the memory of a white rabbit that we saved, together.

The Pogo Factor

(2007)

How Cultural Blindness Has Infected America's View of the World

A book proposal
W. Patrick Lang

In the four years since the United States invaded Iraq, it's become clear that our campaign there has gone terribly awry. We invaded Iraq with too few troops; we destroyed the Iraqi civil administration and military without having a suitable instrument of government ready in the wings; we expelled from public employment anyone with a connection, no matter how tenuous, to the Baath Party—which included most people who could be described as human infrastructure for Iraq. The list of errors goes on and on. Even the Vice President acknowledges that "mistakes were made" (although, presumably, not by him).

But how did the highly educated and powerful American people make such a horrendous, catastrophic series of blunders? As Pogo, the cartoon opossum, once famously said, "We have met the enemy and they is US!" Yes, that's right: We, the American people—not the Bush administration, nor the hapless Iraqis, nor the meddlesome Iranians (the new scapegoat)—are the root of the problem.

It's woven into our cultural DNA. Most Americans mistakenly believe that when we say that "all men are created equal," it means that all people are the same. We generally believe that behind the "cute" and "charming" native clothing, behind the "weird" marriage customs and the "odd" food of other cultures, all humans are motivated by and yearning for styles of life that will be increasingly unified as time and globalization progress. That is what Tom Friedman seems to have meant when he wrote that "the world is flat"; that is, that humankind is being driven by technological and economic change towards a future of cultural sameness. In other words, whatever differences of custom and habit that still exist between peoples will pass away soon and be replaced by a world culture rather like that of the United States in the 21st Century.

To be blunt, our foreign policy tends to be predicated on the notion that everyone wants to be an American. In the months leading up to the start of the Iraq War, it was common to hear seemingly educated people say that the Arabs, particularly Iraqis, had no way of life worth saving and would be better off if all "that old stuff"—their traditions, social institutions, and values— were done away with, and soon. The U.S. armed forces and U.S. AID would be the sharp swords of modernization in the Middle East.

How did Americans come to believe that the entire world is embarked on the same voyage, and that we are the navigators showing the way to a bright future?

Drawing on the Pogo metaphor, I seek to explain why, thematically showing how our own culture is a rich blend, brewed from such elements as;

- *The Enlightenment and the Influence of Jean Jacques Rousseau.* These tendencies have pushed us toward the belief in the essential unity of mankind and the need to liberate humanity from the "bonds" of traditional attitudes. Implicit in this is a belief in "progress" in human affairs, that what is past after all, is just "history" --a uniquely American attitude towards the past. This has led to a view that mankind is fated to "come together" in a globalized single world culture in which old ways will be relegated to museums. As a result many Americans have little or no interest in history; we believe that events in the past are no longer significant as mankind marches on.
- *Overweening optimism.* The virtually unlimited resources which lay before the early European settlers offered the prospect of an endlessly expanding economic "pie." The previous notion that man's life would be "nasty, brutish and short" has all but disappeared from American society and has been replaced with a view of life that for all problems there are solutions. There is little sense of the "tragedy of man's fate" in America; to the contrary, people in California sometimes seem to see death as an un-natural event.
- *Puritan utopianism.* The settlement of Massachusetts by English Calvinists and the triumph of their cultural heirs in the American Civil War biased the country in the direction of a belief of an earthly Utopia. Among the features of this Puritan tendency to hold "black and white" positions on morality and virtue is the continuing emphasis on the narrative of the early English settlements on the east coast of the country. In what is now "accepted wisdom," the Pilgrims and Puritans of the Plymouth and Massachusetts Bay colonies are held up as models of exemplary virtue and the true

founders of the country even though their colonies were theocracies which tolerated no dissent, selected their immigrants on the basis of wealth which provoked the first English-Indian War (King Philips War) soon after they arrived. On the other hand, "accepted wisdom," taught almost universally in the schools, holds that the settlers at Jamestown, Virginia were crass, lazy wastrels and "good for nothings" that would have died out if it had not been for a "bit of luck." Clearly this attitude of a lack of forgiveness for FELLOW ENGLISHMEN originated in a lack of willingness to tolerate a level of "difference" so small as that between Puritans and Anglicans. This attitude persists to this day and is on display every Thanksgiving when it is widely and falsely proclaimed that the feast of Thanksgiving originated at Plymouth. The New England claim is accepted by nearly all even though the historical record is clear that the custom began at Jamestown.

- *The Demeaning of Native Cultures.* Nothing could be more illustrative of the effect of these "strains" in our thinking than the sorry history of our centuries of struggle against the "native Americans." From the very beginnings of European settlement in Virginia and New England, the settlers showed very little understanding of or sympathy for the Indians. The settlers' viewed the Indian as a savage, to be Europeanized at best or destroyed at worst. The existence of institutions like the Carlisle Indian School which were specifically designed to eradicate Indian ways and to make "white people" out of "red people" speaks volumes about early and continuing settler attitude towards those who were "different."

- *Distrust in local knowledge.* Those few government people who mastered Indian ways and dealt with them as equals rather than as a backward and ignorant race were themselves treated as "suspicious," unsound, or of doubtful loyalty. The US Army officers who commanded the Indian Scouts in the Apache Wars of the 1880s were hugely successful as peace makers and leaders of warriors in battle but they were shunned within the army and were never given any other positions of responsibility. This same ethos continues today. Military or diplomatic officers who master the languages, customs and thinking of foreign peoples are viewed through a lens of mistrust, and are said to have "gone native." At West Point in the last twenty-five years the number of foreign languages required for graduation has steadily diminished even though the army is faced with a wider and wider diversity of foreign adversaries.

- *The China Hands.* A 20th Century example of the fate in store for "area experts" in the US government was the treatment given the "China Hands," the Foreign Service and Army China specialists who reported with deep insight on the likely outcome of the Kuomintang – Communist civil war after World War II. They correctly reported that the Communists under Mao Tse Tung were widely popular and capable within a specifically Chinese context. They predicted that the Communists would win the war. They were right and for their insight they were called communist sympathizers and driven from public life.

- *The Green Berets.* In Vietnam the men of the army's Green Berets were carefully picked for their ability to learn languages and the psychological elasticity needed to adapt to truly alien (in many cases Stone Age) tribesmen and villagers and to lead them in battle. They succeeded in that task only to find that the Big Army (the murder army, as TE Lawrence would have called it) disliked them and their "native ways" and sought continuously to denigrate them and to "trap" them in some violation of the trivia of military law.

    (This attitude penetrates even to the arts in American society. In Francis Coppola's rendering of the Joseph Conrad story "The Heart of Darkness," the tale is set in the central highlands of Vietnam where Colonel Kurtz, an officer described as an intellectual Green Beret with a doctorate from one of the "Ivies," is literally driven mad through exposure to the culture of the Montagnard peoples among whom he lives. His men are driven mad as well, apparently because as "carriers" of the alien culture they are its victims as well as potential agents of infection. To solve this "problem" the army sends yet another Green Beret, this one an intelligence man as well, to kill Kurtz and eradicate the alien cultural infection. The director's cut of "Apocalypse Now" has to be seen to grasp the full import of all this.)

- *And now, Iraq.* In the "run-up" to the 2003 invasion of Iraq, the Bush Administration studiously avoided asking the opinion of the substantial body of men and women who had a deep knowledge of

Iraq, preferring instead to rely on the advice of activists and émigrés who had "agendas" for some particular outcome in Iraq. When asked why the "Old Iraq Hands" were not consulted the response was always the same, "They have gone native." "Going Native" is clearly a very bad thing to most Americans. In Afghanistan from 2003 to the present, senior officers were outraged by the wear of local clothing and the growth of beards by Green Berets even though this minor adaptation to the local scene had paid "big dividends" in working with the tribes.

In America we have been pushed to believe in a melting pot of common thinking. This belief system has been fed to us in the public schools, through Hollywood, and now in the endless prattle of 24-hour news networks. It has become secular religion, a religion so strong that any violation of its tenets brings instant and savage condemnation. So called "neo-conservatism" is merely a self-aware manifestation of the widespread American belief that people are all the same. The repeated assertion by President George W. Bush that history is dominated by the existence of "universal values" is proof in the pudding.

Americans invaded an imaginary Iraq that fit into our vision of the world. We invaded Iraq in the sure belief that inside every Iraqi there was an American trying to get out. In our dream version of Iraq, we would be greeted not only as liberators from the tyrant, but more importantly, from the old ways. Having inhabited the same state for 80 years, the Iraqi people would naturally see themselves as a unified Iraqi nation, moving forward into eventual total assimilation into the unified human nation.

Unfortunately for us and for them, that was not the real Iraq. In the real Iraq, cultural distinction from the West is still treasured, a manifestation of participation in the Islamic cultural "continent." Tribe, sect, and community remain far more important than individual rights. One does not vote for candidates outside one's community unless Baathist, Nasserist, or Communist. But Iraqis know what Americans want to hear about "identity," and be they Shia, Kurd or Sunni Arab, they tell us that they are all Iraqis together.

Finding ourselves in the wrong Iraq, Americans have stubbornly insisted that the real Iraqis should behave as our dream Iraqis would surely do. The result has been disappointment and rage against the "craziness" of the Iraqis. We are still acting out our dream, insisting that Prime Minister Nuri al-Maliki's Shiite sectarian government "unify" the state, imagining that Maliki is a sort of Iraqi George Washington seeking the greater good of all. He is not that. His chief task is to consolidate Shiite Arab power while using the United States to accomplish the deed. To that end, he will tell us whatever we want to be told. He will sacrifice however many of his brethren are necessary to maintain the illusion, so long as the loss is not crippling to his effort. He will treat us as the naifs that we are.

Through our refusal to deal with alien peoples on their own terms, and within their own traditions, we have killed any real hope of a positive outcome in Iraq.

What are the features of the ideological and attitudinal "blinders" that we wear when looking at foreigners and which cause us to ignore the actual differences in alien peoples? I think that they are:

- A belief in the inevitability of social progress.
- A belief that the future of mankind lies in political forms similar to ours.
- A belief that a single world culture is emerging.
- A conviction that 'economic determinism" is the measure of humanity.
- A belief that the "melting pot" phenomenon is universal.
- A relentlessly negative attitude towards religion among our "elites."
- A belief in "American Exceptionalism" as leader of the "progress" of humanity that allows us to do whatever we think right.

Table of Contents

The book will be structured in the following way:

Introduction – A discussion of the varying aspects of human cultural and social patterns among the peoples of the world and the effect that cultural blindness in the history of Europe and Japan has had in making war and suffering a common feature of life in many places, especially in the developing world. This section will provide examples of ways in which this disability has contributed to policy errors which have had a disastrous effect. The notion will be introduced here that the United States is in no way exempt from this phenomenon and may, in some ways be especially susceptible to it because of the unusual origins and development of its own dominant culture (that of New England and the Middle West).

Chapter 1 -- *Origins*. This chapter will develop the historical and philosophical "roots" of the American cultural features described in Chapter 3; The Puritan founding of New England with its Utopian view of the New World as the location of the "New Jerusalem," thought to be a perfected form of human society, the commercial culture of modern America focused on materialism to the exclusion of non-material values, isolation behind two oceans as a factor in the insularity of American thinking, a pronounced tendency to disregard "history" as a source of significant knowledge, an indifference to the study of foreign languages as the repository of other people's group identity, a national preference for the study of what might be called "practical" subjects like the hard sciences, engineering, accounting and the like rather than subjects like the humanities, area studies, and languages.

Chapter 2 – The "mind set" that leads to Cultural Blindness in America will each be discussed in detail. They have been enumerated previously above but to remind, here they are again:

- A belief in the inevitability of social progress.
- A belief that the future of mankind lies in political forms like ours.
- A belief that a single world culture is emerging.
- A conviction that 'economic determinism" is the measure of humanity.
- A belief that the "melting pot" phenomenon is universal.
- A relentlessly negative attitude towards religion among our "elites."

A belief in "American Exceptionalism" as leader of the "progress" of humanity that allows us to do whatever we think right.

Chapter 3 --The evidence of "blindness" to the culture of others will be explored throughout American history. The record of our dealing with the Amerindian nations will be described in the context of incomprehension of the vitality and legitimacy of Indian life. Beginning with the first "Indian war" in New England in 1665, through the "Ghost Dance" war against the Sioux in the 1890s, and the insistence on transforming the Indian into pseudo-Caucasians in places like the Carlisle Indian School will be explored. (Pictures of Indians in European clothes at Carlisle, etc will be included.) The Civil War is another example of cultural misapprehension between regions of the country that persists to this day. American "adventures" in many places in Latin America often resulted in the eventual rise to power of dictators like Duvalier in Haiti and Somosa in Nicaragua. American intervention in the Mexican Revolution exacerbated the struggle among the factions and eventually led to Villa's raid into New Mexico and the subsequent Punitive Expedition in 1916-17. (Author's father served in that campaign) American misjudgments about the nature and motivations of the various "players" in Mexico contributed to the long struggle there. This analysis will be brought forward to the recent past through the use of Vietnam as a prime example of our inability to understand local conditions on the basis of local realities and local custom.

Chapter 4 – The Iraq "Horror story." The complex story of the total misperception of the nature of Iraqi society or perhaps "societies" might be a better word. The US decision to invade and occupy Iraq with the intention of creating a new society in a country liberated from outmoded ways was based on a belief that Iraq was a country inhabited by a unified people who thought of themselves as "Iraqi" before all else and who were essentially secular and "modern" in their thinking. The notion that the Iraqis were quite different and would react to Western and foreign occupation by struggling with each other for power on the basis of their ancient allegiances and group identities was resolutely rejected in policy circles in Washington and derided as "racist." The idea that the Iraqi peoples would not want to be "Americanized" was said to imply an incapacity for democracy. The chapter will describe the present wars in Iraq.

Chapter 5- This chapter will survey the areas of the world likely to become disputed territories and in which the ability or inability of the United States to act effectively and without causing further "wreckage" of countries or regions inhabited by people we do not understand. The Islamic World, Africa, Latin America, and the more "exotic" parts of Eastern Europe are all worthy of description with regard to their underlying social and interpersonal values and the ways in which these societies can easily be misunderstood.

Chapter 6 – How can the United States improve its ability to cope with the outside world with instruments more refined than aircraft carrier battle groups? A basic change of attitude is needed, a resolve to learn about other peoples and to take them and their ways seriously. The study of foreign cultures, their history and values should be more firmly encouraged by the government and armed forces of the United States. In particular the armed forces and intelligence services of the United States should begin to advocate and encourage by promotion to positions of influence those who display the ability to comprehend and deal successfully with foreigners. At present such people are either ignored by the agencies of the U.S. government or are relegated to lowly positions as staff assistants to bureaucratic managers. A failure to take up the cause of cultural awareness in the United States will simply continue to lead us to our next disaster, wherever that may be.

Lessons from Vietnam in How to Flip an Enemy
(Christian Science Monitor July 7, 2006)

Long ago and across the world in Vietnam, I had the job of persuading enemy soldiers to leave their government to join "our side" in the long struggle there against revolutionary socialism. Some of my experiences could be replicated in places such as Iraq and Afghanistan, although the recent news makes me wonder if it's still possible to bring people over to our side.

The names we hear daily in the news – "Haditha," and "Hamandiya" among several others – represent serious investigations into atrocities allegedly committed by American troops. It's impossible to say now what the outcome of these investigations will be. Many of the allegations involve the treatment of Iraqi and Afghan civilians. Some include people who were clearly combatants on the other side in the war.

The responsibility of our soldiers – or anyone's soldiers – to safeguard non-combatants is crystal clear in our law and in international law. The problem of how to deal with enemy fighters is another and more complicated issue.

At the commencement of this war on terror the Bush administration decided that enemy fighters would not be considered "prisoners of war," although they would be afforded comparable protections. This judgment, in my view, has made possible the questionable internment and interrogation facility at Guantánamo, "rendition" of prisoners to countries that are known to torture prisoners, such as Egypt, and a general lowering of standards in the treatment of prisoners in places such as the Abu Ghraib prison complex. From personal experience as a military intelligence officer who dealt with prisoners of war in Vietnam, I can tell you that the rules were quite different.

In Vietnam, enemy prisoners of war were treated in accordance with the Geneva Conventions and were given the POW designation. Many people have seen photographs of American or South Vietnamese soldiers with prisoners from the other side, the Viet Cong and North Vietnamese Army. Although there were undoubtedly instances in which individual Americans abused prisoners, I would defy anyone to provide photographic evidence of such abuse in a facility for the detention of enemy prisoners of war in Vietnam.

The enemies captured in Vietnam were held by US or South Vietnamese military police (MPs), interrogated by US Army or South Vietnamese military intelligence, and then sent to prisoner-of-war camps that were run by the South Vietnamese Army under the tutelage of American MP advisers.

Some exceptions applied. Underground political cadres (communist politicians secretly running a shadow government), for example, were not considered to be prisoners of war because they were neither soldiers nor organized guerillas and thus were not protected by the Fourth Geneva Convention on the treatment of prisoners of war. They were treated as criminals and traitors to the South Vietnamese state.

Enemy intelligence personnel apprehended in civilian clothes were subject to the sanction traditionally reserved for spies. There's the famous picture of South Vietnam's chief of police, for example, shooting a captured North Vietnamese intelligence officer in the street during the 1968 Tet offensive. The South Vietnamese general thought he was acting within his legal rights.

Nevertheless, the great majority of captured enemies, and by that I mean soldiers and guerrillas captured on the battlefield, went to prisoner-of-war camps.

These camps were located throughout the country. They housed thousands of enemy soldiers until the end of the war under conditions that met the standards of the International Committee of the Red Cross, the organization charged with monitoring adherence to the Geneva Conventions.

Part of my job that year was proselytizing in these camps, trolling for those who might want to change sides. I visited a number of these camps in 1972 and did not see anything very objectionable about them. When the war finally ended, these imprisoned soldiers were returned to their own side.

But as in any war, soldiers who are not so firmly anchored to one side can be persuaded to "come over." Often these men are among the most intelligent and experienced, who have come to see war itself as a cynical game played by the powerful at the soldiers' expense.

Hundreds of prisoners decided to change sides during the Vietnam War and join with US or South Vietnamese forces. One of the most useful projects that the "turncoats" served in were the "Kit Carson Scouts." These former enemy soldiers wore our uniforms, bore arms as part of our combat forces, and accompanied our own soldiers in the field. Their knowledge of the enemy's methods and habits proved invaluable. After demonstrating their loyalty to the American forces during the war, many of them came to live in the US.

I talked with a lot of prisoners that year. But one stands out. I was "scouting" in the POW camps for someone suitable for a special project that my unit was "running." We needed an enemy officer – an expert resource – to advise our intelligence analysts. We were notified that there was someone in a facility near Saigon who might be interested. I drove out there to see a North Vietnamese lieutenant.

We spent the day in a whitewashed room, smoking Gitanes (French cigarettes), drinking tea, and chatting. The lieutenant had been a rifle company commander in the 325th NVA Division. He spoke excellent French and had graduated from a good school in the North.

Like me, he had served a previous tour of duty in South Vietnam. He was an Olympic competitor in marksmanship and had been sent to the Olympic Games in Europe after his first combat tour. When he returned home, he was upgraded from a sergeant to an officer and sent back to South Vietnam with the 325th – an outfit akin to the 82nd Airborne Division in our forces. During our chat, we discovered that we had actually fought each other a couple of times in the Central Highlands of South Vietnam in days gone by. This was a kind of bond.

At the end of the day, he said that he wanted to get out of "this place," and that he had no one to go home to in the North. He asked if I thought he could live in California "afterward." He left the camp with me to work with our forces against his former comrades. I hope he made it to the Golden State.

None of this sounds like Iraq. We don't seem to really grasp the variety of our enemies in Iraq. We don't seem to know how to take advantage of that. I hope I am wrong.

- *Patrick Lang is former head of human intelligence collection and Middle East intelligence at the Defense Intelligence Agency.*

Untitled and Undated Memorandum

Until the 9/11 attacks on the United States and the subsequent passage by the US Congress of the "Authorizations for the Use of Military Force" and the Intelligence Reform act of 2004, there had long been a settled order in the internal work and authorities if the US Intelligence Community. Since the creation of the Department of Homeland Security there have been 17 member agencies of the US Intelligence Community.

When there were 16 agencies in the IC, the CIA was very much the master of the situation. American government is funded on the basis of "programs." These "programs" group functions, money and personnel authorizations in aggregates that are both general and specific in that they assign areas of work and allocate specific amounts of money and therefore of people for those tasks.

Before 2004, the head of CIA had "two hats" as we say in America. He was both Director of the CIA as an agency and he was also by authority of the National Defense Acts of 1947 and 1958 the more than titular head of the IC as "Director of Central Intelligence." In this latter capacity the CIA chief controlled almost all the "programs money and personnel spaces for the IC agencies. The specific program controlled by the DCI/CIA Director was called the "General Intelligence Program." From this "pot" of money came all the funds that wet to State Intelligence and Research (INR) the many other agencies and most importantly from the CIA's point of view, the Defense Intelligence Agency. DIA was and is considered by CIA to be the most significant of its rivals in the US government. Control of DIA's funds was a mighty weapon in the struggle to be the pre-eminent US full function intelligence agency. The DCI/CIA never achieved control of US SIGINT in spite of many attempts. The main obstacle to this control was the existence of a completely separate program for Signals Intelligence that was loosely controlled by the Secretary of Defense. There was also a program for Reconnaissance, but the DCI/CIA achieved effective control over that program until 2004 and the community reforms.

Tactical intelligence at the field army, numbered air force and fleet level was not funded in the National Programs system. These activities were funded in the individual armed services programs and budgets and were beyond the reach of the DCI/CIA nexus.

In addition to the control created by DCI/CIA control of the General

Intelligence Program, the DCI/CIA had control of certain supposedly shared community functions of great importance. Among them:

- The National Intelligence Council (NIC). This is a panel of senior analysts who write national estimative papers (NIE) that are then voted on by the heads of the IC agencies and which become the "ground truths" of the US government and are cited as the basis of national policy decisions. Control of this body enabled the DCI/CIA power complex to appoint drafters and to bend estimates to suit the taste of policy chiefs at the political level. It must be understood that CIA is a direct instrument of the presidency of the United States.
- The DCI/CIA had the authority to "coordinate" on the clandestine intelligence operational plans of the other agencies. This effectively enabled CIA to disapprove plans by inaction on requests for "coordination." "Miraculously," many of these disapproved plans were later executed by – wait for the punch line – CIA.
- The DCI/CIA had control of the "Interagency Source Register." All agencies controlling clandestine HUMINT assets were required to submit applications to this register for more "coordination." Not surprisingly, CIA frequently "discovered" that it, as an agency, had a prior "interest" in the individual. This blocked use of the individual by the agency that had submitted the rquest, and, guess what – the source often as later used by CIA.

The Spooks versus the Hawks

(2004)

We won the war. We won the war easily. Saddam Hussein was a fascist monster, and it is a good thing that his government is gone. The American people are overwhelmingly contented with the decision to go to war in Iraq and happy that the outcome was both swiftly achieved and gloriously done by our armed forces. The authors share that feeling. Thank God that the "Butcher's Bill" was no higher than it was!

Nevertheless, there are certain nagging questions surfacing in Washington about the way in which the decision was made to go to war. These questions have arisen because we (and the British) were persuaded by our governments that there was an "imminent" danger to our people and our countries from the possession by Iraq of chemical and biological weapons in sufficient quantities and kinds to be a direct threat to us at home. There was also an argument made that the government of Iraq was a closely integrated part of the world-wide network of terrorist groups who had shown us how much they were our enemies on 9/11. If Iraq had WMD weapons and was an ally of the terrorists, did it not follow logically that Iraq would give these weapons to the terrorists to use against us? This was the essence of the argument that was made for war against Saddam's regime. Nearly all of us accepted that argument.

Now, we are in control of Iraq and thus far no evidence has been found that Iraq actually had these weapons in the period just before the recent war. It was well established by the UN inspectors in 1991-1998 that the Iraqis had possessed such weapons at the time of the First Gulf War. But, did they have them in the last year? US Army and Marine Corps teams have searched Iraq by going to the places where it was thought most likely that WMD weapons would be found. So far they have found nothing but several canvas sided trailers that were located in the north of the country. These vehicles look like they were designed to produce pathogens for biological weapons but there is no evidence that they were ever actually used to produce anything. They have been tested thoroughly and there are no traces of any such process in them. To press the search farther throughout the country a 1400 member team is being sent from the US to try to assemble a complete picture of these programs through massive interviews with Iraqis and examination of the tons of documents that we captured from the Iraqi government.

Is this important? Yes! It is important for two reasons:

First because Tony Blair's government is threatened by a lack of proof that the claims that were made about the presence of WMD weapons in Iraq were true. The British Labor Party, and indeed the British public were unwilling to go to war in Iraq until they were convinced by the government's arguments that Iraqi WMD threatened them. Now, Blair is accused of falsifying the evidence in order to follow America's lead. There is going to be an investigation in Parliament. His government could fall.

Second, the credibility of the Bush administration and of American Intelligence is at stake. It is increasingly apparent that long established and prudent procedures for "vetting" the reliability and veracity of sources of information and the data itself were ignored in reaching the conclusions that were "sold" to the Congress and the Citizens of the United States concerning Iraq's activities and weapons holdings. It now seems that some policy staff people abrogated to themselves the task of independently evaluating and analyzing the data provided them by the Intelligence Agencies to reach their own conclusions about such questions as the presence or absence of WMD in Iraq, the connection of Iraq to Al-Qa'ida, the enthusiasm of the Iraqi people for American "liberation" and similar questions.

There seem to be very few people with any real experience of Intelligence work among those who took this task upon them. They appear to be mostly former Congressional staffers and academics. Only last week, a senior adviser of the Bush administration maintained on a national news show that "we had the right to separately evaluate the data… and we found many things that the Intelligence agencies had missed." Few professionals in the Intelligence World would dispute that right. Traditionally it has been the function of Intelligence to DESCRIBE EXISTING REALITY and the function of policy makers to CREATE A NEW REALITY. When the policy makers take it upon themselves to do both they become judge, jury and executioner and an important Red Line has been crossed. Between these functions there is an essential tension that should continue to exist if sound decisions are to be made.

Were we deceived? Was George W. Bush deceived? Was Tony Blair deceived? Probably not deliberately, but we will not know the ultimate truth until the inspection of Iraq is ended.

Webb's Dog-Tags

(October 20, 2006)

Jim Webb doesn't want his friends to talk about his combat record. He thinks it is unseemly to trade on one's service to country for political gain. It is like him to use that word. He is an old-fashioned patriot and warrior. For the same reason, he never talks about George Allan. It would be unseemly. Politics in the United States has degenerated mightily during my lifetime. We used to have leaders like Harry Truman who really did believe that the "buck" stopped with him. Senior military leadership is not what it once was. We once had leaders like George C. Marshall, who, without complaint of any kind, accepted FDR's appeal that he stay in Washington and allow Eisenhower to command the Normandy invasion. Marshall knew that FDR was effectively denying him future national leadership. He never said a word about it. He maintained a principled silence until his death.

Since Jim Webb won't talk about what he did in Vietnam when the "chips were down," I will. Here is the substance of the citation that describes why he was awarded the Navy Cross in Vietnam.

"...deep in hostile territory, First Lieutenant Webb's platoon discovered a well-camouflaged bunker complex…. First Lieutenant Webb was advancing to the first bunker when three enemy soldiers armed with hand grenades jumped out. Reacting instantly, he grabbed the closest man and, brandishing his .45 caliber pistol at the others, apprehended all three of the soldiers. … He then approached the second bunker and called for the enemy to surrender …. Continuing the assault, he approached a third bunker and was preparing to fire into it when the enemy threw another grenade. Observing the grenade land dangerously close to his companion, First Lieutenant Webb simultaneously fired his weapon at the enemy, pushed the Marine away from the grenade, and shielded him from the explosion with his own body. Although sustaining painful fragmentation wounds from the explosion, he managed to throw a grenade into the aperture and completely destroy the remaining bunker." It is unseemly to talk about this? The Navy Cross is the country's second highest medal for battlefield courage.

Think about this. This very young man led his forty-five marines into a fortified enemy position. Three enemy soldiers suddenly appeared. He personally captured the three of them. Then, he moved to a second bunker and in spite of what has just happened, called on them to surrender. The risk in this was appalling. Not many of us would have taken the chance of waiting to see what these new enemies would do. I would not have. In attacking a third bunker, Webb used his own body to shield one of his men from the blast of an enemy grenade. I am surprised that he did not receive the Medal of Honor.

Unseemly to talk about this? Think about the complete lack of focus on self that these actions exemplify. Do we not need leaders like this?

My God. I pray that we will always have leaders like this who can unflinchingly do their duty, and then, a generation later persist in principled silence and self-sacrifice in the way that Jim insists must be.

Senator Allen is reported to treasure the "dog tags" of a constituent, a man who was killed in Iraq. The man's mother gave Allen the identity tags. Soldiers everywhere will appreciate Allen's sentiment in this matter, but it should be kept clearly in mind that Jim Webb has his own "dog-tags."

Webb's "dog-tags" were not given to him. He paid for them in blood.

PART II

Studies in Islam

This section features a series of essays and lectures by the author on the history and internal dynamics within Islam. They are based on both his academic studies (Col. Lang and his wife founded the Arab language and Arabic Studies program at West Point) and his years of interaction as Military Attaché and advisor to several Middle East countries and as Defense Intelligence Officer for the Middle East and North Africa.

Twelver Shiism and Political Power
(November 2, 2005)

In a number of different settings, I have recently heard the opinion voiced that Ithna'ashari (Twelver) Shia 'Ulema (scholars) have traditionally chosen to hold themselves apart from political power in whatever state they have inhabited and that they believe in something akin to the Western notion of a proper separation of church and state. Usually, the same speaker or writer will accompany this with a description of the late Ayatollah Khomeini as a "heretic" for holding a different view of this matter. I find these positions to be inadequate in both statements for two broad reasons:

Historically, Shiism began as a movement of the underdog in Iraq in the first century of the Islamic era. The Arabians who defeated the Sassanian Persians at the Battle of Qadisiyah under the Bedouin general Muthanna believed that the spoils of empire were rightly theirs. In Iraq they established garrison towns like Kufah and settled down there amid a captive Mesopotamian population to enjoy the fruits of victory. To divide the "loot" they devised a list of the "entitled" called the "Diwan." One's placement on this list determined how large an annual subvention one received. The higher you were on the list, the bigger the share. This position was determined by a number of factors. Most important of these were the date of your acceptance of Islam (the earlier the better) and secondly the level of your prominence in Meccan, Medinan or other Arabian society. In conformity to one's position, a regular payment was received from the treasury (beit al-mal) of the community.

Over time more and more of the conquered population were converted to Islam, accepting in the process the many intangible benefits brought by being a member of the Islamic community. Unfortunately for them, this did not generally include inscription in the "Diwan" or the payments from the public purse that went with this. As a result, the converted, "mawali" in Arabic felt cheated of what they thought to be their rightful share of the money. This led to great bitterness among the "mawali" against the Arabians and especially against the "Ummayad" Arabian dynasty of Caliphs soon established in Damascus. This bitterness led to adoption by the Mawali of the cause of the rights of the family of the Prophet whom they believed had been wrongly deprived of the succession to the leadership of the Islamic politico-religious community, the "Umma."

In the early period the family of the Prophet was represented by the

Caliph Ali who the Shia incorrectly believe was murdered in Najaf by agents of the Damascus (Sunni) crowd, then by the subjugation of Hassan, Ali's son and the Prophet's grandson. The "grand finale" for the Mawali (who were also known as "Shiat Ali – "The party (Shiat) of Ali") was the battlefield death of Hussein, Hassan's younger brother at Karbala at the hands of the Sunni general 'Umar ibn Sa'd (of malodorous memory). Following Hussein's death, the "Shiat Ali" (Party of Ali) were beaten into submission by the Arabian Sunni 'Ummayad Caliphs ruling from Damascus and remained a more or less permanent underclass in the 'Umma until the 16th Century C.E. Sunni Caliphs came and went, first the 'Ummayads, then the Abbasids ruling from Baghdad. Throughout this period, the Shia 'Ulema were deprived of political power, not because they preferred to be without political power, but because they were not able to seize it.

Islam in its pure form envisions a world theocratic state in which all aspects of life are integrated into a whole, a "seamless garment." These Shia of the Middle Ages (al-Qurun al-Wusta) were people living as best they could in the direction of this ideal. In this period there lived nine more leaders of the Shia community whom they considered to be "divinely selected." They were descendants of the Prophet and thought to be vessels of special grace from God. The Shia would have liked nothing better than to install these "Imams" as they called them in supreme political power, but they lacked the means. The Sunni 'Ummayad, and Abbasid Caliphs stood in the way as did a variety of Sunni Turkish Sultans who often wielded the real power behind the Caliphs. Faced with this situation, the Shia retreated into development of their religious sciences within the "Ghettos" of Najaf and Karbala and accepted the status quo with what grace they could muster.

There were a couple of episodes in the Middle Ages that were exceptions to this "rule." One involved the existence in Egypt for a time of a "Caliphate" set up as a rival to the Sunni Abbasid Caliphate in Baghdad. The rulers of this "schismatic" group were Shia of the "Sevener" variety. This is a kind of Shiism which reveres in a special way the seventh of the "divinely appointed" Shia Imams. This dynasty ruled for around two hundred years and roughly co-existed in time with the Crusader Kingdom of Jerusalem with which it often made common cause against other Muslim powers. This dynasty was eventually destroyed by the great Sunni Kurdish Sultan Saladin (Yusuf Salah al-Din al-Ayyoubi). The second major "exception" was the period of power of the "Buyid" or "Buwayhid" dynasty of Turkish strongmen in the Abbasid Caliphate. These people were originally nomads from Central

Asia who invaded what are now Iraq and Iran and who reduced the Sunni Caliphs in Baghdad to the status of "puppets." The "Buyids" were Shia and for a time they threatened to make Shiism the dominant form of Islam. The Abbasid Caliph al-Ma'mun was "persuaded" by the "Buyid" warlord of his time to designate the Shia Imam of that time as his successor as Caliph but unfortunately for Shia aspirations the Imam died before al-Ma'mun and history moved on.

The next major political opportunity for the Twelver Shia "clergy" came at the beginning of the 16th Century C.E. in Persia, now Iran. At that time a dynasty arose of local power that aspired to separate Persia from the larger world of Ottoman Turkish dominated Islam under their own regional rule. These were the Safavids. Because Islam claims universal authority and seeks a universal state under God's law, it is always necessary for Islamic rebels to declare the Islamic "purity" of their cause and the defects of their overlords' "submission" in Islam. Without such a claim to "authentic" Islam they would be thought (even by themselves) not to be true Muslims. With such a claim, rebellion can be seen not to be rebellion, but instead to be a "restoration" of true religion. With this in mind, the Safavids decided that all Persians living in their domain should become Shia and therefore not subject to the decrees of the "heretical" and schismatic Ottoman Sultan in Istanbul. Within a remarkably short time very nearly the entire population of Iran became Twelver Shia and so they have remained ever since.

One might think that this would have been a fine chance for the Shia "clergy" to take power in Iran to assure that God's law should be properly applied, but, alas, this was not to be. The Safavid Shahs found Shiism to be a useful political tool, but they had no intention of sharing power with an "other worldly" collection of religious scholars and judges and made sure that such people were adequately "compensated" but had no real power at all except in whatever matters of personal status came before the Sharia courts. Faced with the brute power of the state the Shia "clergy" once again retreated into their contemplation and codification of such matters as Koranic exegesis. Once again, it was not a question of the "clergy" abjuring worldly power. No, it was a surety that the Safavids, and their successors the Qajars and Pahlavis denied any such power to them.

In what is now Iraq, Ottoman Sunni power prevailed until the end of the First World War when British forces occupied that part of the Ottoman Empire and eventually made it into the modern state. In the course of that transformation the British made a deliberate decision to create a country that would not give power to the Shia "clergy," but instead would install a Sunni Arab dominated government headed by an Arabian prince of Sharifian descent. This decision enraged the Shia 'Ulema and within a few months they led a rebellion against British rule which shook the empire. Their resistance to the very concept of continuing secularist and Sunni power never ended throughout the era of Hashemite royal government and then successive "lay" nationalist, communist and Baathist regimes. Their present restiveness should not surprise anyone familiar with their history.

Thus, the matter lay until the late Shah in Shah Riza Pahlavi weakened by illness and American pressure to "reform" was forced from office by a revolution inspired if not led by the late Ayatollah Ruhollah Khomeini. The form of clerical government that he created endures in Iran to the time of this writing.

To sum up the historical record with regard to the political ambition of the Twelver Shia 'Ulema, they never had governmental power until the establishment of the Iranian Islamic republic because they were never able to seize it. If they are confronted with a vacuum of secular power in Iraq today, there is no reason from history to believe that they will not want it.

Khomeini as "heretic."

Sunni Islam is all about Law. This is the majority form of the religion (85% of all Muslims) and it holds that the "Roots of the Law" ('usul fiqh) are essentially four in number: Quran, Hadith (the traditions of the practice of the Prophet and the early Islamic community, Qiyas (analogy from existing case law), and Ijma' (consensus among reputable scholars of the religious sciences).

There is some dissent about this last "root" since Hanbali and Wahhabi Sunni Muslims would limit the right to form consensus to those who actually knew the Prophet in his lifetime. This necessarily limits Hanbali and Wahhabi contemporary interpretations of the law. There is, or was, a fifth "root" which is no longer readily available to Sunni Muslims. This was called "Ijtihad" (This means a scholar's effort to reach an original opinion on some point of law based on the other "roots of the law"). A scholar who could do that would be called in Arabic a "Mujtahid." There are no such persons in the world of Sunni Islam today because Sunni Muslims hold that the religious sciences were so perfected in the first centuries of the Islamic era that for a person to be capable of Ijtihad today that person would have to possess perfect mastery of those sciences. As a practical matter, this means that marked change is very difficult in Sunni Islam and occurs only in a slow and evolutionary way. In expression of this phenomenon, Sunni Muslims say that the Gate of Ijtihad" is closed, perhaps forever. This conviction is so firmly held that "innovation" (Bida' in Arabic) is said to be equivalent to heresy.

This question of "Ijtihad" is one of the major ways in which Shiism (especially the majority Shia Twelver Usuli faction in Iraq and Iran) differ from the Sunnis. These Shia judge that not only is the "Gate of Ijtihad" still open but that the function of the Mujtahid is essential to the continuing relevance and development of the Islamic faith in the modern world. As a result, Twelver Shia Islam possesses an elaborate system of education and virtual certification of religious scholars with the goal of producing senior "clerics" who are "qualified" and recognized Mujtahids. The most senior of these Mujtahids bear the title of "Ayatollah," ("Sign of God" in Arabic). Each of these Ayatollahs is considered to be a "reference point for emulation," (marja' at-taqlid in Arabic) and every pious Shia Muslim is required to follow the practice and teaching of one such although the opinion of an Ayatollah does not have authority after his death unless endorsed by a living Mujtahid of sufficient stature.

Since neither major form of Islam (Sunni or Twelver Shia) have any concept or theory of hierarchy among "clerics" each scholar is free to have whatever opinion he finds worthy concerning points of law and governance of the Islamic community.

In Sunni Islam this freedom is limited by the closure of the "Gate of Ijtihad." Radically new opinions are not accepted in Sunni Islam by the Ijma' (consensus) of leading scholars because Ijtihad is no longer a real possibility and so they can readily be held to be incorrect or simply outside Islam. This would be a virtual definition of heresy.

In Twelver Shiism with its living tradition of Ijtihad the situation is radically different. "Certified" Mujtahids, especially Ayatollahs are free within Islam to theorize on legal, social and religious matters as much as they want. Their peers may not agree with their judgments and that is a serious matter. The individual Mujtahid may hold minority views, but it is a mistake to say that because his views are not universally endorsed by the consensus of his fellow Mujtahids he is so far in error as to place him outside Islam or in Western theological terms, in heresy.

This is precisely the case with the late Ayatollah Ruhollah Khomeini. He was a Philosopher (Kalam in Arabic) by specialization. This was his field of study not Jurisprudence as many have supposed. In the course of his long life, he developed many interesting and innovative doctrines for the development of Islam. The most famous of these is his concept of the "Rule of the Religious Scholar" (wilayet al-faqih in Arabic). According to this teaching of his, the community should be ruled by the clergy. This Iranian revolution of 1979 created such a government, and it endures to this time.

A good many of Khomeini's peers and fellow Mujtahids did not share his belief in the correctness of this doctrine and denied him their Ijma'. This denial simply meant that they differed with him in this important matter. It did not mean that they or he were heretics. To think that this lack of total consensus of support for Khomeini's thinking placed him outside Islam reflects a basic ignorance of Usuli Twelver Shia belief.

Varieties of Islamic Faith
(December 14, 2016)

Who are Muslims? What do they believe? Are their ideas and traditions so alien there cannot be reconciliation between them and Christianity? Are they united in their beliefs and attitudes? Are they uniformly and permanently hostile to the West? In the last five years, these have become important questions for us all. Once, the nature and theology of Islam were the concern of Orientalist scholars, but no more.

Roots. Islam appeared suddenly in the seventh century after the birth of Christ, emerging in a world long ravaged by war between the Christian Byzantine and the Zoroastrian Sassanian Persian empires. These two great powers had fought to a state of mutual exhaustion and were incapable of resisting armies of desert Arabs, who, driven by drought, overpopulation and faith in a new revelation brought to them by Muhammad — a merchant of the city of Mecca — swept north, east and west from the Arabian Peninsula.

According to Islamic teaching, the angel Gabriel facilitated Muhammad's reception of maxims, which when compiled constituted the final revelation from God to a sinful world. This was the Quran, the central Islamic scripture.

For Muslims, Muhammad is the last in a long series of prophets that includes the prophets of the Old Testament and Jesus of Nazareth, whom Muslims revere as a messenger of God.

The new faith was sternly monotheistic, admitting the legitimacy of

Judaism and Christianity, but holding that the Jewish tradition had been superseded by the "descent" of the Quran while Christians had misunderstood the New Testament, distorting it in such a way that they believed Jesus was one element of a triune God. Muslim intensity on this issue led many of the Church Fathers, who encountered Muslims in Syria and Egypt, to believe Islam was not a new religion, but a Christian heresy, specifically the "Arian" heresy. This was the view of St. John of Damascus, who lived at the court of the Umayyad caliphs.

Religious sciences. Exposure to the intellectual culture of the Hellenistic world and Zoroastrian Persia soon provided philosophical structure and theological support to the new faith. During the first centuries of Islamic presence in the Near East, the religion existed in a great state of flux, driven in various directions by the influence of Greek rationalism and Persian mysticism.

In this period, it appeared for a short time that mainstream Islam would be dominated by scholars — the Mu'taziliin — who sought to wed rationalism to Islamic revelation in such a way as to make the faith an endlessly adaptive "living" system. In much the same period, the mysticism that calls itself "Sufi" ("wooly" in Arabic in honor of the "habits" of its adepts) developed to fulfill the human need for personal experience of the infinite.

Both these experiments ended in tragedy for their proponents. The power of the majority traditionalists and scriptural literalists eventually proved too much for the Mu'taziliin, who were driven from office and honor with much bloodshed and suffering. Today, their teachings survive in a clear form only among the Zeidi Shia (also called Shiite) people of north Yemen.

The mystics met a similar fate in which torture and crucifixion often occurred. Their crime lay in believing that they personally experienced God. For the literal minded, this seemed an obvious impossibility and blasphemy: Man is insignificant and flawed while God is transcendent and perfect. Sufi mysticism continues, with a large number of devotees, but it has survived only because its adherents have accepted the concept that what they experience is not God, but rather his reflection.

Seamless garment. In its unadulterated form, the Islamic faith is essentially medieval in character. It views the world in much the same way the peoples of the West viewed life before the Renaissance, the Protestant Reformation and the Council of Trent. It envisions human existence as a "seamless garment," in which all the aspects of life are united and viewed through the prism of "submission" to the will of God. Business, family life, inheritance, personal status, politics, and war are all seen as governed by the same attitudes and laws. As a result, Muslims do not readily accept ideas that seek to separate various spheres of human activity.

The separation of church and state, for example, is not a concept readily accepted by pious Muslims, and it is often true that the zealous among them experience little remorse in the application of personal or state retribution against those seen as "impious" or "disrespectful" of God and his law. The now infamous *fatwa*, or religious edict, against the author Salman Rushdie was a good example of this as was the Danish cartoons incident last year. In both cases, death was the remedy suggested by some Islamic authorities.

A religion of law. After the initial age of development and ferment, the Islamic idea system stabilized into the forms that continue to dominate Islamic groups:

- Islam became a religion of laymen, a religion without an ordained clergy or hierarchy. Those who are often referred to as such in the West are usually religious scholars; they are scholars of the law, not clergy.
- Islam became a religion without sacraments, a religion in which family and life cycle events (like marriage) are governed by rulings and contracts rather than sacramental grace.
- Islam became a religion of law, a system in which the formulation of divinely sanctioned law was the primary and defining activity of the religion. Forms of Islam that moved away from this definition of the faith have sometimes been tolerated, but only that.

Due to this emphasis on law, the juridical and scholarly processes to formulate Sharia, or divine law, by any group became central to the life of the Islamic community.

Islamic law is created through the application of "tools," known in Arabic as *usul fiqh*, the roots of law. These tools, which are employed by a virtual army of religious experts, are:

- Quran *(Qur'an)*. For the great majority of Muslims, the Quran is the uncreated word of God, a document that has existed in the mind of God from all eternity in its present language. It is in some sense an aspect of the mind of God. The Quran's usages, admonitions and anathemas, indeed its very language, are sacred. With this status, it is inevitable the Quran should be a primary source for the formulation of law.

- Tradition *(hadith)*. These are canonically accepted collections of accounts of the early practice of the Islamic community and of the prophet Muhammad. Typically, a tradition consists of the story of what the community is said to have done and then a description of those who repeated this story from the time of the event until the collection was compiled. Some Islamic groups prefer one collection of *hadith* while others prefer another. The general word in Arabic for "practice" is *sunna*.

- Analogy *(qiyas)*. In the first centuries of Islam, it was thought throughout the Islamic world that individuals learned in the Quran and tradition could, through personal effort, arrive at new and unprecedented interpretations of these documents that would create new law. This root of the law was called "ijtihad."

As the system matured, however, most Muslim scholars came to believe the possibilities for fruitful original interpretation of scripture and tradition had been exhausted. Ijtihad could no longer be used to find new meaning in the raw materials of revelation.

The use of ijtihad continued within the minority Shia community as the purview of scholars certified as "mujtahids" or "ayatollahs." In the Sunni vision of Islam, however, the gate of ijtihad has been considered closed and unavailable for a thousand years. This was an awkward development; the interpretation of scripture and law in courts lay at the very heart of Islamic life. It is possible, but difficult, to find detailed guidance in specific cases within the canon of Quran and tradition, but the multiplicity of events in daily life, many of which were without precedent in the time of Muhammad, required some help in finding a satisfactory jurisprudential outcome.

Eventually, it was decided that, even if the gate of ijtihad was closed, it was still possible to reason from analogy to previous case law to find a judgment sanctioned by revelation. This feature of Islamic law formulation is called *qiyas,* or analogy. This tool of the Islamic legal scholar remains central to the process.

- Consensus *(ijma')*. Because Islam is a religion of laymen, there are no definitive sources of authority in theology *(kalam)*. Instead, groups form in response to the rulings and teachings of noted or certified scholars. These groups may be of any size or ethnicity. The group accepts the authenticity of the ideas of an individual scholar or that of a school of study and for that group the consensus surrounding the teaching of the group becomes the "real" Islam. The views of other groups are measured and judged by their similarity or deviation from the accepted consensus.

  Consensus groups can be of any size. They can be as numerous as the inhabitants of the Ottoman Empire or as few as the followers of Osama bin Laden. The present consensus among the Islamic Jihadi movement that *jihad* — the struggle for the faith — necessitates permanent armed struggle against the *kuffar*, or the unbelievers, is a good example of the way in which consensus over a key issue of law and theology can create a group identity so strong that it excludes all those Muslims who do not share this consensus and defines them as "outside Islam" and subject to the ultimate sanction of death.

The application of these tools to the formation of Islamic law, and the group identity that grows from consensus among those who believe their particular group to be the custodians of the true Islam, is central to the history and present existence of a great variety of Islamic sects and related communities, some of which are only distantly Islamic in their beliefs.

There are other factors that influence the formation of Islamic states and political groupings. Ethnicity, geography, economics, military rivalries; these are all significant. But in the context of the medieval mindset that tends to cause the Muslim to see all elements as inseparable parts of the same divinely ordained whole, the role of religious consensus is central to identity and often serves as justification for separation and hostility, where the true causes may lie elsewhere.

Without effective central authority and under the pressure of the centrifugal impetus of varying consensus, Islam has tended to evolve in the direction of ever proliferating understandings of the nature of Islam. That process continues and leads to widely differing understandings on the part of Muslims of the nature of Islam and its requirements for salvation.

Some of the groups and their origins (from a Western point of view):

Sunni. This is by far the largest sect in Islam and was the original form of the religion. About 70 percent of all Muslims are Sunni, who live in large numbers from Morocco to Indonesia, from Central Asia to the Indian Ocean.

Sunni Islam is distinguished by its conviction that the roots of law no longer include the possibility of original interpretation of scripture. There are four mutually recognized schools of Sharia within Sunni Islam: Maliki, Shafa'i, Hanafi and Hanbali. The differences among these schools of law are not thought by Muslims to amount to sectarian divisions, but to something analogous to the corpus of varying case law available to lawyers in different state jurisdictions in the United States. Sunni Muslims who accept these schools are distributed in roughly cohesive geographic areas with a good deal of overlapping.

- Adherents of the Maliki school live almost entirely in western North Africa.
- Perhaps the oldest school, the Shafa'i, is found throughout the Islamic world, but is concentrated in the Levant.
- The Hanafi school benefits from having been the imperial court faction of the Ottoman Empire. Hanafi adherents are widely distributed throughout the lands of the former empire.
- Found in Saudi Arabia and Qatar, the Hanbali school differs from the other three in that it recognizes only two roots of the law: the Quran and tradition. This refusal to accept consensus and analogy as bases for case law causes Hanbali courts and Hanbali followers to be prone to severe and inflexible opinions that lead toward the extremism often a characteristic of fundamentalist belief in any religion.

Hanbali teachings and opinion are heavily influenced by the writings of the medieval scholar, Ibn Taymiyya (died 1328), who was in large part the originator of the concept of "Salafism." This doctrine looks backward to the early figures of the Islamic community as models for behavior and practice and as a basis for the purification of the faith.

Based on this teaching, the Wahhabi movement was founded in the 18th century in what is now Saudi Arabia. Largely suppressed by Ottoman and Egyptian forces, the movement was revived in the 19th century and became the endorsed form of Islam within the Saudi state. The extremist Jihadi groups inspired by Osama bin Laden are in a direct line of descent from the Wahhabi variant of Salafist Islam as well as other Salafist extremists whose place of origin was in Egypt.

Shia. When the newly converted Muslim armies of desert Arabs conquered Mesopotamia in the seventh century, millions of Persian-speakers — in what is now southern Iraq — were brought under Arab Muslim control. Over an extended period of time, nearly all converted to Islam.

For a century, the Arabs ruled as an occupying army, excluding Persian-speaking Muslims from participation in the list (*diwan*) of those who received a share in the annual income of the Islamic community. This was thought to be unjust. When a dispute arose among the Muslims regarding the right of succession to the caliphate, the oppressed of southern Iraq predictably chose to support the descendants of Muhammad rather than their oppressors, the Umayyad dynasty of caliphs.

Since Islam embraces the idea of theocracy and the universal unity of belief, it has always been a feature of Islamic history that, an Islamic population who wishes to revolt against an Islamic government, frames its cause in religious terms to make the revolt one in which the rebels are restoring "true" Islam against sinners and deviants.

This appears to have been the case in the original Shia (also called Shiite) revolt against what is now called the Sunni majority. To this day, Shia populations are quick to think of themselves as an oppressed underclass bullied by the stronger and more numerous Sunnis.

This is often seen as reflecting Shia weakness in the larger Islamic world rather than in particular settings, like Iraq. Given the mechanisms of group formation previously discussed, it should not be surprising that the Shia populations have divided and re-divided themselves many times along "fault lines" of doctrine and ethnic advantage.

There are now many different Shia or Shia-descended groups, all of which are oriented toward the special status given to those who come directly from the family of the Prophet Muhammad from his offspring. The historical figures in that line of descent are all referred to as "Imam," as opposed to the Sunni tradition of naming their leaders "Caliph."

Various Shia groups think this line of descent ended after 5 imams (the Zeidis in Yemen), 7 imams (the Ismailis, who live mainly on the Indian subcontinent) or 12 imams (the Imami Shia in Iraq, Lebanon and Iran). In some cases they believe the last of the line has been "hidden" from the world for centuries waiting for the time of return in glory to "judge the living and the dead." There is a widely held belief in Islam (both Sunni and Shia) that a messiah (*mahdi*) will come to assure the ultimate triumph of Islam. This notion of the messiah is often conflated with that of the "Hidden (12th) Imam" in such a way that one man is expected to be both. In the Shia tradition, it is thought the messiah/Hidden Imam will return with Jesus of Nazareth and that together they will judge the world.

Sufis. For many humans, law and obedience to law is not enough solace in dealing with the daily travail of life. For many Muslims, the traditional Islamic orientation toward a man/God relationship mediated by religious lawyers has never been enough comfort. In response to this, Muslims developed forms of mysticism that remain enthusiastically supported in most parts of the Islamic world. Islamic mystics of this kind are called "Sufis," so named for the woolen "habits" worn by some of their "brothers."

Only the Hanbali/Wahhabi/Salafist tendency in Sunni Islam firmly rejects Sufi mysticism as impertinent blasphemy. For other Muslims, however, Sufism is not an alternative identity, but a special devotion added to their more conventional observances.

There are many orders, or *tariqas*, among the Sufis. Some, such as the Qaderis and the Naqshbandi, are very old. They all posses a special liturgy, or *thikr*, and form brotherhoods that are not necessarily the quiet groups sometimes described by their friends in the West. In the 19th century, Sufi brothers fought the Imperial Russian armies for decades, fought the Soviet Army in Afghanistan and continue to fight the Russian Army in Chechnya. There, as in the Balkans, they have made common cause with their Wahhabi adversaries. What the result of that will be, only time will tell.

Ibadhi. This is the prevalent form of Islam in the Sultanate of Oman. Ibadhism is probably descended from the Khariji revolt, which took place shortly after the death of the Prophet Muhammad (632). The Ibadhis do not accept that idea, but, it is, nevertheless, probably the case.

The Ibadhis are neither Sunni nor Shia and consider both to be unbelievers. They do not believe the Quran is the uncreated word of God, but believe Muhammad to have written it inspired by God. The Ibadhi refusal to accept the validity of other views of Islam is undoubtedly the result of isolation and the innate divisiveness of the consensus process of group formation in Islam.

Deobandi. This is an extreme form of Sunni orthodoxy that developed in India in response to the presence and influence of the British colonial government. Like other Salafist idea systems, Deobandis look to the older forms and documents of Islam, believing that, over the centuries, Islam has been corrupted.

The Taliban practice a simplistic form of revivalist Islam based on Deobandi teachings. The Taliban learned this form of the Islamic faith in Islamic religious schools, or *madrasah*, run on the basis of an uneasy cooperation between Deobandi teachers and Wahhabi money.

Schismatics and heretics. There are other groups that derived from Islam, but are, in their present form, of doubtful Islamic identity.

- Druze, an esoteric sect, form a minority population in Lebanon, Syria and Israel. The Druze faith originated as a variant form of Twelver Shiism, but over time, elements of Gnosticism and other influences from Greek philosophy have permeated the sect's beliefs.

  The Druze often employ the Islamic practice of dissembling, known as *takkiya*, to protect their institutions and people from curiosity and hostility. Most Muslims do not accept the Druze as fellow believers unless political necessity requires it.
- The Alawi is yet another esoteric sect derived from Shiism. In this case, the Shia "root" of the sect lies in the Fatimid dynasty in Egypt at the time of the Crusades.

  The Alawis make up about 10 percent of the population of Syria, but enjoy great power there, having been given authority by the French in the belief that a minority population would have to ally itself to the colonial administration to survive. The end of colonialism after World War II spoiled that plan but left the Alawis in a position of influence.

  The Alawis do not accept converts. They hold very un-Islamic beliefs that involve the incarnation of God in Ali, the son-in-law of the Prophet Muhammad. For these and many other reasons of heterodox belief, Alawis are not considered Muslim by Orthodox Sunnis and Shia. In spite of that, the Syrian parliament was forced to declare the Alawi as Islamic; the Syrian constitution requires that the president must be Muslim.

- Living on the fringes of Middle Eastern theological life groups such as the Yazidi and Bahai. The Yazidis are a Kurdish minority who practice an ancient religion only distantly related to Islam. The Bahai religion, although derived from the teachings of a Persian Shia divine, have wandered in the direction of accepting all belief as valid — far from the Islamic fold — that it is anathema in such places as Iran.

The very nature of the Islamic faith, with its lack of a governing religious authority and reliance on group consensus for legitimization of Islamic identity, insures that the continuing proliferation of splinter groups, large and small, is inevitable and will result in variations in doctrine and practice until the "last days."

Wahhabism and Jihad

(America Magazine, November 14, 2004)

In the weeks since the heinous attacks on the World Trade Center in New York and the Pentagon we have heard a great many people say that these crimes were committed by people who embrace a "perverted version of Islam," or by those who have "hijacked Islam." The statement is often made that Islam is a religion of gentleness and peaceful behavior and that no true Muslim would commit such acts. In the present situation it is necessary to generalize in this way. Coalitions must be built and maintained across the world, but generalizations are always defective in some way.

It is true that ordinary Muslims seek to live in peace with their neighbors and that they are enjoined in their scriptures and traditions against the very kinds of behavior that killed so many on 11 September. Suicide is forbidden in the Qur'an (Koran), as is war made upon women and children and the innocent in general. Nevertheless, the impression has been created that Islam is a pacifist religion rather like 21st century Christianity which has all but abandoned Aquinas' doctrine of "The Just War."

In fact, Islam is not a pacifist religion. It has never been a pacifist religion. The prophet Muhammad led his armies in person against the enemies of the emergent Islamic revelation. His successors (caliphs) did the same in the early days of expansion The Caliph Omar himself accepted the surrender of Jerusalem when it was captured by force of arms from the Byzantines.

Subsequent history shows clearly that Islamic states and peoples have never been strangers to the sword.

Nevertheless, it is true that the Islamic tradition contains within it a powerful tendency and admonition toward humane attitudes toward life and benevolence toward all mankind. This tendency is most clearly found in the teachings and influence of many of the Sufi (mystic) Orders to which a great many Muslims belong. An example of the kind of thinking typical of the Sufi element in Islam is this recent statement by Prince Hassan of Jordan, himself a member of the Naqshbandi Order. "Respecting the sanctity of life is the cornerstone of all great faiths. Such acts of extreme violence, in which innocent men, women and children are both the targets and the pawns, are totally unjustifiable. No religious tradition can or will tolerate such behavior and all will loudly condemn it."

If this is the thinking of a prominent Muslim, indeed a lineal descendant of the Prophet Muhammad himself, then who attacked us? We were attacked by those who hold the beliefs and way of life of the Sufis and ordinary Muslims in contempt as not really Islamic at all, by those who have always been prepared to kill if they could not persuade. We were attacked by the Wahhabis engaged as they always are in the pursuit of the central element of their belief, the Jihad, the Holy War.

Sunni Islam is a religion of laws, of legal schools and jurisprudence. God is master of the universe for Sunnis. He has made law for man to live by, for man to submit to. (Islam means submission in Arabic) There are four great schools of the religious law in Sunni Islam. All of these were founded in the Middle Ages and are named for the scholars who inspired a particular way of looking at scripture and tradition. One of these schools is named for a man named Ibn Hanbal who believed that the law should be seen in a very "boiled down," literalist way that left little room for interpretation, adaptation or modernity. This was not a very popular way of thinking about the law since the passage of time and different circumstances required adaptability.

The Hanbali school of law would probably have died out, discarded by believers as too extreme for "real life" except that in the 18th century, a scholar named Muhammad Abd al- Wahhab who lived in what is now Saudi Arabia embraced it and convinced a desert chieftain named Ibn Sa'ud to accept his version of Hanbalism as the official faith of what eventually became Saudi Arabia. This faith, popularly known as Wahhabism, rejected the right of all other Muslims to believe and practice Islam in their own ways. It particularly condemned all the different Sufi mystical brotherhoods for their attempts to experience God personally rather than through the rigid law of the Hanbali school. It continues to condemn all other Muslims. It cites the Qur'an's description of war made against unbelievers in the first centuries of Islam to justify, indeed, to require and demand, unceasing war to the death against other Muslims and especially against non-Muslims.

This is the Jihad, a moral obligation of every true Muslim, but the Wahhabi way is an insistence on an understanding of Jihad that other Muslims have long left behind them. For the great majority of "The Faithful," Jihad has long been divided into the "Greater Jihad" and the "Lesser Jihad." The lesser Jihad is the Jihad of war, death, and blood. The greater Jihad is the inner struggle of every pious Muslim to bring himself closer to God through self-denial, charity, and a moral life.

This was not, and is not, the Wahhabi way. For them, the unbeliever, and the non-Wahhabi Muslim must accept their view or suffer the consequences. The followers of this cult, generally condemned as heretics, did their best to spread their rule by force across the Arabian Peninsula until the Ottoman Turkish governor of Egypt sent his army into the area and utterly crushed them. From that time in the late 18th century until the creation of modern Saudi Arabia at the beginning of the last century Wahhabism was a little known and marginal footnote in Islamic history. The Arabian Peninsula was unified by force of arms by Abd al-Aziz al-Sa'ud, the first king of Saudi Arabia. This process was largely completed by 1925. In the new Saudi state, Wahhabism was the official faith, the only faith sanctioned by the state. This remains the case. Eventually, the constant threat of rebellion caused the state to allow the Shia people of the Eastern Province to have their own mosques, but to this day no Christian, Jewish or other religious establishment is allowed in the Kingdom.

In the early years of the existence of the Saudi state, the Jihad doctrines of Wahhabism were ruthlessly enforced by the Ikhwan (Brotherhod) Bedouin armies which brought the Kingdom into being. A good example of this is the treatment given by the Ikhwan tribes to other Bedouin tribes living in Iraq and Jordan. Believing that they had a divine mission to accomplish, the Ikhwan tribes raided constantly into those countries, crossing borders that had no meaning for them to kill peaceful shepherds, their families, and livestock. No quarter was ever given to women and children. This is an abomination in both Islamic tradition and Arab customary law. ('urf). These large- scale atrocities only came to an end when the governments of Iraq and Jordan adopted the tactic of pursuing the Ikhwan into Saudi Arabia to deal with them. The Saudi government then sought to disarm the Ikhwan tribes and faced a revolt by the zealots in the tribes who denounced the king as "no true Muslim." This revolt was severely put down and its leaders executed.

In the aftermath of the Ikhwan revolt, the Saudi government sought to moderate its policies and practices, so as to make it possible to interact productively with the outside world. The Saudi government has followed this path of relative moderation ever since. This became particularly important with the discovery of huge deposits of petroleum in the Kingdom before the Second World War. A kind of alliance with the United States in that war created a relationship which although it has never been formalized by treaty has stood the test of time. While the Saudi government has pursued its long-term alignment with the United States, very different currents have run beneath the surface of society in that country. The Al-Sa'ud royal family created the Kingdom by force of arms. They are descended from desert warlords of the central region of the peninsula (the Najd). They are not descended from the Prophet Muhammad as are the kings of Jordan and Morocco. In their subjects' eyes they derive their legitimacy from their support and adherence to Wahhabi Islam. Because of this it has been very difficult for the royal government to restrict the teaching of Wahhabi doctrines in divinity schools, and universities or to prevent the preaching of these doctrines in the public mosques of the country. It has also been impossible for the government to prevent the export of vast sums of private Saudi money to support Wahhabi missionary works abroad.

A similar flow of private money from several Gulf states has always "accompanied" Saudi funds. What kind of pious missionary works have they accomplished? Schools have been founded across the Islamic world, in Europe and the United States. Mosques have been built and endowed in many places. Sheikh Hisham Kabbani recently wrote to the State Department that because mosques are not government regulated in the United States, as they are in the Islamic World, 80% of U.S, mosques are endowed by Wahhabi groups and have prayer leaders selected by the same groups. This means that the moral formation of American Muslim youth is in their hands.

In the fifties, President Nasser of Egypt suppressed the "Society of the Muslim Brethren," (the Ikhwan Muslimeen) and drove them underground. The Muslim Brethren were the oldest and in many ways one of the most murderous of extremist groups. Soon, thereafter, private money from the oil rich economies of the Gulf "rescued" the Muslim Brethren from extinction and was used to build them into a great force in the world. In the decades since then, the Egyptian Muslim Brethren have become a worldwide network of Wahhabi Ikhwan cells and societies with many linkages to all other Wahhabi terrorist groups. They are one of the largest components of the Al-Qa'ida network created by Osama bin Laden.

The Wahhabi Ikhwan Muslimeen fought ferociously in Afghanistan against the Soviets. They fought there with pious volunteers from all over the Islamic World. Osama bin Laden fought there. His leadership was first noticed there. At the end of the Afghan War against the Soviets, America turned away from Afghanistan, turned away from the six non-Wahhabi Mujahideen armies who had done the bulk of the fighting. America turned away and did nothing while in the refugee camps in Pakistan, the Wahhabi Taliban movement was born and took power in Kabul.

How did they take power? They had money, lots of money and they had the continuing single-minded support of the worldwide Wahhabi movement. The Wahhabi movement believes that the Islamic World is corrupt and that it is the West which has corrupted it. They believe deeply that existing governments in their countries must be brought down to make way for a "pure" Islamic life. They believe that the United States is the ultimate enemy, "The Great Satan." They will do whatever is needed to eliminate the United States as an obstacle to their dreams.

Al-Qaeda and the Jihadis
(August 23, 2006)

The Al-Qaeda that most Americans imagine does not exist. It is largely a figment of our imaginations and fears, a "boogie-man" that does not exist in the form that we dread, and it never existed in that way. Al-Qaeda is not an "organization" in the Western sense of the word. It is a movement, a historical phenomenon and a set of ideas offered to Muslims across the world.

This does not mean that there are not violent and dangerous Jihadi terrorists in the world. There are, but they are not members of a sprawling and tightly organized secret "army" of Islamists who operate in obedience to orders from Osama bin Laden. There is no cave in the Pakistan/Afghanistan border country that has a sign in Arabic over the door that reads "Al-Qaeda Headquarters." There is no central command for the Jihadis.

Obviously true? If this is obvious, then why do we hear, over and over again the same endlessly repeated questions every time there is a terrorist incident; "Is this group Al-Qaeda?" "Was this operation Al-Qaeda?" "Was this group a franchise of Al-Qaeda?" These questions are posed by journalists, government officials, and supposed "experts."

All these questions betray a basic lack of comprehension of how authentically Islamic activities are conducted. This lack of comprehension wastes time and effort and it distracts from effective operations against the Jihadis.

Islamic groups typically form around the personality and pronouncements of a leader. There are no clergy in Islam. There is no hierarchy. The acceptance by followers of the opinions of a leader is the basis of group identity. Osama bin Laden directly controls a relatively small group of "hard core" Jihadis who have accepted his views on the nature of Islam and its enmity to the influence of the West. This group has certain operational characteristics which are well-known: long term planning, simultaneity of operations, etc. Beyond that directly controlled group, Bin Laden and his Al-Qaeda provide inspiration and example to discontented Muslims across the world who harbor deep resentments against what they see as the injustice and excessive power of the West and its policies. Bin Laden used to provide "seed money" for the growth of such groups. He still provides training when he can, but he does not control them in the sense that Saddam Hussein controlled the government of Iraq.

The Arab governments are largely the product of western influence in the colonial period. The Jihadi groups are not like that. They form in response to appeals to widely felt grievances and take what they want from a "menu" of ideas offered by well-known Islamic teachers both past and present and from the operational example of present leaders like Bin Laden.

The recently discovered British based plot to destroy airliners is a good example. This Jihadi group clearly decided to follow the example of Al-Qaeda in its well known "Bojinka" plan. That plan envisioned the near simultaneous destruction, through the use of liquid explosives of a large group of airliners over the Pacific. The British Jihadi group copied most of the features of this Al-Qaeda plan, but there is no evidence that the British Jihadi group was in any way directed or "pushed' by Bin Laden's Al-Qaeda to attempt a "re-run" of this plan. In the great majority of Jihadi actions and attempts at attacks there is no evidence of "control" of the involved groups by Bin Laden's Al-Qaeda.

Nevertheless, each incident of Jihadi aggression against the West continues to be an occasion for an all-out search for Al-Qaeda "command" of the operation.

We obviously want to believe that the Jihadi phenomenon is a tightly commanded network. Our reasons for wanting to believe that are clear. We want an enemy who can be decisively defeated by destruction of the organization, preferably by decapitation. We want an enemy whose ways of thinking mirror our own. An enemy who does not think or "organize" as we do require us to learn to think like that enemy. This is difficult. It is much easier to "opt out" intellectually by saying that they are merely "crazy."

A lack of comprehension of the most basic things about our enemies continues to hamper our ability to defeat them. We have to learn to put ourselves in their "shoes." We have to learn to be able to "walk their path" in our minds.

Al "Kayda" or "Al Ka'eeda," which is it?
(July 10, 2005)

That is a joke, folks. The endless discussion of this jihadi organization would, to me, be more impressive if the participants were interested enough in understanding the group to have made SOME effort to understand it well enough to learn to pronounce its name correctly rather than adopting the vulgarism of "Al Kayda." The British favor "Al-Ka'eeda." That isn't correct either but at least it shows effort.

The News media driven obsessive discussion of the internal map of the jihadi world has been re-started by London's carnage. This always seems to center on the degree of "de-centralization" of the supposed de-centralization of al-Qa'ida (Al-Kayda) which we are often told was once a tightly organized, vertically commanded terrorist network but which under pressure from the Forces of Retribution have "morphed" into a "franchised," "second generation," "wannabe," "spin-off," "sleeper-cell" grouped, "Al-Qaida 2.0."

BULL!!!

The only thing that the kind of discussion described above proves is that the participants no more understand Islamic jihadism now than they did before Islam came into their lives on 9/11. Al –Qa'ida has not changed. Islamic jihadism has not changed. What has changed is the still deeply flawed perception that ill-informed and wishful people in the West have of the jihadi phenomenon.

Arab and Islamic activities do not naturally organize themselves into the kind of Christmas tree shaped, authority and responsibility driven, chain of command obsessed patterns that dominate Western thinking about organization. Such patterns are now seen in parts of the Islamic World, but they are always evidences of acculturation toward the West (Globalization, if you wish). Such efforts fit the larger cultural pattern poorly and, as a result, often fail or become a kind of sad mockery of the good intentions of their promoters.

Islamic jihadism in the present era was NEVER organized on the Christmas tree model. It is the "filter" of the minds of subject matter ignorant; analysts, newsmen and professors of the pseudo disciplines of political science and international relations that made it seem so. The jihadi movement grew over the last decades in response to the relative disparity of power, wealth and "muscle" possessed by the West and the US as the obvious symbol and leader of the West and the total unacceptability of this situation to many Muslims who believe that it is unnatural and contrary to God's will that this should be so. This is a hard saying for many in the West. Why? The reason is that the great majority of Westerners of whatever religion, or lack of religion, no longer BELIEVE in the way that such Muslims believe. We say we believe but our belief is largely a matter of public observance and life-cycle rituals like baptism, marriage and funerals. There are Westerners who still believe in the way the jihadis do, but they are generally viewed with suspicion and secretly feared by most of us.

Jihadism is about SALVATION. It is about the aspiration of some Muslims for a "short cut" to paradise. It IS NOT about economic deprivation or political oppression. It is not even about the various "provocations" that the West has offered to the Islamic World in the last century. Those "provocations" act as further irritants and "accelerators" as a fire investigator would say, but they are not at the root of jihadism. The reaction of HAMAS the Palestinian national resistance and terrorist group in denouncing the London bombings is illustrative.

"They kill in pursuit of salvation?" is the question I heard Larry King ask the other night. YES!! They do, and any Christian or Jew who is honest must admit that our ancestors did the same thing over and over in history. We killed because we thought God wanted it or to protect the people of God.

As I have written elsewhere, jihadism is an "influence," a state of mind which translates belief into action, action which can make any number of Muslims volunteer to kill themselves after walking away from job, family and long earthly life. It is a state of mind that rejoices in the opportunity and which relatives, spouses and friends accept and welcome with the "martyr." A desire for personal salvation through "testimony" (shihada) is not something which leads to a desire to fit into a large and well-articulated group. This has been true in the enemy we are fighting.

There is not one Al-Qa'ida. There never was. There are hundreds of such groups, large and small. There always were. Why do we insist on the centrality of Al-Qa'ida? I suspect that it is because we do not want to admit to ourselves that the "tendency" to jihadism is as widespread as it is. There is something like a billion Muslims. If .1% of them are at present in a jihadi way of feeling and acting, that is a million souls….. If there are even a few percentage points who are "reserve" sympathizers, then our task in fighting them will be of long, long duration. No wonder we cling to the idea of Al-Qa'ida.

When we learn to do that, we will defeat them.

PART III

Short Stories from the Crusades Era

Unlike most of his classmates at Virginia Military Institute (VMI), Col. Lang did not earn his degree in engineering. He studied English Literature, which provided him with insight into the human condition which served him well throughout his career in intelligence. It also kindled a love of historical fiction. This section includes a series of short historical fiction, set during the long period of the Crusades.

"The Most Beautiful Men in the World"

(Anna Comnena Writing of the Normans), (June 21, 2021)

1097 AD, Constantinople

"Now the man was such as, to put it briefly, had never before been seen in the land of the Romans, be he either of the barbarians or of the Greeks (for he was a marvel for the eyes to behold, and his reputation was terrifying). Let me describe the barbarian's appearance more particularly – he was so tall in stature that he overtopped the tallest by nearly one cubit, narrow in the waist and loins, with broad shoulders and a deep chest and powerful arms. And in the whole build of the body he was neither too slender nor overweighted with flesh, but perfectly proportioned and, one might say, built in conformity with the canon of Polycleitus... His skin all over his body was very white, and in his face the white was tempered with red. His hair was yellowish, but did not hang down to his waist like that of the other barbarians; for the man was not inordinately vain of his hair, but had it cut short to the ears. Whether his beard was reddish, or any other color I cannot say, for the razor had passed over it very closely and left a surface smoother than chalk... His blue eyes indicated both a high spirit and dignity; and his nose and nostrils breathed in the air freely; his chest corresponded to his nostrils and by his nostrils... the breadth of his chest. For by his nostrils nature had given free passage for the high spirit which bubbled up from his heart. A certain charm hung about this man but was partly marred by a general air of the horrible... He was so made in mind and body that both courage and passion reared their crests within him and both inclined to war. His wit was manifold and crafty and able to find a way of escape in every emergency. In conversation he was well informed, and the answers he gave were quite irrefutable. This man who was of such a size and such a character was inferior to the emperor alone in fortune and eloquence and in other gifts of nature."

Thus, Anna Comnena described Bohemund of Taranto in the "Alexiad."

Anna was the daughter of the Byzantine Emperor Alexius Comnenus. She was a well-known historian and chronicler even in her time and the author of the "Alexiad," a lengthy history of her father's reign, times and deeds. She was well educated in Greek literature and history, philosophy, theology, mathematics, and medicine. And from the contemporary portraits of her, one would have to judge her "a looker." She had been taught the French language and was often employed by her father as translator. He knew the self-serving dishonesty of many translators and he believed correctly that he could trust his 14-year-old daughter. She was clearly smitten with Bohemund, an Italian Norman of the House of Hauteville and from her description of him who could blame her?

As is usually the case in her part of the world, life was difficult. There had earlier been a series of strong soldier emperors who had empowered the largely Armenian nobility of Anatolia. Under these rulers: Nikephoras Phokas, John Tzimiskes, Basil II (the Bulgar blinder) the empire had been secured all the way to eastern Anatolia, far up in the Balkan peninsula and most of Southern Italy. The military nobility was respected and well-funded.

And then the rot set in. The Arab historians wrote that luxury softens and weakens successive generations of ruling dynasties. That is what happened to the Byzantines. Security made people soft. A great many restrictions and rules were placed on the military governors of the east, civilian courtiers were favored by the imperial government, military budgets were cut.

The inevitable happened. A formidable enemy appeared. These were the Seljuk Turks. Newly emerged from the Asian steppe gradient they decided to challenge the Byzantine governors of eastern Anatolia.

At Manzikert in 1071 they defeated the Emperor Romanus IV. His force outnumbered the Turks two to one but half his people deserted when the fighting started. They were local, untrained levies and foreign mercenaries. After that the Seljuks flooded into Anatolia and within 15 years or so Anatolia was Roman no more even though the population were still majority Greek speaking and Roman Christian.

Anna's father came to power in 1081after a long career in government. He was obsessed with the need to recover territories lost to the Seljuks in the East and in southern Italy to the Normans.

These were the selfsame Normans who came to Anna's father in 1097 seeking his blessing and support in reconquering the Levant from the Turks and other assorted Muslims. Jerusalem was the goal.

After years of largely fruitless struggle, Anna's father decided that he needed help from the West. This was a painful decision. It would require him to beg for help from the pope, the only effective leader of western Europe.

For several hundred years there had been a deep split and animosity between eastern and western Christianity. The issue seems trivial to modern men, something about the use of images in worship. But in that time, it was enough to imperil the possibility of help from western lords.

More clever than the "furry" semi barbarians whom he "led" like a herd of cats, Pope Urban preached an "armed pilgrimage" to recapture the Holy Sepulcher and indeed all the Holy Land from the defilement of infidel rule.

That worked. The pious, both rich and poor, signed up for the glory of God. The merely ambitious looked to their main chance in terms of lands to be had by those who had no land. For some there was a bit of both motivations.

The Crusade of the Princes assembled outside Constantinople early in 1097. There were 15000 heavy cavalry and 55000 well skilled professional infantry. None of these were anything like the peasant rabble that had crossed the Bosporus into Asia a few months earlier led by their fanatic preachers.

There were truly noble men among the "princes," men noble in character. Count Raymond of Toulouse, who gave up his holdings and swore not to return from Palestine, Duke Godfrey of Bouillon, who borrowed against everything in his duchy in Belgium to bring enough men to the fight, and we should also remember all the simple, landless men at arms who went east to fight for God and his indulgence of their past sins.

There was also Adhemar, a bishop who was the papa legate. He was theoretically in command, but no one paid much attention to him.

The emperor Alexius was a clever man. He was feeding all these creatures from the West, men he thought of as crude and unlettered. For them to have much chance of success, they would need a lot of his continuing support; food and fodder, his Pecheneg constabulary as guides and reconnaissance force, siege engines. The list was endless.

In return, he wanted an oath on scripture that whatever lands were recovered would be ruled as part of the empire. There was a good deal of complaining at that. The nobles finally took a form of the oath, all except Raymond of Toulouse who told Alexius that what he and the emperor should do is make a pact to act in unison against Bohemund when it became necessary. Alexius agreed.

At the meeting with the aforementioned Bohemond, Alexius sat and watched the interplay between the "blond god" and his teen-aged daughter.

When the man had left, she hesitated a moment while her father waited to see how addled she was. She blushed and finally said, "you can't trust him, you know. He will betray you in a heartbeat."

The emperor smiled. "My lovely girl, we will use him so long as he is useful. I have not forgotten what he did to us in Apulia in Italy. I am pleased to see that you do not lose control of yourself…We will see you well married, and soon…"

Good to his word, Alexius married her off to a distinguished soldier and historian. The couple raised six children. When her husband was killed in combat against the Bulgars, she entered a convent endowed by her mother and remained there for the rest of her life. She must have often thought of Bohemund.

The next month the Byzantine navy began to ferry the Alexius' forces and the Crusader army across the Sea of Marmara to Asia.

Dorylaeum

(June 21, 2021)

The Crusader army of nobles and their men came to Nicaea. The city had been in Seljuk hands since the Manzikert debacle in 1071. It was the capital of the Sultan of Rum, Kilij Arslan. He happened to be away when the Crusaders invested the city. It was still a Greek speaking Orthodox Christian place. The crusaders sat down, dug lines of circumvallation to wall the city in and started mining and bombardment operations. These Franks were professional fighters by trade. The Byzantines watched in surprise as the Western Europeans constructed a variety of siege equipment: battering rams with overhead cover, rolling towers for the assault, catapults, trebuchets, and onagers.

As I have recounted, there had been an earlier wave of Crusaders. They had come months before, traveling light and hungry. These had been the masses of "little people." They were not soldiers. They were the peasants and small-town people who had heard Pope Urban's appeal for a pilgrimage to Jerusalem. Coming from and through the Rhine Valley and led by fanatic preachers they had worked themselves into a frenzy over the Jewish population of the towns. Taking to heart the description in the St. Matthew Gospel of the responsibility of the Jews of Jerusalem for the death of Jesus at the hands of the Romans, they looted, burned and murdered their way toward the Holy Land. When they reached Constantinople, the emperor shipped them across the water to the countryside of northwest Anatolia. There, they resumed the local looting and rapine by which they had sustained themselves as they came south through the Balkans. In response the Turks killed the men *en masse,* and enslaved the women and children as *ghanima* or "booty" in the same way that the jihadis of ISIS treated their non-Muslim captives in the 21st Century.

The Frankish nobles and their men at arms learned the details of this sad story while in position around Nicaea and were consequently even more eager to get at the Seljuk Turkish force occupying the city. This became evident to the Turks when the remnants of attempted relief columns straggled into the city with wild tales of the ferocity of the Frankish ambushes that had killed or driven off the majority of their comrades.

Adding to the effect was the exhibit before the walls of the city of Turkish prisoners who were given the opportunity to abjure Islam. Those who did not were mocked, anointed with pig blood, and then beheaded.

As with the Turks, the fanatic behavior of the Franks marks them as spiritual kin of the 21st Century Islamic jihadis.

The Turkish garrison decided that if the Franks took the city there would be little chance of quarter and so, proceeding logically, they surrendered the town to the Byzantine emperor's forces and representative.

This enraged the Western Europeans, most especially Bohemund, the apple of Anna's eye. She would have been intrigued by his rage against her father.

The Frankish force was not really one army. It was a number of bands of men at arms, each following and loyal to its feudal lord. The only group among the Crusaders resembling an "army," as the present author understands the term, was the Byzantine army force sent along by the emperor to safeguard his interests.

The Byzantine general "minding" the Frankish princes was an interesting man. The name by which he is known in history is Tatikios. He was a close friend of Anna, the emperor's daughter and kept her informed of the "doings" of the Frankish wild men. Born a Turk, he was raised in the household of the Comneni as a captive slave and a playmate of Alexius. He fought for his childhood friend in the long struggles for the throne and in campaigns against the Bulgars, Pechenegs and Normans. Any thought that he was anything like a slave had long been gone in his role as the emperor's favorite general.

Bohemund made a nuisance of himself, ranting against the emperor's "treachery" and it was decided by a council of war, headed by the papal legate, Bishop Adhemar to send him ahead with an advanced guard to "prepare the way" for the main body which would follow a day behind. He would have 2,000 heavily armored cavalry and 8,000 archers and pikemen. The princes probably wanted to be free of Bohemund for a few days. He would have Tatikios as guide and some of the Byzantine soldiers as well. The main force would have four times that many soldiers in all.

To divide your force in the face of an enemy of unknown position and strength is folly. This is the sort of thing that an idiot like George Custer would do. It often has fatal results unless one is very, very lucky.

Glad to be off on his own, away from the grownups, Bohemund marched his advanced guard southeast in the direction that Tatikios indicated would lead to a substantial body of water. This is always a necessity if one has ten thousand men and thousands of horses to water.

Pitching camp on the north bank of the river near the ancient city of Dorylaeum (modern *Eskishehir* – "Old Town" in Turkish). Bohemund did not bother to entrench. I suppose he thought the main body would arrive before he needed that security. This was a serious error.

The Seljuk Turks controlled most of Anatolia. Only Armenian Cilicia in the Southeast was still Christian territory. The Turks showed up in the middle of the night. They had been brought to this area by Killij Arslan, their sultan. His scouts had established the location and strength of the two crusader groups. He wanted Nicaea, his capital, back and to make that happen he planned to devour Bohemund's advanced guard and then, having done that, to encircle and crush the main body. He had about the same number of men and horses as Bohemund but possessed a great advantage in having two thousand horse archers. These fighters could charge at you, shoot a couple of times with their stubby little bows, and then race away to re-group for another attack.

They attacked in the pre-dawn twilight, leaving their baggage and non-combatants behind, a half mile or so north of Bohemund's camp. The Frankish crusaders were completely surprised as were the Byzantines with them. They had posted no adequate security and the first they knew of the Seljuk onslaught was a hail of arrows and the Turks riding in among the tents to cut down one and all who were unfortunate enough to stagger out into the dawn. The crusaders lost a lot of horses either taken from the horse lines in the confusion or shot down by the archers.

Bohemund faced defeat on the spot and a nasty end at the hands of the friends of those he had executed on their knees outside Nicaea, but he and Tatikios finally got the armored knights and men at arms into a dismounted line of defense with his own archers sheltered behind them where they could shoot from a somewhat protected position. His foot archers had more range and that tended to inhibit close in Turkish attacks but he had already lost many men and horses.

His knights had initially tried to mount and charge but that had gotten a lot of them killed or captured when surrounded by the more mobile Turks.

Early in the fight Bohemund sent a couple of "gallopers" south across the river and then northwest to tell the main body what had happened and to plead for help.

His men fought very hard with their backs to the river losing men and animal continuously from the arrows. The chroniclers mention that the soldiers' women cared for the wounded and carried water from the river throughout the day. "The colonel's lady and Molly O'Grady are sisters under the skin."

It has always been thus.

After several hours of this, Raymond of Toulouse arrived on the scene with fifty of his men. They fought their way through the heathen, dismounted and took their place in the line.

A few hours later Bishop Adhemar, the papal legate, arrived with several hundred men. Strictly by chance he came upon the Seljuk encampment and charged into it, his men looting and ravaging as they went. Adhemar was a clergyman *san pareil*. He always fought alongside the knights.

The word spread quickly among the Seljuks that their baggage, spare horses and camp followers were lost. They were disheartened by the stiffness of the Frankish resistance, however haphazard the early defense had been and with this news their morale collapsed.

Virtually as one man, the horse archers left the field, streaming away to the east. Kilij Arslan had no choice but to go with them.

The crusaders then turned their attention to the abandoned enemy foot soldiers and massacred them en masse on the field. There were several thousand Turkish dead, killed as more and more heavy Frankish cavalry came on the field.

Bohemund, Tancred, Raymond, Tatikios, Bishop Adhemar and Hugh, Count of Vermandois consulted on the spot.

"How far will they run?" Bohemund asked the Byzantine general.

"They are stunned by their failure, and will run far," was the answer. "They will run all the way to their home villages far in the east to the north of Armenian Cilicia. The sultan will be lucky if they do not kill him. They do not accept failure."

"Will there be resistance as we move toward Antioch?" asked Bishop Adhemar.

"No," Tatikios responded. "My Pechenegs will clear the way to Armenian territory where you will be welcomed with a warm embrace… if you behave yourselves." He laughed at the thought.

"What will you do," Adhemar asked.

"Ah, gentlemen, I will report to my master, Alexius that we should be grateful to you for restoring a vast swath of territory and a multitude of our people to Christian, Roman control. We will re-occupy our lost domain. Personally, I hope he does not send me back to you. You are too impulsive for my taste, but he will send someone."

"We want YOU," Adhemar answered. "We know you. What do you want to do?"

"Ah, there are islands in the Aegean that need my attention."

"I am going home," said Hugh of Vermandois. "I did not want to come. My wife insisted. I do not need to be this holy."

They all laughed.

Hugh was an ancestor of the present author. He did go home. His wife hounded and humiliated him until he signed on for the Second Crusade. This time, he died of his wounds in Anatolia, not far from Dorylaeum.

She was undoubtedly proud of him.

Melisende and Fulk

1041 AD

"But did you love him, mother?"

She laughed. "Perhaps not, but we certainly lusted together. You are proof of that."

"You were of different generations," he responded after a moment, perhaps seeking to shield her feelings.

"He was a great man, your father. I was almost a girl when we were married. I expected a cold marriage for reasons of state but he would have none of that ..."

"And now he is gone, dead in a stupid mishap with a horse who could not stay on its own feet. I am glad the hunters killed the animal."

She looked unhappy. "The mare was a gift from my Armenian kin, your Armenian kin. He would not have been pleased with her death, stabbed with a boar spear."

"His brains coated the ground," he objected.

They sat in the palace of the King of Jerusalem in what was now her son's capital. The rosy stone walls were hung in black.

Her husband Fulk's Templar brethren filled the surrounding rooms in their mourning

She disliked them. Their austerity made them unacceptable to an Armenian gentlewoman. She could never really comprehend how a robust, worldly, sensuous man like Fulk could have once been of their number even if for but a year or so.

She smiled. I don't know how he gave up women and their bodies, even for a year, she thought. "They are necessary to the defense of the realm," she muttered to her son, the new king.

He grimaced in return. "I prefer the Hospitallers or better yet, the levies of our barons."

"Yes, but the pope loves the knights of the temple and just as importantly, Bernard of Clairvaux is their patron. Why he wrote their rule is a mystery…"

"Could we not look to the emperor?" he asked.

"Not unless you wish to accept the Comneni as your sovereigns and abjure Catholicism," she replied. "That would lose us all support in the West. At times I have thought that would not be a bad thing. The foreign nature of new arrivals from the West is frightening. They come to conquer and destroy, We half Westerns know that is the path to final destruction of what we have built."

"How old are you now, mother" He asked.

"Thirty-eight." She was a lovely, ripe bodied woman even when dressed in widow's garb of black silk. She showed little of the blond coloring of Northern Franks like her father Baldwin or her husband.

"Your father was fifty-one. I expected many more years of his strong, wise help."

The boy looked at her with the half-suppressed yearning of an adolescent.

She contemplated him. He looked so like his father. "We will get you married soon. You will take great comfort in that. Perhaps a Roman princess of the Comneni? It seems I will be regent for a while so I will be near you. We must keep you off battlefields for several years, my king."

He looked resentful. "Will our Christian faith shield us here, mother?

Sighing, she responded, "Your father made me hopeful, but our meager numbers compared to the Muslims makes me think we may have reached the limits of our grasp of the land. At least the Muslim peasants do not hate us. They would rather live under us than their own kind. The rapaciousness of the emirs knows no limits. You must do everything you can to encourage immigration of the burgher class from the West."

"Yes, mother."

A Voyage to Aigues-Mortes

"The Franks Are Mighty Men. May God Curse Them."
Usama ibn Munqidh

The two men were Savoyard. They were knights from the mountain region wedged betwixt what would be the countries of Italy, Switzerland, and France.

Their names were Jean de Grailly and Otto de Grandson.

In some unimaginable future time, their valleys would be assigned by history to the French Republic, But just now, they had survived one of history's most ferocious small battles and were physically and emotionally expended.

The year was 1291 AD, and they would live to talk about the fall of Acre. The burning town could still be seen astern on the horizon. Smoke hung like cloud above its walls.

These soldiers had campaigned together in Europe, and both had been on Crusade earlier in life, but something, something had drawn them back to Outremer, something awesome in the power of its grip.

Perhaps, it was the sheer menace of the reported situation in the Holy Land. Perhaps it was the incompetent fecklessness of the Lusignan kings and their inability to keep order among the lay nobility and the military religious orders like the Teutonic Knights, Knights Hospitallers, Leper Knights and the Guardians of the Holy Sepulcher. There were also a few hundred of King Henry II's own soldiers as well as men who went to Acre to sign up to fight for the money. Those were tough times in Europe.

For much of the near 200-year existence of the Kingdom of Jerusalem, Egypt and Syria had been ruled by descendants or successors of Saladin. Saladin himself was a religious fanatic but his heirs simply wanted to reign quietly in as much luxury as could be had. If that meant friendly diplomatic, trade, and military relations with the Crusader states even to the point of alliance against third party Muslim states, so be it. Such truces were allowed by and sanctioned by Islam if thought to be advantageous to the 'umma, the world community of the faithful. Such a truce is called a hudna and is renewable.

But all good things come to an end, and the end was spelt mamluk in this case. From the 9th century onward, the various Egypt based Muslim dynasties had relied on slave soldiers, children bought from among Turkic, Balkan and Caucasian peoples, and forcibly converted to Islam. They fought with the conviction of those well proselytized and assured of salvation. As was often the case in Islamic states the ruling dynasty weakened in character with time. Ibn Khaldun, the North African philosopher of history, captured this process well in his "Kitāb al-'Ibar wa-Dīwān al-Mubtada' wa-l-Khabar fī Ta'rīkh al-'Arab wa-l-Barbar wa-Man 'Āṣarahum min Dhawī ash-Sha'n al-Akbār" or simply the "Muqqadimah."

Not surprisingly, the slave soldiers eventually took power from their "masters." They then completed organization of a society which was clearly a country and people "occupied" by an army, a country in which the military sciences were closely studied and that study well applied. We should remember that these were the men who defeated the Mongols at Ayn Jalut.

Within a few decades a sultan came to power in Cairo who decided that his popularity with both the slave soldiers and the religious scholars would be enhanced if the remaining annoying Crusader city on the Palestine coast was eliminated.

This was al-ashraf khalil. Born in 1260, he was 31 years old when he more or less casually decided to capture Acre.

As a man educated in war, al-ashraf Khalil knew what to do next. He tasked his supply people to create a chain of supply dumps on the road to Acre and when they were complete, 20,000 men marched north along the coast road and he with them. He and the more than eager assault force arrived before Acre on the 6th of April. There was a large artillery train consisting in the main of trebuchets. These are large siege engines used to batter at curtain walls while miners tunneled beneath seeking to collapse them. al-ashraf Khalil took his time and made straight the way for the men in the assault force although they did not seem concerned about their fate. His own attitude seemed to be that there were many men like these available in Egypt and those who died as shuhada would be on their way to paradise with all forgiven them.

This was much like the behavior of the 9/11 "martyrs" some of whom partied through the night before their deaths because they believed that God would forgive their sin.

The people of the city of Acre understood that. At the fall noble women and their female servants were seen on the quays offering rich jewels and indeed their bodies if the seamen offshore or at the quays would transport them somewhere, anywhere that might be safe for they knew their fate if taken as booty by jihadis.

By May 18 all was ready. Several of Acre's 12 towers had collapsed. These had been built as gifts from pious pilgrims. There were not really enough men to hold all the walls, especially considering the breaches in the curtain walls and the fallen towers. The Crusaders decided to leave the gates open as sally ports.

This decision was the occasion for the chance meeting at a gate of de Grailly and de Grandson who was at the gate to plan a mounted raid on the mamluk siege artillery that very night. The Crusaders were raiding forward of the walls every night and doing considerable damage but not enough.

De Grandson heard someone speaking Savoyard French. He turned to find his old comrade, de Grailly, speaking to several men in their mother tongue. "What are you doing here?" de Grandson said. "You are supposed to be in Europe finding someone to come save our collective asses."

De Grailly could only laugh grimly. He was the seneschal of the Kingdom of Cyprus and Jerusalem. No one of any significance would be coming from Europe. King Henry had sent him to Europe looking for help. There was no enthusiasm in the West for a renewed crusading reinforcement. The pope was at daggers drawn with most of Europe and only a handful wanted to help him with what was essentially still a papal project. Few would be coming. Now his sovereign lord had sent him to Acre to see for himself what the situation might be.

"What are you up to at this gate?"

"The Templars have loaned me 300 knights and sergeants. We are going to make a mounted sortie starting here at 2 in the morning and try to burn their damned trebuchets.

"How are you going to light'em up?"

"We have some wagons. We found a sailor from the Genoese fleet who knows how to make Greek Fire… We are going to 'liberate' the draft animals out there somewhere in the dark. No point in feeding them. They will be better off on their own, afterward."

"You are taking me with you, right? I am the king's representative…"

"How about these?"

De Grandson was referring to the dozen men of the French Regiment with de Grailly. King Louis of France maintained this body of veteran troops in the service of the king of Cyprus and Jerusalem. King Henry had sent them to Acre to try to keep his seneschal alive long enough to see if it would be safe to come visit the doomed.

The raid was made in a blessedly moonless darkness. They lit the fires and left the siege machines burning. It did not prove a damned thing. The mamluks repaired the machines and carried on smashing breaches in the double walls.

The next day King Henry II arrived from Limassol to visit this bastion of his kingdom in Asia. Someone provided a horse and he rode about the city and along the inside of the walls peering out at the mamluks. Having made up his mind, he sent an emissary to al-ashraf Khalil offering to surrender the city

The sultan responded that he was not interested. His men would enjoy the pillage of the city too much for him to deny them the booty.

Henry returned to Cyprus having told de Grailly that he knew it was useless to argue for him to leave with him. "But," he said, "I will leave you a ship so that you will have a chance to escape, if you choose. I will leave a galley so that you are not trapped by an onshore wind. Why haven't all these people left?" And with that he was gone.

A week later, May 18th to be precise, al-ashraf khalil was ready. He deployed his 20,000 men all along the walls and when the word was given, they poured through the breaches and through the open gates.

The issue was never in doubt. By midday the mamluks had taken half the city, and were pushing forward on parallel streets, pushing toward the harbor.

Around 10 AM the Teutonic Knights asked al-ashraf khalil for a truce that would let them depart for Europe unarmed. The sultan calculated that he was losing more men than he had expected and that he might as well let them go to what would become East Prussia, and so he agreed.

The Templars tried for the same deal, but al-ashraf khalil knew the depth of the hatred felt by the mamluks for the Templars and refused.

He reckoned that there would be enough loot and human booty to slake the hunger of his men from among the inhabitants of the city.

De Grailly, his men and Otto de Grandson fought in the line of battle until it became clear that if they did not fall back, they would be cut off from the harbor and possible escape. At around 1 PM De Grailly decided that it was time to sauve qui peut and get as many of his men and beasts out as possible. His party were all mounted on big European war horses, and he intended to save as many as he could or leave them dead on the quay. His escort from the French Regiment were armed with crossbows and swords. He told them to watch the rooftops and cross streets for marksmen.

Fortunately, the mamluks were busy with their orgy of destruction and murder. Down the intersecting streets they could be seen enjoying themselves.

On one street a group could be seen cutting the throats of a group of monks, Benedictine perhaps. Down another a group of nuns and other women were being introduced to the life they would lead henceforth. Some might be ransomed, but they would be few.

Half a dozen women ran out of a house at their approach. "Save us! May God save us!" One of them was clearly the lady of the house and the others were her servants and relatives.

"Get in the middle," de Grailly told their leader. "And lead us to the harbor!"

The mamluks were steadily closing in from both sides. De Grailly's little party shot a few to make them back away from their path.

And suddenly they were at the long stone quay that lined the harbor. The king had sent a galley designed for horse transport. It had a hinged contraption like a drawbridge covered with creosote. The captain had placed his vessel stern to the pier. The rowers moved the ship astern toward the pier until they could drop the bridge safely. Archers on the ship could now cover the walls and streets entering the harbor.

"Get on board! Up the bridge! Go!" de Grailly roared. With that the women, men and horses poured up and over the bridge. There was a ramp on the inside, a ramp down into the horse well. He was the last on board.

By then the soldiers on board had shot several mamluks.

De Grailly nodded to the captain and the man began to raise the drawbridge even as his rowers moved the ship away from the dock headed for the breakwater and the open sea.

An hour later, having peered carefully around to make sure there were no blockading mamluk ships, de Grailly and de Grandson were on the stern peering aft at Acre burning on the horizon. They had ensured that man and beast were watered. Both were busy wetting down the planking in the horse well.

"Two days to Limassol?" de Grandson asked without taking his eyes off the cloud on the horizon.

"Yes."

"Then what?"

"Then I tell King Henry that I am leaving his service and ask for a ride for you, me and her to Aigue-Morte. This tub makes regular trips there to keep the supply of horses up on Cyprus. I ran all that sort of business for Henry."

"Her?"

"The noblewoman. She asked an hour ago. She has family in Toulouse. Why not. She says we can stay with her kin."

"Will Henry let you go?"

"He doesn't have much choice. I will make sure everyone knows I am back before our meeting"

De Grandson turned to look back at the cloud. He laughed. "Ah well, farewell to Outremer." With that he went to see what there was to eat on the little ship.

"The knights are dust. their good swords rust.
Their souls are with the saints we trust"
Sir Walter Scott

PART IV

The Iraq War

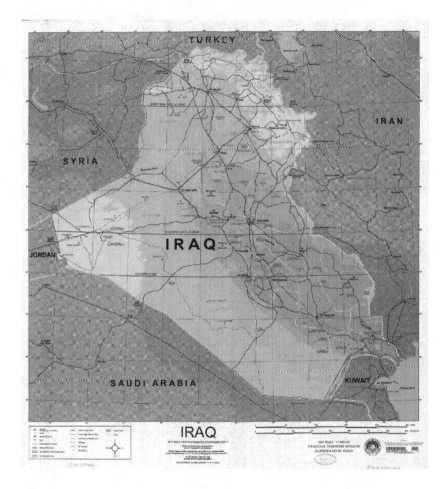

This section begins with a comprehensive essay on the events and personalities that led the United States into the Iraq war, based on a deeply flawed and manipulated intelligence process and executive deliberation. Some of the essays included in this section could have been included in Part I on the intelligence process. Having served as an advisor to the Iraq armed forces during the Iran-Iraq war, Col. Lang had a unique insight and deep concern about the consequences of the U.S. action, which reflect in each of the essays selected for this section.

Drinking the Kool-Aid

(Middle East Policy Journal, June 1, 2004)

Throughout the author's long service life in the Department of Defense, first as an Army officer and then as a member of the Defense Intelligence Senior Executive Service, there was a phrase in common usage that is hard to forget. The phrase was "I will fall on my sword over that," meaning that the speaker had reached a point of internal commitment with regard to something that his superiors wanted him to do and that he meant to refuse even though this would be career suicide. The sense of this phrase was that the speaker preferred career death to the loss of personal integrity, indeed personal honor.

This phrase is no longer so widely in use. What has taken its place is far more sinister in its meaning and in its implications for the public service of the United States. "I drank the Kool-Aid," is what is now said. All those old enough remember the Jonestown tragedy; remember this phrase all too well. For those too young to remember it is easy to tell the tale. Jim Jones, a self-styled "messiah" figure from the USA, lured hundreds of innocent and believing followers to Guyana where he built a village, isolated from the world, where his utopian view of the universe was the only possible view. He controlled all news entering the town, regulated all discourse and expression of opinion and shaped behavior to his taste. After a time, his paranoia grew unmanageable, and he "foresaw" that "evil" forces were coming to threaten the "paradise" that he had created. He decided that these forces were unstoppable and omnipotent, and that death would be preferable to living under their control. He called together his followers in the town square and explained the situation to them. There were a few survivors and they all said afterward that within the context of the "group-think" prevailing in the village, it sounded quite reasonable. Jim Jones then invited all present to drink from vats of Kool-Aid containing lethal doses of poison. Nearly all did so, without physical coercion. Parents gave their children the poison and then drank themselves. Finally, Jones drank. Hundreds died, many hundreds.

In the upper ranks of the armed services of the United States and in the intelligence services, this phrase has now come into wide use. "I drank the Kool-Aid," "He drank the Kool-Aid," etc. What does this mean? It signifies that the person in question has given up personal integrity and has succumbed to the prevailing "group-think" that has typified policy making in recent years and that this person has become "part of the problem, not part of the solution."

What was the "problem?" The problem was, and is, that the sincerely held beliefs of a small group of people who think they are the "bearers" of a uniquely correct view of the world, sought to dominate the foreign policy of the United States in the first Bush 43 administration, and succeeded in doing so through a practice of excluding all who disagreed with them from government. Those they could not drive from government they bullied and undermined until they, too, had drunk from the vat.

What was the result? The war in Iraq was the result. It is not anything like over yet, and the body count is still mounting. As of March 2004, 554 American soldiers dead, several thousand wounded, more than 15,000 dead Iraqis (the Pentagon is not publicizing the number of Iraqi deaths). PBS' recent special program on Frontline concerning Iraq mentioned that senior military officers had said of General Franks "he had drunk the Kool-Aid." Many, many serving intelligence officers have told the author that they too drank the Kool-Aid and as a result consider themselves to be among the "walking dead," waiting only for retirement, and praying for an early release that will allow them to go away and try to forget their dishonor and the damage they have done to the intelligence services and therefore to the Republic.

What we have on our hands now is a highly corrupted system of intelligence and policymaking, one twisted to serve specific group goals, ends, and beliefs held to the point of religious faith. Is this different than the situation would have been in previous administrations? Yes. The intelligence community, and by this I mean the information collection and analysis functions, not the "James Bond" covert action activities, which should properly be in other parts of the government. The intelligence community has as its assigned task the business of describing reality as best it understands it. The policy staffs and politicals in the government have the task of creating a new reality, more to their taste. Nevertheless, it is "understood" by the government "pros" as opposed to the zealots that a certain restraint must be observed by the policy "crowd" in dealing with the intelligence folk because without objective truth, decisions are based on subjective drivel. Wars result from such "drivel." We are in the midst of one at present.

How did it come to this? Actually, signs of this impending disaster were clear from the beginning of this administration. Insiders knew it all along. Statements made by the Bush Administration often seem to convey the message that Iraq only became a focus of attention after the terrorist attacks on 9/11. The evidence is otherwise, but the story of how we got to where we are is so long and convoluted that it is probably best to follow it in a roughly chronological way.

Sometime in the spring of 2000, Stephen Hadley, now Condoleeza Rice's deputy at the National Security Council (NSC) briefed a group of prominent Republican Party policy-makers on the national security and foreign policy agenda of a future George W. Bush Administration. Hadley was one of a group of senior campaign policy advisors to then-Texas Governor Bush, known collectively as "the Vulcans." The group, in addition to Hadley, included Condoleezza Rice, Paul Wolfowitz and Richard Perle, and had been assembled by George Shultz and Dick Cheney, beginning in late 1998, when G.W. Bush first launched his Presidential bid.

Hadley's briefing shocked a number of the participants according to Dr. Clifford Kiracofe, who spoke to several of them, shortly after the meeting. Hadley announced that the "number one foreign policy agenda" of a Bush Administration would be Iraq and the unfinished business of removing Saddam Hussein from power. Hadley also made it clear that the Israel-Palestine conflict, which had dominated the Middle East agenda of the Clinton Administration, would be placed in the deep freeze.

Dr. Kiracofe's account of the pre-election obsession of the Vulcans with the ouster of Saddam Hussein is corroborated by former U.S. Treasury Secretary Paul O'Neill's memory of the first meetings of the Bush National Security Council, which he attended in late January and early February of 2001. Ron Suskind's book, "The Price of Loyalty," based on O'Neill's memory and notes, tells us of an NSC meeting, ten days into the Bush Administration, at which both the Israel-Palestine and Iraq situations were discussed.

Referring to President Bill Clinton's efforts to reach a comprehensive peace between the Israelis and the Palestinians, President Bush declared, "Clinton overreached, and it all fell apart. That's why we're in trouble. If the two sides don't want peace, there's no way we can force them. I don't see much we can do over there at this point. I think it's time to pull out of the situation."

Next, Condoleezza Rice raised the issue of Iraq and the danger posed by Saddam's arsenal of weapons of mass destruction. A good deal of the hour-long meeting was taken up with a briefing by CIA Director George Tenet on a series of aerial photographs of sites inside Iraq that "might" be producing WMD. Tenet admitted that there was no firm intelligence on what was going on inside those sites, but at the close of the meeting, President Bush tasked Secretary of Defense Donald Rumsfeld and Joint Chiefs of Staff Chairman Gen. Hugh Shelton to begin preparing options for the use of U.S.

ground forces in the northern and southern no-fly zones in Iraq, to support an insurgency to bring down the Saddam regime. As author Ron Suskind summed it up: "Meeting adjourned. Ten days in, and it was about Iraq." Rumsfeld had said little, Cheney nothing at all, though both men clearly had long entertained the idea of overthrowing Saddam." If this was a decision meeting, it was strange. It ended in a presidential order to prepare contingency plans for war in Iraq. Surely, this was not the first time these people had considered this problem. One interesting thing about the people at that meeting is that there were no people present or in the background who had any real and substantive knowledge of the Middle East. It is one thing to have traveled to the area as a senior government person. It is another to have lived there and worked with the people of the region for long periods of time. People with that kind of experience in the Islamic World are strangely absent from the Bush Team. As Team Bush approached putting its game plan together for the Arab and Islamic Worlds, most of the government's veteran experts in the Middle East were largely shut out. The Pentagon civilian bureaucracy of the Bush administration, dominated by an inner circle of think-tankers, lawyers, and senate staffers virtually hung out a sign, "Arab-speakers Need Not Apply," apparently in an attempt to purge the process of Americans who might have inadvertently developed sympathies for the people of the region.

Instead of including such "veterans" in the planning process, the Bush Team opted for amateurs brought in from outside the Executive Branch of the government who tended to share the views of many of President Bush's earliest foreign policy advisors and mentors. Because of this hiring "bias," what the American people got in the end relative to the Middle East was a very theoretical and somewhat artificial planning process dominated by "insider" discourse among old colleagues and old friends, who ate, drank, talked, worked, and planned only with each other. Most of these people already shared attitudes and concepts of how the Middle East should be handled. Their continued association only reinforced their mutually held beliefs. This created an environment in which any shared belief could become sacrosanct, in which any group belief could become "holy" and unchallengeable. A situation like this is, in essence, a war waiting for an excuse to happen. If there is no "imminent threat," one can be invented, not as a matter of deliberate deception, but rather as an artifact of group self-delusion. In normal circumstances, there is a flow of "new talent" into the government that melds with the "old timers" in a process both dynamic and creative. This does not seem to have happened in the Bush 43 Administration. Instead, the newcomers behaved as though they had seized control of the government in a "silent coup." They tended to behave in such a way that civil servants were made to feel that somehow, they were the real enemy, barely tolerated and under suspicion. There seemed to be a general feeling among the newcomers that professional intelligence people somehow just did not "get it." To add to the discomfort, the new Bush Team began to do some odd things.

"The Information Collection Program"

Early in the Bush 43 Administration, actions began that clearly reflected a predisposition to place regime change in Iraq at the top of the foreign policy agenda. Sometime in January 2001, the Iraqi National Congress (INC), the opposition group headed by Dr. Ahmed Chalabi, began receiving U.S. State Department funds to begin an effort called the "Information Collection Program." Under the Clinton Administration, some money had been given to Iraqi exiles for what might be called agit-prop activities against Saddam's government but the INC (Chalabi) had not been taken very seriously because they had a bad reputation for spending money freely, with very little to show for it. The CIA had concluded that he and his INC colleagues were not to be trusted with taxpayer's money. Nevertheless, Chalabi had longstanding ties to a group of well-established anti-Saddam American activists who were installed by the Bush Administration as leading figures of the politically appointed civilian bureaucracy in the Pentagon and in the Office of the Vice President.

Those ties paid off. The "Information Collection Program," launched in the early months of the Bush Administration, was aimed at providing funds to the INC for recruiting defectors from Saddam's military and secret police, and making them available to American intelligence, but what the program really did was to provide a steady stream of raw information useful in challenging the collective wisdom of the intelligence community on the many points on which the "War with Iraq" enthusiasts disagreed with the intelligence agencies. If the president and Congress were to be sold the need for war, information had to be available with which to argue against what was seen as the "lack of imagination" and "timidity" of regular intelligence analysis. To facilitate the flow of such "information" to the President, a dedicated apparatus, centered in of the Office of the Vice President, created its own intelligence office, buried in the recesses of the Pentagon, to "stovepipe" raw data to the White House, to make the case for war on the basis of the testimony of self-interested émigrés and exiles.

At the time of the first Gulf War in 1991, I was the Defense Intelligence Officer for the Middle East in the Defense Intelligence Agency. This meant that I was in charge of all Defense Intelligence Agency substantive business for the region. In discussions at the time of the victorious end of that campaign and the subsequent Shia and Kurdish revolts in Iraq, it became abundantly clear that the same people who later made up the "war party" in the Bush 43 Administration were completely un-reconciled to the failure of US forces to overthrow the Saddamist regime. In spite of the lack of UN sanction for such an operation and the probable long-term costs of the inevitable American occupation of Iraq, the group later known as the "neocons" seemed deeply embittered by the lack of decisive action to remove the Iraqi dictator. Soon after the dust settled on Operation Desert Storm, the first Bush Administration helped launch the Iraqi National Congress (INC). The INC was initially an umbrella of anti-Saddam groups largely composed of Kurdish and Shi'ite organizations. In the beginning the CIA provided seed money as a result of presidential direction, and a private consulting firm, the Rendon Group, provided the initial public relations support. To this day, one of the Rendon advisors to the INC, Francis Brooke, serves as the INC's chief Washington lobbyist.

Chalabi's American connections played a dominant role in the INC's evolution over the next dozen years. At the University of Chicago, Chalabi had been a student of Dr. Albert Wohlstetter, a hard-line utopian nuclear war planner, who had been the dissertation advisor to another University of Chicago PhD, Paul Wolfowitz. Wohlstetter had also been a mentor to Richard Perle. In the summer of 1969, Wohlstetter arranged for both Wolfowitz and Perle to work for the short-lived Committee to Maintain a Prudent Defense Policy, a Washington-based group co-founded by two icons of American Cold War foreign policy, Dean Acheson and Paul Nitze. Wolfowitz and Perle remained close collaborators from that time forward.

Chalabi, an Iraqi Shia Arab, had fled Iraq in 1958, just after the overthrow of the Hashemite royal government. His father and grandfather had held cabinet posts in the British-installed Hashemite regime. Before coming to the United States to obtain a doctorate, Chalabi lived in Jordan, Lebanon and Britain. He returned to Beirut after obtaining a PhD, but in 1977, he moved to Jordan and established a new company, the Petra Bank, which grew into the second largest commercial bank in the Hashemite kingdom.

Twelve years later, the Jordanian government took over the bank, and charged Chalabi, who fled the country, with embezzling $70 million. In 1992, Chalabi was tried and convicted, in absencia. He was sentenced to 22 years at hard labor. One of the persistent stories concerning the Petra bank scandal is that Chalabi's bank was involved in arms sales to Iran during the Iran-Iraq war, and that Saddam Hussein having discovered this pressured King Hussein of Jordan to crack down on Chalabi.

Shortly after his hasty departure from Jordan, Chalabi, with the backing of his "neocon" allies in Washington, most notably, Paul Wolfowitz, Richard Perle, and Professor Bernard Lewis helped launch the INC. Chalabi had been first introduced to Perle and Wolfowitz in 1985 by their mutual mentor, Albert Wohlstetter. Bernard Lewis met Chalabi in 1990, and soon thereafter asked his own allies inside the Bush 41 Administration, including Wolfowitz's Pentagon aide Zalmay Khalilzad, to help boost the Iraqi exile. Another future Bush 43 Iraq war player also met Chalabi about that time. Gen. Wayne Downing was first introduced to Chalabi in 1991. At the time, Downing commanded the Joint Special Operations Command (JSOC) at Fort Bragg, North Carolina.

In November 1993, Chalabi presented the newly inaugurated Clinton Administration with a scheme for the overthrow of the Saddam Hussein regime. Dubbed "End Game," the plan envisioned a limited revolt by an insurgent force of INC-led Kurds and Shi'ites in the oil regions around Basra in the south, and Mosul and Kirkuk in the north of Iraq. The "End Game" scenario hoped that, at the first sign of revolt against Saddam, there would be a full-scale insurrection by military commanders, which would overthrow the Saddam clique, and install a Washington and Tel Aviv-friendly, INC-dominated new regime in Baghdad. The plan was based on a belief that Iraq was ripe for revolt and that there were not units in the armed forces that would fight to preserve Saddam's government. Since the same units had fought to keep Saddam in power during the Kurdish and Shia revolts of a few years before, it is difficult to see why the sponsors of "End Game" would have thought that. A limited effort to implement "End Game" ended in disaster in 1995 when the Iraqis did fight to defeat the rebels and the Iraqi Army killed over 100 INC combatants. From that point on, both the CIA and DIA considered Chalabi to be "persona non grata" and wanted no more to do with him. The CIA also dropped all financial backing for Chalabi, as the INC, once an umbrella group of various opposition forces, degenerated into little more than a Chalabi "cult of personality," gathered together in London, where Chalabi and his small group of remaining INC loyalists retreated.

In spite of this, neoconservatives inside the U.S., largely in exile during the Clinton Administration, succeeded in influencing the Congress enough to obtain the passage of "The Iraq Liberation Act of 1998," largely to revive Chalabi's "End Game" scheme. Now retired, Gen. Downing, along with retired CIA officer Duane "Dewey" Clarridge, of Iran-Contra fame became military "consultants" to Chalabi's INC and then drafted their own updated version of the Chalabi plan, now dubbed "the Downing Plan." It was different in name only. The Downing-Clarridge plan insisted that a "crack force" of no more than 5,000 INC troops, backed by a group of former U.S. Army Special Forces soldiers (Green Berets), could bring down the Iraq Army. "The idea from the beginning was to encourage defections of Iraqi units," Clarridge insisted. "You need to create a nucleus, something for people to defect to. If they could take Basra, it would be all over." It is difficult to understand how a retired four-star Army general could believe this to be true.

In subsequent Congressional testimony, then-Central Command head Gen. Anthony Zinni (USMC) denounced the Downing scheme in no uncertain terms, warning that it would lead to a "Bay of Goats," adding that, by his most recent counts, there were 91 Iraqi opposition groups. None of them had "the viability to overthrow Saddam." Elsewhere, he mocked Chalabi and the INC as "some silk-suited, Rolex-wearing guys in London." Despite CIA and uniformed military repudiation of "End Game," the "Downing Plan," and other variations on the same theme, the neoconservative group continued to crank out advocacy for Chalabi's proposed revolution.

On Feb. 19, 1998, a group of "neocons" calling themselves the "Committee for Peace and Security in the Gulf," issued an "Open Letter to the President," (This was BEFORE the passage of the "Iraq Liberation Act.") calling for the implementation of yet-another revised plan for the overthrow of Saddam. The letter was remarkable, in that it adopted some of the very formulations that would later be used by Vice President Dick Cheney, and other current Administration officials to justify the preventive war in Iraq that commenced on March 20, 2003. The letter stated, "Despite his defeat in the Gulf War, continuing sanctions, and the determined effort of UN inspectors to root out and destroy his weapons of mass destruction, Saddam Hussein has been able to develop biological and chemical munitions... While Iraq is not unique in possessing these weapons, it is the only country, which has used them – not just against its enemies, but its own people as well. We must presume that

Saddam is prepared to use them again. This poses a danger to our friends, our allies, and to our nation." Equally as striking as the statements about Saddam's WMD arsenals, were the recommendations in the letter. Chapter and verse, the document called for the implementation of the Downing Plan with a few added wrinkles. After demanding that the Clinton Administration recognize a "provisional government of Iraq based on the principles and leaders of the Iraqi National Congress (INC)," the letter called for the creation of INC-controlled "liberated zones" in the north and south of the country; the lifting of sanctions in those areas and the release of billions of dollars of frozen Iraqi government funds to the INC; the launching of a "systematic air campaign" against the Republican Guard divisions and the military-industrial infrastructure of Iraq; and the prepositioning of U.S. ground force equipment, "so that, as a last resort, we have the capacity to protect and assist the anti-Saddam forces in the northern and southern parts of Iraq." The letter was co-authored by former Congressman Stephen Solarz (D-NY) and Richard Perle; and the signers included some people simply sympathetic to the cause of Iraqi freedom and a pantheon of Beltway "neocons," many of whom would form the core of the Bush Administration national security apparatus. Among the signers were: Elliot Abrams, Richard Armitage, John Bolton, Stephen Bryen, Douglas Feith, Frank Gaffney, Fred Ikle, Robert Kagan, Zalmay Khalilzad, William Kristol, Michael Ledeen, Bernard Lewis, Peter Rodman, Donald Rumsfeld, Gary Schmitt, Max Singer, Casper Weinberger, Paul Wolfowitz, David Wurmser and Dov Zakheim. Some of these gentlemen may have had cause to reconsider their generosity in signing this document. This was in February 1998. A month after the release of the letter, Paul Wolfowitz and Gen. Wayne Downing briefed a group of U.S. Senators on the INC war scheme. The senators at the meeting may also have cause to regret their subsequent sponsorship of the "Iraq Liberation Iraq." This law clearly set the stage for renewed fighting in the Middle East in 2003.

The Bush-Cheney 'Clean Break'

A core group of "neoconservatives," including "Vulcans" Paul Wolfowitz and Richard Perle, came into the Bush Administration fully committed to the overthrow of the Saddam Hussein regime in Baghdad as the number one foreign policy priority for the United States, but they found it necessary to spend much of the first nine months of the Bush Presidency in bureaucratic combat with the State Department, the Joint Chiefs of Staff, and the CIA, who all remained unconvinced that Saddam Hussein posed any kind of serious threat to American strategic interests. At the first NSC meeting of the new administration, Colin Powell argued that the existing sanctions regime against Iraq was ineffective, and he promoted the idea of a change to "smart sanctions," in order to zero in on vital military technologies that might enable Saddam to rebuild his military machine which had been devastated by Desert Storm, a decade of sanctions, "no-fly zone" bombing sorties, six years of UN inspections, and the 1998 Operation Desert Fox 70-hour bombing campaign.

Arguments like this were hard to deal with for those who were so completely convinced of the necessity of a new government in Baghdad. Colin Powell cast a mighty shadow on the American political scene and his military credentials were formidable. If there had not been a cataclysmic event that tipped the balance, it is possible that the "war party" would never have won the struggle to have their point of view accepted as policy. It was the attacks on New York and Washington on September 11, 2001, that provided the "neocons" with the opportunity to turn their dreams into reality. In a war cabinet meeting at the Presidential retreat at Camp David, Maryland four days after the 9/11 attacks, Deputy Defense Secretary Paul Wolfowitz made an appeal for an immediate American military invasion of Iraq, in retaliation for the terrorist attacks. Wolfowitz argued that attacking Afghanistan would be uncertain. He worried about 100,000 American troops being bogged down in mountain fighting in Afghanistan indefinitely. In contrast, he said that Iraq was a brittle, oppressive regime that might break easily. He said that Iraq was "doable." He estimated that there was a 10 to 50 percent chance Saddam was involved in the September 11 terrorist attacks. (This, of course is a judgment that he was not involved) The U.S. would have to go after Saddam at some time if the war on terrorism was to be taken seriously." Wolfowitz's pitch for war against Iraq, rather than against the Afghan strongholds of Osama Bin Laden's Al Qaeda, was rejected at the Camp David session, and two days later, on September 17, President Bush signed a two-and-a-half page directive, marked "Top Secret," which spelled out the plan to go to war against Afghanistan. The document also ordered the Pentagon to begin preparing military options for an invasion of Iraq.

Instantly, the "neocon" apparatus inside the Pentagon and in the Office of Vice President Dick Cheney seized upon the opportunity, represented by the authorization. On September 19, 2001, the Defense Policy Board (DPB) convened a closed-door meeting to discuss Iraq. "Vulcan" Richard Perle chaired the DPB. In the past, the board had been recruited from defense experts from both parties, and with a broad range of views. In contrast, Perle's DPB had become a "neocon" sanctuary, including such leading advocates of war on Saddam as former Speaker of the House Newt Gingrich, former CIA Director R. James Woolsey, (a Democrat but nevertheless a long standing member of the "neocon" group) former arms control advisor Ken Adelman, former Undersecretary of Defense Fred C. Ikle, and former Vice President Dan Quayle. Wolfowitz and Defense Secretary Donald Rumsfeld attended the Sept. 19 session. The speakers at the event, who aggressively advocated U.S. military action to overthrow Saddam Hussein, were Ahmed Chalabi and Dr. Bernard Lewis.

One consequence of the DPB meeting was that former CIA Director Woolsey was secretly dispatched by Wolfowitz to London, to seek out evidence that Saddam Hussein was behind the 9/11 attacks and the earlier 1993 attack on the World Trade Center. Part of Woolsey's mission involved making contact with INC officials, to get their help in further substantiating the link between hijacker Mohammed Atta and Iraqi intelligence. This theory was the brainchild of Laurie Mylroie, a scholar completely "in tune" with "neocon" thinking. According to news accounts at the time, Woolsey's actions drew the attention of police officials in Wales, who contacted the U.S. embassy to confirm that Woolsey was on "official U.S. government business," as he claimed. It was only then that Secretary of State Colin Powell and CIA Director Tenet found out about Woolsey's mission.

By October 2001, Undersecretary of Defense for Policy, Douglas Feith, had established a two-man intelligence cell inside his office with the job of combing the intelligence community's classified files to establish a pattern of evidence linking Saddam Hussein to Al Qaeda and the 9/11 attacks. The permanent, statutory agencies of the national intelligence community could not support such beliefs on the basis of what they saw in their own files, and so some other means was sought to obtain the conclusion that the Iraqi government had been involved in 9/11. The team's mission was to cull the massive data holdings of the intelligence database and to "uncover" intelligence reports accumulated on the subject of Iraq-Al Qaeda links. The issue of whether or not the intelligence agencies considered these reports to be true was thought immaterial. Not surprisingly, some of the sweetest cherries picked in the data searches came from informants provided by the INC's "Information Collection Program." The team in Feith's office was later more formally constituted as the "Policy Counter terrorism Evaluation

Group." This kind of single-minded intensity in pursuing his goals was nothing new for Feith.

In July 1996, Douglas Feith had been a principal author of a study prepared for Israeli Prime Minister Benjamin Netanyahu. This paper advocated abrogation of the Oslo Accords, and the "launch" of a new regional balance of power scheme based on American-Israeli military dominance with a subsidiary military role for Turkey and Jordan. The study was produced by the "Institute for Advanced Strategic and Political Studies" (IASPS), a Jerusalem based Likud Party-linked think tank, and was called "A Clean Break: A New Strategy for Securing the Realm." In it, Feith and company wrote, "Israel can shape its strategic environment, in cooperation with Turkey and Jordan, by weakening, containing, and even rolling back Syria. This effort can focus on removing Saddam Hussein from power in Iraq – an important Israeli strategic objective in its own right –as a means of foiling Syria's regional ambitions." The study group leader was Richard Perle. Other members of the team included Charles Fairbanks Jr., a longtime friend of Paul Wolfowitz, since their student days together at the University of Chicago; David Wurmser, an American Enterprise Institute Middle East fellow; and his wife, Meyrav Wurmser, who headed the Washington, DC office of the Middle East Media Research Institute (MEMRI). Her boss in that group was a retired Israeli intelligence officer, Yigal Carmon. On July 8, 1996, Richard Perle presented the "Clean Break" document to Netanyahu, who was visiting Washington. Two days later, the Israeli Prime Minister unveiled the document as his own regional foreign policy design in a speech before a joint session of the U.S. Congress.

The initial team, selected by Feith, to conduct the "cherry picking" data search mission in the Pentagon, consisted of "Clean Break" co-author David Wurmser and Michael Maloof. Maloof was a career Pentagon bureaucrat, who had joined forces with Perle during the Reagan years, when Perle was a Pentagon official. At that time Maloof was a deputy to Dr. Stephen Bryen. The existence of the Wurmser-Maloof unit was kept a secret within the Pentagon for more than a year. Only on Oct. 24, 2002, did Defense Secretary Rumsfeld formally announce that he had commissioned what the Washington Post called "a small team of defense officials outside regular intelligence channels to focus on unearthing details about Iraqi ties with Al Qaeda and other terrorist networks." The unveiling of the "Policy Counter terrorism Evaluations Group," as Pentagon officials dubbed it, coincided with a move by Rumsfeld to directly takeover the financing and management of the INC's

"Information Collection Project" from the State Department, which had developed serious reservations about maintaining an "off the reservation" intelligence operation.

Rumsfeld defensively told the Pentagon press corps on Oct. 24, 2002 "Any suggestion that it's an intelligence gathering activity or an intelligence unit of some sort, I think would be a misunderstanding of it." But former CIA case officer and American Enterprise Institute fellow Reuel Marc Gerecht, a relatively late recruit to the "neocon cause, could barely conceal his enthusiasm in discussing the group, "The Pentagon is setting up the capability to assess information on Iraq in areas that in the past might have been the realm of the agency. (CIA) They don't think the product they receive from the agency is always what it should be." Gerecht was then consulting with the "Policy Counter terrorism Evaluation Group." In September 2001, the State Department Inspector General issued a scathing audit of the INC, charging that the group had failed to account for how it was spending its U.S. government cash. "The Information Collection Project" was singled out as one of the particular problem cases. According to the audit, there was no accounting for how informants were paid, or what benefit had been derived from their work. As the result of the audit, the State Department placed severe restrictions on the INC, suspended some payouts, and insisted that an outside auditor co-sign for all funds drawn by the group.

It was not until June 2002 that the State Department loosened the restrictions on the INC's cash flows. By then, the drive for a war against Iraq was in high gear inside the Pentagon civilian bureaucracy, and Feith and company sought direct control over the INC, (as opposed to the State Department) particularly the informant program.

No Saddam-Al Qaeda Ties

The overwhelming view within the professional U.S. intelligence community was (and is) that there was no Saddam Hussein link to the 9/11 terrorists. Admiral Bob Inman, who served in both Democratic and Republican administrations as head of the Office of Naval Intelligence, Director of the National Security Agency, and Deputy Director of the CIA, bluntly stated, "There was no tie between Iraq and 9/11, even though some people tried to postulate one... Iraq did support terror in Israel, but I know of no instance in which Iraq funded, direct, deliberate terrorist attacks on the U.S. By contrast, we know with certainty that Iran funded the bombing of the Marine barracks in Beirut. So if you're looking for a country funding attacks on Americans, Iran would have been the next priority."

Vincent Cannistraro, who headed the CIA's Counterterrorism Office before his retirement in 1990, maintains close ties to the intelligence community to this day. He also debunks the Saddam 9/11 claims. "The policy makers already had a conceit they had adopted without reference to current intelligence estimates. And those conceits were basically: Saddam was evil, a bad man, he had evil intentions, and they were greatly influenced, of course, by some of the neoconservatives' beliefs that Saddam had been involved with the sponsorship of terrorism in the United States since as early as 1993, with the first World Trade Center bombing; what Laurie Mylroie had articulated in her book, and which the neocons such as Woolsey and Richard Perle and Paul Wolfowitz had all adopted." He continued, "They threw in the World Trade Center..." None of this is true, of course, but these were their conceits, and they continue in large measure to be the conceits of a lot of people like Jim Woolsey." This, he added, is not the view of the intelligence community. "No, no, no, look, the FBI did a pretty thorough investigation of the first World Trade Center bombing and while it's true that their policy was to treat terrorism as a law enforcement problem, nevertheless, they understood how the first World Trade Center bombing was supported... and had linkages back to Osama Bin Laden. He was of course, not indicted... because the FBI until recently believed that you prosecuted perpetrators, not the sponsors. In any event they knew there was no Saddam linkage. Laurie Mylroie promoted a lot of this, and people who came in [to the Bush Administration], particularly in the Defense Department, Wolfowitz and Feith, were acolytes, promoting her book, The Study of Revenge," particularly in the "Office of Special Plans," and the Secretary's Policy Office. In any event, they already had their preconceived notions... So the intelligence, and I can speak directly to the CIA part of it, the intelligence community's assessments were never considered adequate."

The Office of Special Plans

Sometime before the 9/11 attacks, Vice President Cheney dispatched one of his Middle East aides, William Luti, over to the Pentagon, as Deputy Undersecretary of Defense for Near East and South Asian Affairs (NESA). Luti, now a retired Navy Captain, should be thought of as a completely loyal member of the neocon group. Dr. Albert Wohlstetter had recruited Luti, to the neocon camp. They had met in the early 1990s, when Luti was part of an executive panel of advisors to the Chief of Naval Operations.

Parenthetically, the author once received what must have been an exploratory recruiting visit from Dr. Wohlstettor and his wife, Roberta. In 1992, the Wohlstettors unexpectedly arrived at my doorstep in the Pentagon with the news that a mutual friend, now a senior personage in the Pentagon, had told them to visit me. There followed an hour and a half long conversation involving European and World history, philosophy and a discussion of the various illustrious people who were friends and associates of the Wohlstettors. Roberta Wohlstetter went so far as to show me various books that they and their friends had written. An unspoken question seemed to hang in the air. After a while they became impatient with my responses and left, never to return. Clearly, I had failed the test. At the time, I only vaguely knew who these people were and did not really care, but since they have become so important to this story I have asked various "smart" people who might have received similar visits, and found that this was not such an uncommon thing. An old academic colleague of Wohlstettor has also told me that the couple had done similar things in the university setting.

In any case, Luti landed a job as a military aide to Speaker of the House Gingrich (R-Ga.) from 1996-97. There, he worked with Air Force Col. William Bruner, another active duty military officer on loan to the Speaker. Still on active duty when the Bush 43 Administration came into office, Luti worked in the Vice President's Office, as part of a shadow "National Security Council" staff, under the direction of Cheney's chief of staff and chief policy aide, I. Lewis "Scooter" Libby.

Libby was a Yale Law School protégé of Paul Wolfowitz. Beginning in the 1980s, Libby followed Wolfowitz into the Reagan and Bush 41 Administrations. When he was not working for Uncle Sam and Uncle Paul, Libby was the law partner/protégé of Richard Nixon's personal attorney, Leonard Garment. Under his direction, for a period of 16 years, on and off, Libby was the attorney for fugitive swindler, and Israeli Mossad protégé, Marc Rich. In the first Bush Administration, Libby served with Wolfowitz in the policy office of then-Defense Secretary Cheney, where he gained some notoriety as one of the principal authors, along with Wolfowitz and Zalmay Khalilzad, of the draft 1992 "Defense Planning Guidance" that advocated preventive war and the development of a new arsenal of mini-nuclear weapons, to be used against Third World targets thought to be developing arsenals of weapons of mass destruction.

Sometime midway through 2001, Luti retired from the Navy, and took a civilian Pentagon post as head of NESA. Under normal circumstances, NESA is a Pentagon backwater, responsible primarily for arranging bilateral meetings with military counterparts from a region stretching "from Bangladesh to Marakesh" – i.e., from South Asia to North Africa. Before the recent war, the NESA staff worked daily with the "Defense Intelligence Officer for the Near East, South Asia, and Counterterrorism." This was the most senior officer in DIA for that region and the person responsible for seeing that NESA was well provided with intelligence information. During the early Luti period at NESA, the DIO was Bruce Hardcastle. There were "DIOs" for each of the major regions of the world, Hardcastle happened to be the man for the Middle East. I knew Hardcastle and respected his work. He had been a middle level analyst in DIA when I held the job of DIO for the Middle East.

Abruptly, last year, the Defense Department dismantled the entire DIO system. It now seems likely that frictions that developed between Luti and Hardcastle were a significant factor in this destruction of a very worthwhile intelligence analytic system. Historically, the DIO oversaw all of the regional analysts and assets of DIA, but reported directly to the Director of the DIA, avoiding bureaucratic and managerial duties while retaining responsibility for all analysis within his or her geographic domain. The roots of the friction between Hardcastle and Luti were straightforward: Hardcastle brought with him the combined wisdom of the professional military intelligence community. The community had serious doubts about the lethality of the threat from Saddam Hussein, the terrorism links, and the status of the Iraqi WMD programs. Luti could not accept this. He knew what he wanted. This was to bring down Saddam Hussein. Hardcastle could not accept the very idea of allowing a desired outcome to shape the results of analysis.

Even before the Iraq desk at NESA was expanded into the "Office of Special Plans," in August 2002, Luti had transformed NESA into a "de facto" arm of the Vice President's office. While the normal chain of command for NESA ran through Undersecretary for Policy Feith, and up to Deputy Secretary Wolfowitz and Secretary Rumsfeld, Luti made it clear that his chain of command principally ran directly up to Scooter Libby, Cheney's chief of staff. We are lucky enough to have a description of this relationship from a participant in the business of the office itself.

Lt. Col. (Ret.) Karen Kwiatkowski (USAF) who served as the North

Africa desk officer at NESA from June of 2002 to March of 2003 provides an interesting perspective by a member of NESA. She had served previously in the Pentagon at the Office of the Air Force Chief of Staff. She says she "was shocked to learn that Luti was effectively working for Libby. "In one of the first staff meetings that I attended there," she recalled recently, "Bill Luti said, 'Well, did you get that thing over to Scooter? Scooter wants this, and somebody's got to get it over to him, and get that up to him right away.' After the meeting, I asked one of my co-workers, who'd been there longer, 'Who is this Scooter?' I was told, 'That's Scooter Libby over at the OVP. (Office of the Vice president). He's the Vice President's chief of staff.' Later I came to understand that Cheney had put Luti there."

Kwiatkowski learned that OSP personnel were participating, along with officials from the DIA and CIA, in the debriefings of Chalabi-delivered informants. John Trigilio, a DIA officer assigned to NESA, confirmed it to her, in a heated discussion. "I argued with him (Tregilio) after the President's Cincinnati speech [in October 2002]. I told him that the President had made a number of statements that were just not supported by the intelligence I had access to. He said that the president's statements are supported by intelligence, and he would finally say, 'We have sources that you don't have.' I did not take it to mean top-secret intelligence. I took it to mean the sources that Chalabi was bringing in for debriefing." "Trigilio did participate," she continued. "He told me he participated in a number of debriefs, conducted in hotels downtown, or wherever, of people that Chalabi brought in. These debriefs had Trigilio from OSP, but also CIA and DIA participated." "If it (the information) sounded good, it would go straight to the OVP, or elsewhere. I don't put it out of possibility that the information would go straight to the media because of the (media) close relationship with some of the neoconservatives. So this information would make it straight out into the knowledge base, into the realm of common knowledge, without waiting for intelligence (community analysts) to come by with their qualifications, with their qualifiers, and reservations."

NESA/OSP apparently carried the "cherry picking" methods of the smaller "Policy Counter terrorism Evaluation Group" to a new level of effectiveness according to Lt. Col. Kwiatkowski. "At the OSP, what they were doing was looking at all the intelligence that they could find on WMD. That was the focal point, picking bits and pieces that were the most inflammatory, removing any context that might have been provided in the original intelligence report, that would have caused you to have some pause in believing it, or reflected doubts that the intelligence community had, so if the intelligence community had doubts, those would be left out." Quoting her again, "They would take items that had occurred many years ago, and put them in the present tense, make it seem like they occurred not many years ago…. But they would not talk about the dates, they would say things like; 'he has continued since that time' and he could do it tomorrow, which of course, wasn't true" "And then the other thing they would do would be to take unrelated events that were reported in totally unrelated ways and make connections that the intelligence community had not made. This was primarily in discussing Iraq's activities and how they might be related to Al Qaeda or other terrorist groups that might be against us, or against Israel." "These kinds of links would be made, and they would be made casually, and they would be made in a calculated way to form an image that is definitely not the image that anyone reading the original reports would have. The summaries that we would see from Intelligence did not match the kind of things that OSP was putting out. So that is what I call propaganda development, it goes beyond the manipulation of intelligence to propaganda development." A number of people have made the observation that Lt. Col. Kwiatkowski did not have sufficient access to have seen what was going on with intelligence materials. The previous paragraphs would seem to disprove that idea.

Kwiatkowski also knows a lot about Luti's efforts to exclude DIO Bruce Hardcastle from the briefings to foreign military officials. Luti ordered that Hardcastle was not to be included in briefings on Iraq, its WMD, and its links to terrorism. Instead, the Iraq desk of NESA and later the Office of Special Plans, would produce "talking points" which, Luti insisted, were to be the only briefings provided on Iraq. "With the talking points," she says, "many of the propagandistic bullets that were given to use in papers for our superiors, to inform them, internal propaganda, many of those same phrases and assumptions, and tones, well, I saw them in Vice President Cheney's speeches and the President's speeches. So I got the impression that those talking points were not just for us, but kind of a core of an overall agenda for a disciplined product, beyond the Pentagon. Over at the Vice President's Office and the Weekly Standard, the media, and the neoconservative talking heads and that kind of thing, all on the same sheet of music."

Lt. Col. Kwiatkowski identified Abram Shulsky as the principal author of the NESA/OSP talking points on Iraq. Shulsky was one of the Pentagon "defense intellectuals" who had been involved on the periphery of intelligence work since the late 1970s, when he first came to Washington as an aide to Sen. Daniel Patrick Moynihan (D-NY). He also worked for Sen. Henry "Scoop"

Jackson (D-Wa.) Shulsky shared a common background with Paul Wolfowitz. Both men had graduated from the University of Chicago and had studied under Dr. Leo Strauss. In 1999, Shulsky, along with his fellow Chicago alumnus and Strauss protégé, Gary Schmitt, founder of the "Project for the New American Century" (PNAC), wrote an essay entitled, "Leo Strauss and the World of Intelligence," which attacked American intelligence community icon Sherman Kent, for failing to understand that all intelligence work ultimately comes down to deception and counter-deception. For Shulsky, (as expressed in his article) the goal of intelligence is to serve the needs of policy makers in making possible the attainment of policy goals. Intelligence, he wrote, "Was the art of deception," and Shulsky seems to have set out to use the OSP as the means for providing the Bush Administration policymakers all the ammunition they needed to get their desired results. Interestingly, neither Shulsky nor the great majority of the people employed at one time or another by all these "ad hoc" intelligence groups were people with any previous experience of intelligence work. They were former congressional staffers, scholars, and activists of one kind or another. They were people embarked on a great adventure in pursuit of a goal, not craftsmen devoted to their art.

Subverting and Subduing the Intelligence Professionals

Supporting the statements of Kwiatkowski and others about the pipeline of unevaluated information that flowed straight into the hands of Vice President Cheney and other key policy makers, there is extent a June 2002 letter from the INC's Washington office addressed to the Senate Appropriations Committee, which argues for the transfer of the "Information Collection Program" from the State Department to the Defense Intelligence Agency's Defense HUMINT Service. (A service which I was instrumental in founding) In a clumsy act of indiscretion, the letter's author explained that there was already a direct flow of information from the INC into the hands of Bill Luti and John Hannah, the latter being Scooter Libby's deputy in Cheney's office.

Armed with the INC product, Vice President Cheney made a series of visits to the CIA headquarters at Langley, to question "Agency" analysts, who were producing assessments that did not match the material that had been funneled to him through Luti and Hannah. The Vice President also made personal visits to many members of the Congress, to persuade them, in the autumn of 2002, to grant the President the authority to go to war with Iraq. One leading Democratic Senator says that Cheney sat in his office, and made what now appear to be greatly exaggerated claims about Saddam's nuclear weapons program. The fear of Saddam possessing a nuclear bomb compelled the Senator to vote in favor of granting the war powers.

Part of the "Saddam bomb plot" tale came from Dr. Khidir Hamza, an Iraqi nuclear scientist who defected in 1994, and settled in the United States through the assistance of the INC. Hamza initially went to work for the "Institute for Science and International Security," a think tank headed by a former UN weapons inspector, David Albright. According to a May 12, 2003 New Yorker interview by Seymour Hersh with Albright, Hamza and his boss drafted a 1998 proposal for a book, that would have exposed how Saddam's quest for a nuclear bomb had "fizzled." There were no takers. But, two years later, Hamza co-authored a very different book, with Jeff Stein, vastly exaggerating Saddam's nuclear weapons program. This, despite the fact that, in 1995, Saddam Hussein's son in law, General Hussein Kamel, who was the head of Iraq's weapons agency, escaped to Jordan with a large collection of Iraqi government documents that showed how little was left of Iraqi WMD programs. Kamel was interviewed by a team of UN weapons inspectors, headed by Rolf Ekeus, the chairman of the UN teams, and he confirmed that the inspections had, in effect, uprooted most of what was left of the Iraqi WMD program, after the 1991 Gulf War.

It was telling that, in the more than two-year run-up to the March 2003 invasion of Iraq, nobody in the Bush Administration sought to commission a National Intelligence Estimate (NIE) on Saddam Hussein's WMD programs. Perhaps, it is not surprising that they did not want such an estimate. An estimate, if conducted over a period of months, would undoubtedly have revealed deep skepticism about the threat posed by Saddam's weapons program. It would have exposed major gaps in the intelligence picture, particularly since the pullout of UN weapons inspectors from Iraq at the end of 1998, and it would have likely undercut the rush to war. It was only as the result of intense pressure from Sen. Bob Graham (D-Fla.), the chairman of the Senate Select Committee on Intelligence, that the intelligence community was finally tasked, in September 2002, to produce an NIE on Saddam's WMD programs. The report was to be rushed to completion in three weeks, so it could reach the desks of the relevant Congressional committee members before a vote on war powers authorization, scheduled for early October, on the eve of the midterm elections. As the NIE went forward for approval everyone knew that there were major problems with it.

The issue of the Niger yellowcake uranium precursor had been a point of controversy, since late 2001, when the Italian secret service, SISMI, reported to their American, British and Israeli counterparts, that they had obtained documents on Niger government letterhead, indicating that Iraq had attempted to purchase 500 tons of yellowcake. The yellowcake lead had been reported to Vice President, by his CIA daily briefing officer, and Cheney had tasked the CIA to dig deeper. Obviously, if the case could be made that Saddam was aggressively seeking nuclear material, no one in Congress could justifiably oppose war. The story proved to be a hoax. In February 2002, the CIA dispatched former Ambassador Joe Wilson to Niger to look into the report. Wilson had served in several African countries, including Niger, and had also been the U.S. "charge d'affaires" in Baghdad, at the time of the Iraq invasion of Kuwait. He knew all the players. After several days of meetings in Niger, he returned to Washington and was debriefed by the CIA. The yellowcake story simply did not check out. Case closed. Contrary to Wilson's expectations, the Niger story, or variations on it, continued to creep into policy speeches by top Administration officials. Although CIA Director George Tenet personally intervened to remove references to the discredited African uranium story from President Bush's early October 2002 speech in Cincinnati, Ohio promoting the overthrow of Saddam Hussein, the Niger yellowcake fake information appeared in a December 19, 2002 State Department "fact sheet" on Saddam's failure to disclose his secret WMD programs. As we all know, President Bush's January 2003 State of the Union speech contained the now infamous 16 words, citing British intelligence claims about Saddam seeking uranium in Africa.

For Greg Thielmann, who retired in Sept. 2002 from his post as director of the Strategic, Proliferation and Military Affairs Office at the State Department's Intelligence Bureau, the issue of the aluminum tubes was an even more egregious case of policymakers' contamination of the intelligence process than the Wilson "yellowcake" affair. His position is that, "What was done with the aluminum tubes was far worse than what was done with the uranium from Africa. Because the intelligence community had debated over a period of months and involved key scientists and engineers in the National Laboratories – and foreigners as well – in a long and detailed discussion. The way I would have characterized it, if you had asked me in July 2002, when I turned over the leadership of my office, there was a growing consensus in the intelligence community that this kind of aluminum was not suitable for the nuclear weapons program. So, I was really quite shocked to see – I was just retired – to see the National Intelligence Estimate say that the majority of agencies came to the opposite interpretation, that it was going into the nuclear weapons program."

Even with this "majority" view, Thielmann points out that anyone at the White House or the National Security Council, who was genuinely seeking the truth, would have seen through the subterfuge and drawn the proper conclusion. "If they had read the NIE in October, it is transparent that there were different views in the intelligence community. They could have read, for example, that the Department of Energy and the State Department INR believed that the aluminum tubes were not going into the nuclear weapons program, and instead, were going into conventional artillery rockets. And, if one assumes a modicum of intelligence understanding at the NSC, they should know that one agency that is most able to judge on this would be the Department of Energy. They control all the laboratories that actually over the years have enriched uranium, and built centrifuges. So that's really where the expertise of the U.S. government lay on this question. We were, from the State Department INR, we were sitting as a jury, listening to this long debate between CIA and the other experts. We started out agnostic and then over time, became very confident in the Department of Energy version of events, because they could answer the logical questions. They were, after all, the best people to analyze."

Thielmann also had an important observation about the "Office of Special Plans," and the other intelligence boutiques that Cheney and Rumsfeld and Wolfowitz had established inside the Pentagon's policy shop. "I did not know these guys. I didn't even know the names of these people. They were sort of non-players. They did not exist. It was a stealth organization. They didn't play in the intelligence community proceedings that our office participated in. When the intelligence community met as an intelligence community, there was no OSP represented in these sessions. Because then, if they did that, they would have had to subject their views to peer review, and they didn't want to do that. Why do that when you can send stuff right into the Vice President?"

The NIE Contamination

Two other major INC-foisted fabrications made their way into the NIE, and, from there, into policy speeches by top Bush Administration officials, including the President, the Vice President, and the Secretaries of Defense and State.

The first involved claims that Iraq had mobile biological weapons labs that could produce deadly biological agents. The declassified version of the October 2002 NIE stated that "Baghdad has mobile facilities for producing bacterial and toxin BW agents; these facilities can evade detection and are highly survivable. Within three to six months, these units probably could produce an amount of agent equal to the total that Iraq produced in the years prior to the Gulf war." The same claim was a dramatic highlight of Colin Powell's February 5, 2003, presentation before the UN Security Council.

But a subsequent review of the intelligence files – long after the NIE had been produced – revealed that the sole source for the mobile lab story was an Iraqi military defector, a major, who had been produced by the INC via the "Information Collection Program." The CIA and DIA had both given warnings about the defector, after concluding that he was a "fabricator." But, as CIA Director Tenet would later admit in a February 2004 speech at Georgetown University, those warnings fell on deaf ears. The fabrication judgment was shown to be correct after the U.S. invasion when two of the mobile labs were captured. They were, as other Iraqi sources had claimed, mobile facilities for producing hydrogen for weather balloons.

A somewhat different fiasco occurred on the issue of the equally inflammatory claim that Iraq had unmanned airborne vehicles (UAVs), outfitted to deliver biological and chemical weapons. Allegations about the UAVs surfaced in early September 2002, prompting both CIA Director Tenet and Vice President Cheney to visit House and Senate leaders, the day Congress reconvened after the Labor Day recess, to present their new "smoking gun" argument for war. The UAV story appeared in President Bush's Oct. 7, 2002, speech in Cincinnati, Ohio. It was also featured in Colin Powell's UN Security Council presentation four months later. Powell warned the Council then that "Iraq could use these small UAVs, which have a wingspan of only a few meters, to deliver biological agents to its neighbors, or, if transported, to other countries, including the United States."

Yet, the declassified version of the Oct. 2002 NIE, while reporting that "Baghdad's UAVs could threaten Iraq's neighbors, US forces in the Persian

Gulf and if brought close to, or into, the United States, the US Homeland," also noted that "The Director, Intelligence, Surveillance and Reconnaissance, US Air Force, does not agree that Iraq is developing UAVs primarily intended to be delivery platforms for chemical and biological warfare (CBW) agents. The small size of Iraq's new UAV strongly suggests a primary role of reconnaissance, although CBW delivery is an inherent capability." Indeed, the specifications of the Iraqi UAVs, known to US Air Force Intelligence, proved that they were ill suited for CBW dissemination. According to several news accounts, even the formulation that "CBW delivery is an inherent capability" was foisted upon the Air Force during the negotiating sessions over the final wording of the NIE.

The subversion of the intelligence process was a death by a thousand tiny cuts, a cumulative process of badgering, in which the pipeline of disinformation, from the INC, through OSP, to the desk of the Vice President played a decisive role.

Cannistraro puts it this way: "Over a long period of time, there was a subtle process of pressure and intimidation, until people started giving them what was wanted, maybe not as completely as they wanted, but you certainly looked hard for answers that you could give them that they wanted. When the Senate Intelligence Committee interviewed under oath, over 100 analysts, not one of them said, 'Well, I changed my assessment because of pressure;' none of them would admit to that, and no decent analyst would do exactly that. But the process is much more subtle than can be described by saying, 'I was intimidated into giving this answer.' I think the environment was conditioned in such a way that the analyst subtly leaned toward the conceits of the policy makers… The intelligence community was vulnerable to the aggressiveness of neoconservative policy makers, particularly at the Pentagon and at the VP's office. As one analyst said to me, 'you can't fight something with nothing, and those people had something. And whether it was right, or wrong, or fraudulent or specious, it almost didn't make any difference, because the policy makers believed it already, and if you didn't have hard countervailing" evidence to persuade them, then you were at a loss.' And I think that was the kind of situation we saw."

Cannistraro also has this to say on the issue of the OSP "stovepipe." "This stuff did not pass go, did not get sanctioned or coordinated or endorsed by the intelligence community. It went directly to the policy makers and found its way into their speeches. As we know, and Chalabi himself admitted it, a lot of this information was specious… Did that play a major role? Clearly it played a major role. Don't forget the "Iraq Liberation Act" authorized something like $100 million to fund the opposition. The principle beneficiary was the INC, Chalabi. So he got a big chunk of money from that first appropriation, and with it, the INC hired Richard Perle as a lobbyist to get more money, continuing money, to the point that even in the current intelligence budget, there's apparently over $3.5 million allocated for the INC. It was an incestuous relationship. What our money bought us was a constant stream of fabricated information, as well as some that was just of dubious origin, but some were actually fabricated. In many cases, the INC coached defectors what to say to the intelligence people, whether it was DIA or CIA. And what happened? Not only did this stuff get into policymakers' speeches, such as the Vice President's speeches. It got in, it seeped into the premiere intelligence product that the community makes, which is the NIE – the premiere product prior to the invasion of Iraq. To the point that information from a known fabricator, even though it had been red flagged by the DIA, got into this Estimate itself. So this means that the process of producing the most prestigious and influential intelligence estimate the government is capable of, was corrupted."

Lt. Col. Dale Davis (USMC-ret.) concurs that the intelligence process was badly subverted by a "political operation." Davis, through March of this year, headed International Programs at Virginia Military Institute. He is a fluent Arabic speaker and has served throughout the Arab world. Davis initially said that he did not think that the intelligence analysts were pressured, "per se." "I clearly believe that the reason the Administration and Rumsfeld set up OSP was because they weren't getting the answers that they wanted out of the intelligence community, so they created an organization that would give them the answers they wanted. Or at least, piece together a very compelling case by rummaging through all the various intelligence reports and picking out the best, the most juicy, but quite often the most flimsy pieces of information."

On the issue of the corruption of the process, Davis says, "it's very subtle. The Vice President doesn't have to say, 'You're an idiot, redo this report.' For him, it is sufficient to use the weight of his office in a very subtle and mild way during a briefing with an analyst, an intelligence analyst, to get across the message that this isn't appropriate. By creating the OSP, Cheney was able to say, 'Hey, look at what we're getting out of OSP. How come you guys aren't doing as well? What is your response to what this alternative analysis that we're receiving from the Pentagon says? That's how you do it. You pressure people indirectly."

The Countdown

"Why on earth didn't [Saddam] let the
inspectors in and avoid the war."

> Sen. Pat Roberts, Chairman, Senate
> Select Committee on Intelligence,
> quoted in a New York Times column
> by Paul Krugman, February 6, 2004

Sen. Patrick Roberts of Kansas is the Republican Chairman of the Senate
Select Committee on Intelligence, which is today investigating the misuse
of intelligence prior to the Iraq war, the failures of intelligence, the Iraqi
National Congress, and the Office of Special Plans. The answer to his question
is simple:

Saddam {did} let the inspectors in, at a level of cooperation that was
unprecedented.

The question that Senator Roberts should really be asking is, "Why didn't
it matter"?

It should have been a warning to the U.S. Congress that it was a very
bad sign of things to come, when the man who had been convicted of lying
to Congress during the "Iran-Contra Affair"-- Elliot Abrams -- was put in
charge of the Middle East section of the National Security Council staff. One
under-estimated talent of the "neocon" group in the run up to this war was
its ability to manipulate Congress. They were masters of the game, having
"made the team" in Washington in the 1970s on the staffs of two of the most
powerful Senators in recent decades: New York's Senator Patrick Moynihan,
and Washington's Senator Henry "Scoop" Jackson. The "old boys club" --
Abe Shulsky at OSP, Undersecretary of Defense Paul Wolfowitz, Assistant
Secretary of Defense for Policy Doug Feith, Middle East Desk Officer at the
NSC, Elliot Abrams, Defense Policy Board Chairman Richard Perle -- had
not only worked together in their early government years in these two Senate
offices, but they had stayed together as a network through the ensuing decades,
floating around a small number of businesses and think-tanks, including the
American Enterprise Institute, and the openly neo-imperialist Project for a
New American Century (PNAC). The neo-cons were openly contemptuous of
Congress, as they were of the U.N. Security Council. And a number of tricks
and manipulations of the Congressional process have now been exposed. But

was the trickery planned? Was it a well-orchestrated obfuscation, an accident, or coincidence? What is the evidence?

First, there was the consistent refusal to provide witnesses and information to the U.S. Senate, especially regarding the projected costs of the war, and the lack of opportunities to question key players, such as Gen. Jay Garner, who was appointed by the Defense Department to be the first head of the U.S. provisional authority in Iraq. There was also the subtle hiding of the objections of the Department of Energy and the State Department's Bureau of Intelligence and Research (INR) in the NIE of October 2002. One Congressional source explained that the classified NIE was made available in its entirety to only a select few members of Congress. There were verbal briefings, and an elaborate process to access the document in a secure location. But, it was never clear that the 27-page unclassified version that was available to every office was missing any crucial information.

There were also false statements to Congress about providing the U.N. inspectors {all} the intelligence that might have helped them locate the Iraqi Weapons of Mass Destruction, and programs. Sen. Carl Levin of Michigan has accused the Administration, and especially CIA Director Tenet of withholding information because "the truth" -- that the U.S. had withheld the locations of 21 high- and middle-priority sites -- might have slowed down the drive for war. "The truth" might have convinced Congress to take action to delay military action until the inspections were completed.

The March 7, 2003, appearance by the UNMOVIC (Blix) and IAEA (Baradei) chairmen before the UN Security Council was a disaster for the "neo-conservatives." The Iraqis and Saddam Hussein had "accelerated" cooperation with the United Nations, said Dr. Hans Blix, the chairman of UNMOVIC. Blix told the Council that Iraq had made a major concession -- they had agreed to allow the destruction of the Al Samoud ballistic missiles. "We are not watching the breaking of toothpicks," Blix said. "Lethal weapons are being destroyed. "The destruction undertaken constitutes a substantial measure of disarmament -- indeed, the first since the middle of the 1990s."

The Al Samoud, a massive missile, 7 meters long, weighing two tons with its warhead, was being destroyed, without the slightest obstruction, or even complaints from the Iraqis. Major Corrine Heraud, a French woman who served as the chief weapons inspector for UNMOVIC in this operation, and who had also served, beginning in 1996 with UNSCOM, says that the level of cooperation from the Iraqis was unprecedented -- something that she never would have expected, and did not encounter during the 1996-98 inspections.

Each single missile cost more than $1 million, estimates Maj. Heraud, who also cautions that this would be equivalent to a much higher amount in Western dollars, considering the difficulty that Iraq encountered in buying materials and parts, due to the U.N. sanctions.

Yet, to President George W. Bush, the destruction of the Al Samoud, a missile that is often mistaken in photographs for the better-known SCUD missile, was meaningless. The missile destruction, said Bush, was a "campaign of deception." For the UN inspectors, Bush's words were a shock. "We didn't know what to make of this," an UNMOVIC official said.

"Blix came down hard on the Iraqis, and we actually were in the process of destroying all these Al Samoud missiles," says Greg Thielman the former head of the WMD section of INR. "As soon as the Iraqis agreed to do that I kind of sighed a big sigh of relief. I thought "the UN inspectors are working; we've stared Saddam down, we've forced him to do what he desperately didn't want to do, in the most active, in that area, of activity that was of most concern to us." Thielman believes that the al Samoud incident shows that the Administration was so intent on war, that this compliance with the inspections "made no difference."

But it was after the next presentation, that by IAEA chairman, Mohammed El-Baradei, that "all hell broke loose" in Washington. El Baradei in his statement sank the U.S. intelligence community's prestigious "National Intelligence Estimate," President Bush's State of the Union address, and Colin Powell's Feb. 5 address to the UN Security Council with one blow. El Baradei was calm in what he had to say. "With regard to uranium acquisition, the IAEA has made progress in its investigation into reports that Iraq sought to buy uranium from Niger in recent years," he began. "Based on thorough analysis, the IAEA has concluded, with the concurrence of outside experts, that these documents, which form the basis for reports of recent uranium transactions between Iraq and Niger -- are in fact, not authentic." The Niger "yellow cake" documents were forgeries. Then El Baradei told the press that an IAEA staff member had in fact used the common search engine, Google, to determine, within hours that the Niger documents, which had been passed on to the U.S. Embassy in Rome through an anonymous source, were fakes! Members of Congress then began to grumble. In light of the contradictions, a bill was introduced, demanding that the Administration disclose the intelligence reports that were the basis for the statements made by Bush, Cheney, Rumsfeld and Powell about the Iraqi WMD threat. It was locked still locked in committee when the war began.

The destruction of the Al Samoud missiles continued. It was not only missiles, reports UNMOVIC chief weapons inspector Corrine Heroud, it was engines, launchers, training missiles, and missiles still in production that were destroyed. Heroud, called "The Terminator," in her native France, for her expertise in destroying missiles described the delicate process of disarming the missiles, then crushing them, over and over, till they "were a pancake," that was then buried and encased in concrete

How would the White House respond to these evidences of effective work by the UN in Iraq?

In the final weeks of the countdown for war, the Administration's actions resembled nothing so much as some of the madder scenes from "Alice in Wonderland." The fact that the documents the Administration had used to "prove" that Iraq was working on nuclear weapons were forged, only led to greater insistence that Iraq was a danger. The absence of discovery of WMD by the UN inspectors was only greater evidence that the Iraqis were the greatest deceivers in history and that they had succeeded in concealing their location. The destruction of the Al Samoud missiles was just further evidence of a "grand deception."

George Tenet has now told us, on February 5, 2004 -- exactly one year after he and Colin Powell drank the Kool-Aid at the U.N. Security Council -- that there was no imminent danger. The Administration spin-doctors immediately responded to this statement by saying that nobody from the Administration ever claimed there was an "imminent danger."

On March 7, 2003, Mohammed El Baradei spoke to the U.N. Security Council in an open session watched by tens of millions of Americans, and by countless Congressional and government offices.

He said:

"In conclusion, I am able to report today that, in the area of nuclear weapons -- the most lethal weapons of mass destruction -- inspections in Iraq are moving forward."

"One, there is no indication of resumed nuclear activities in those buildings that were identified through the use of satellite imagery as being reconstructed or newly erected since 1998, nor any indication of nuclear-related activities at any inspected sites."

"Second, there is no indication that Iraq has attempted to import uranium since 1990."

"Third, there is no indication that Iraq has attempted to import aluminum tubes for use in centrifuge enrichment. Moreover, even had Iraq pursued such a plan, it would have encountered practical difficulties in manufacturing centrifuges out of the aluminum tubes in question."

"Fourth, ... there is no indication to date that Iraq imported magnets for use in a centrifuge enrichment programme."

"After three months of intrusive inspections, we have to date found no evidence or plausible indication of the revival of a nuclear weapons programme in Iraq... I should note that, in the past three weeks, possibly as a result of ever-increasing pressure by the international community, Iraq has been forthcoming in its co-operation, particularly with regard to the conduct of private interviews and in making available evidence that contribute to the resolution of matters of IAEA concern."

On March 16, 2003, the neo-cons stuck back with the heavy artillery. Vice President Dick Cheney appeared on "Meet the Press. When pressed by Tim Russert about Iraq's nuclear danger. Cheney retorted, "We know he has been absolutely devoted to trying to acquire nuclear weapons. *And we believe he has, in fact, reconstituted nuclear weapons.* I think Mr. ElBaradei frankly is wrong. And I think if you look at the track record of the International Atomic Energy Agency and this kind of issue, especially where Iraq's concerned, they have consistently underestimated or missed what it was Saddam Hussein was doing. I don't have any reason to believe they're any more valid this time than they've been in the past."

On March 17, 2003, President George W. Bush went on national television to tell Saddam and his sons, "They have "48 hours" to get out of town." No new evidence or reason was given. It was the ultimate imperial moment.

On March 19, 2003, the bombs began to fall.

Book Reviews:
Cobra II and Iraqi Perspectives Report
(June 22, 2006)

It is an unusual thing to find two works of history published at roughly the same time which clearly should be reviewed together, but these two works of research on the Gulf War of 2003 and its aftermath are inextricably linked. They are linked in their study of the same historic events but differentiated by their focus on the different viewpoints provided by the two combatant "sides."

"Cobra II" is a massively detailed account of what happened on the American and coalition "side of the hill" before, during and after Operation Iraqi Freedom while the "Iraqi Perspectives Report" was written by a team of scholars at the "Institute for Defense Analyses" (IDA) in Washington for the United States Joint Forces Command (JFCOM). The "Iraqi Perspectives Project Report" is the other side of the "Cobra II" coin. It recounts the events and personalities on the Iraqi "side of the hill." Michael Gordon and Lieutenant General (Ret.) Bernard Trainor had a copy of the classified version of the "Iraqi Perspectives Project" report, and it informed their view of events within the Iraqi government. This use of the IDA paper as source material binds the two documents even closer together than they might have been otherwise. The commercially available version of the IDA paper is what is reviewed here rather than the classified edition. This is probably not a major issue in judging the value of the work because the classified supplements to government documents rarely contain anything of crucial significance. They usually exist because the sourcing of some available material is such that it can not be de-classified and for completeness the authors choose to write a supplementary chapter or chapters which can identify the sources specifically.

The IDA team traveled extensively in Iraq, interviewed prisoners and other Iraqis who were former senior officials, both military and civilian in the Saddam government and examined mountains of captured documentation. Their mission was to learn what the real situation had been in Iraq before the US led coalition invaded and occupied the country in March 2003. What they learned is most disquieting:

- Saddam had ended his Weapons of Mass Destruction (WMD) programs in the 1990s under the pressure of UN inspectors and economic sanctions.
- Saddam had informed his general staff of the non-existence of these weapons only at a very late date in the progress toward war with the United States.
- Saddam was convinced that the United States did not want the burden of the occupation of Iraq and for that reason would not go to war "on the ground" against him.
- He believed that Iraq could "shrug off" any amount of precision weapons attack by the United States.
- Saddam's priorities in defense had little to do with the United States.

- He was primarily concerned with the possibility of a renewal of hostilities with Iran and for that reason positioned the bulk of his conventional forces to defend against attack from the east.
- Saddam's second most serious threat concern was that of internal security and defense against a renewal of the Shia revolt which had occurred in the south of Iraq after the First Gulf War. To that end, he fostered the creation of party and personal paramilitary militias during the decade of the 90s. The most prominent of these was the "Saddam Fedayeen" organization which existed everywhere, but most strongly in the Shia majority areas of the south.
- Fear of both the Regular Iraqi Army and the conventional Republican Guard led him to "starve" these military forces of equipment and funds throughout the 90s. As a result, the conventional forces of Iraq did not train or conduct command post exercises throughout the 90s. This caused a steady degeneration in combat capability tending toward zero after 2000.
- No significant operational planning occurred during the period under discussion and plans which had been written previously by the military were "scuttled" for reasons of internal security. For example, the idea of defending Baghdad in depth inside the city was abandoned for fear of the Iraqi Army.
- Saddam never had any intention of damaging Iraqi infrastructure, especially the oilfields in the north or south. He thought of himself as the "guardian" of these assets.
- There were no preparations by the government to conduct widespread guerrilla resistance in the event of the occupation of Iraq.

In short, Iraq had prepared no adequate defense of its territory and was incapable of resistance to coalition forces except through the medium of irregular and improvised attacks on coalition forces supply lines.

It is manifestly clear from the Gordon and Trainor book, that the Bush Administration already had the goal of the overthrow of Saddam Hussein when it took office in January, 2000. A number of major and minor figures in the new administration had been involved in neoconservative initiatives against the Iraqi government, often in cooperation with figures of the Israeli Likud political party. These had culminated in several now famous policy papers which were proposed for implementation against the Iraqi government. These were often abetted by fantasist military and paramilitary figures like General Wayne Downing and Duane Claridge who during the 90s advocated an invasion of Iraq with a small force of mercenaries and anti-Saddam enthusiasts in the hope that the Iraqi masses would rise against the regime. The neoconservatives and their uninformed allies in the Congress wrote the Iraq Liberation Act of 1998 for the specific purpose of funding such schemes with US Government funds. Much of the money found its way into the hands of the Iraqi National Congress, an exile group headed by Ahmad Chalabi, a fluent and facile advocate for the notion that Iraq was a basically secular and homogeneous state inhabited by a population that waited only for liberation from the dictator to flower as an outpost of Western civilization and an ally in the heart of the Arab World for the United States. It was confidently expected that the resulting democracy would make peace with Israel and thus start a chain reaction of modernization and peace making that would revolutionize the East. This flight of the imagination was accompanied by a pathetically naïve belief that Muslims were not inhabitants of another cultural continent, with which most were content, and that these Muslims would joyously fall in with neoconservative dreams and would abandon all but the more picturesque, harmless and culinarily inventive aspects of their own culture. Gordon and Trainor imply that this view may have been overly optimistic.

In the absence of specific stimulus for implementation of these schemes, there would probably have been little opportunity for the historic experimentation with cultural modification that has taken place since the invasion and occupation of Iraq in 2003.

The Jihadi assault on the United States on 9/11 changed that. Within a day or two the more vocal "clergy" in the neoconservative "church" (notably Paul Wolfowitz) began to urge an invasion of Iraq upon the president of the United States. He rejected that advice in favor of a direct attack on the Al-Qa'ida base area in Afghanistan, but as Gordon and Trainor demonstrate returned to the subject of Iraq well before the job of eradicating the Taliban and Al-Qa'ida were finished there. The job is yet unfinished and is going badly.

Planning guidance to the armed forces was given to the uniformed military by the president and the secretary of defense. They were told to plan for an invasion and liberation of Iraq. The planning would be carried out by United States Central Command (CENTCOM) under General Tommy Franks. Gordon and Trainor make it clear that at this point many of the threads that have led to the present discomfort in Iraq began to come unraveled.

- There had been a much revised, updated and approved Operational Plan (OPLAN) for Iraq for many years. It envisioned the employment of a force of several hundred thousand troops for the task of conquering and subduing Iraq.
- Secretary Rumsfeld rejected that plan. He had been for many years a leading figure in a "circle" of former junior officers, defense academics and political figures like him who had long contemplated the inefficiencies and ineptitudes of the senior officers of the armed forces, especially those of the Army. This group considered themselves to be prophets without honor in the Pentagon and Rumsfeld's accession to the ministerial chair there was clearly a great opportunity to affect the public good. The reformist group believed that large ground forces with their ponderous artillery, numbers, logistics, artillery and associated "dinosaur" generals were a thing of the past. They envisioned a future for warfare that would be dominated by small ground forces, minimal armor and artillery supports and a concomitant small logistical requirement. They especially believed that this would be true in a world which operated on the basis of the sort of "carefully crafted" and perfectly executed plans which featured in the academic seminars and "war games" which they frequented. The traditional military habit of building in redundancy and sufficient force to deal with unforeseen events was viewed by them as evidence of a lack of sophistication and inferior intellect. There are always allies to be found in any bureaucracy for radical change which ridicules leaders "at the top," and junior men like that were found in the Army who assured the White House and Rumsfeld that Iraq could be dealt with two or three brigades of armor. This is less than 20,000 men. They should be ashamed.
- As Gordon and Trainor make clear, Secretary Rumsfeld interfered in operational planning for Iraq to an unprecedented extent and pursued his vision of an expeditionary army, an army that would be virtually a constabulary army at the expense of the planning for the Iraq campaign. Over the last forty years the armed forces worked out a computer assisted planning system for preparing for large operations overseas. It is called the "Joint Operational Planning System" (JOPS). This system systematically prepares the needed logistical and deployment plans needed to execute any approved operational scheme. It produces a variety of documents. Arguably,

the most important is a document called the "Time Phased Force Deployment List" (TPFDL). This computer-generated list depicts all the forces need for the operation and the order and dates for their movement to the theater of war for the use of the commander on the ground. It is the "guts" of the plan. The old "saw" that holds that amateurs want to talk about operations in war and professionals talk about logistics is exceptionally true in the matter of this document.

- Secretary Rumsfeld rejected not just the existing plan for Iraq. He also rejected JOPS as the BASIS OF PLANNING. He insisted that his wisdom was superior to any plan written by Colonel Blimp types and that JOPS "tied his hands" in the exercise of his role as generalissimo. He insisted that the CENTCOM planners could tell him what units they wanted and when and HE would decide what they would get and when. Additionally, he reserved the right to himself to delete PARTS of units from deployment that did not suit him. This is an interesting exercise of power for someone who has no experience of ground warfare and, in fact, has little experience of military affairs other than his two stints as Secretary of Defense, isolated in the ivory tower of his Pentagon offices.

- He was capricious in the exercise of his legal power to insert himself into operational planning matters, giving and withholding assets and authorities on the basis of his whims. As a result, detailed planning at CENTCOM was reduced to a "hit or miss" shambles in which nothing could be predicted with any assurance.

General Franks accepted this. His ground force commander, Lieutenant General David D. McKiernan did not, and Trainor and Gordon make it abundantly clear that he and his staff fought every day for the forces needed for Operation Iraqi Freedom (OIF). They are the real heroes in this story. They stood up to an arrogant and malevolent bully in defense of American interests and the American soldier.

There have now been a vast number of American casualties in Iraq. The ideologues and vapid academics who were the real planners of OIF are responsible for the misery of many of our people. These two books make that clear.

Iraq Fantasy: What the US Government Does Not 'Get' in Iraq

(February 12, 2007)

Where to start? Where to begin in constructing a list of the "mistakes," the errors, the stupidities that have characterized the campaign in Iraq? There have been so many, both great and small, so many, and now we Americans are reduced to sending a "brain trust" of soldier-scholars to "save" us from the cumulative effects of our misdirected energies. We are sending them as followers of a youthful general who is whispered to be an "intellectual," an Odysseus like figure whose magical qualities will, at the last hour, bring about a "happy ending."

Ah! The List! The list of errors:

- We invaded Iraq with too few troops.
- We destroyed the Iraqi government both civil and military without having a substitute instrument of government at hand.
- We expelled from public employment all those with any connection of any kind with the Baath Party. This included most people who could be described as human infrastructure in the country.

But- why go on? Even the Vice President acknowledges that "mistakes" were made, although probably not by him. Why list them all? How did this happen? How did a highly educated, wealthy, powerful people like us Americans make such a horrendous, catastrophic series of blunders/? How? Pogo the cartoon opossum once famously said that "We have met the enemy and they is us!" That sums it up quite well, but I will elaborate on the theme. "What? What did you say?" I can hear the incredulity now. No. It is true. As I have said with ever increasing shrillness over the last few years, WE AMERICANS ARE THE PROBLEM.

How, you might ask, is that? Simple. Most of us Americans believe that all people are the same. We Americans instinctively assume that under the "cute" native clothing, the weird marriage customs and the odd cooking we humans are all basically motivated and yearning for styles of life and futures which will be increasingly unified as time and "globalization" progress. That is what Tom Friedman seems to have meant when he wrote that "the world is flat." He appears to mean that humankind is moving towards a future of cultural sameness on a species wide basis. In other words, whatever still exists in a state of apparent difference of custom and habit among the nations of the earth is merely a vestige that will pass away soon and be replaced by a world culture which seems to be imagined as rather like that of the United States in the 21st Century.

To be blunt, our actions tend to be predicated on the notion that everyone wants to be an American, and that the crazy cavalry colonel on the beach in "Apocalypse Now" was right in declaring that "inside every Gook there is an American trying to get out." In the time of psychological preparation for the Iraq War, it was a common thing to hear seemingly educated people say that the Arabs and particularly the Iraqis had no "way of life" worth saving and that they would be better off if all "that old stuff" were done away with, and soon.

Think about that. How often did you hear something like that said? How often did you think it? How did we come to have this notion, the notion that the entire world is embarked on the same voyage and that we are the navigators showing the way into a bright future?

Our own culture is a rich blend, brewed from such elements as; Enlightenment optimism, Puritan utopianism, a bias toward a Calvinist lack of forgiveness of the sinner, and the "settler's" lack of respect for the weak and "native" peoples of the world. In America, such "threads" have pushed us in the direction of "the melting pot," and an ideology based on the idea that we are all the same, all the same. This "belief system" has been fed to us in the public schools, the movies, television "drama" and now the endless prattle of twenty-four hour a day news networks.

This has become secular religion, a religion so strong that any violation of its tenets brings instant and savage retaliation. That is what "political correctness" is all about. "PCness" is concerned with the suppression of speech offensive to our faith in human oneness, with the dream of worldwide flatness. "Neoconism" is a self-aware manifestation of that dream. There are other such manifestations of the dream. The repeated assertion by President Bush '43 that history is dominated by the existence of "universal values" is certainly one such dream. We invaded Iraq in the sure belief that inside every Iraqi there was an American trying to get out. We invaded the Iraq that fit into our dream. We did not invade the real Iraq.

In our dream of Iraq, we could reasonably expect that we would be greeted as liberators from the tyrant, but more importantly, from old ways. In our dream Iraq, the Iraqi people would "naturally" understand that having lived as citizens of the same state for eighty years they should see themselves as a unified "nation," moving forward into eventual total assimilation into the human "nation." Unfortunately for us and them, that was not the real Iraq.

In the Iraq of the Iraqis, cultural difference from the West was still a treasured manifestation of participation in the Islamic cultural "continent." In the real Iraq, pressure toward assimilation of the existing ethno-religious "nations" had only partially succeeded by 2003. In the real Iraq, tribe, sect, and community were still far more important than individual rights. In the real Iraq one did not vote for candidates outside one's community unless one were a Baathist, a Nasserist, or perhaps, a Communist-- in other words a believer in world "flatness" like the neocons.

In the real Iraq, Iraqis knew what Americans wanted to hear about "identity" and whether Shia, Kurd, or Sunni Arab, they told them what was needed. Finding ourselves in "the wrong Iraq" we have stubbornly "acted out" our faith in our dream, insisting that the real Iraqis should behave as our dream Iraqis would surely do. The result has been frustration, disappointment and finally rage against the "craziness" of the Iraqis. We are still "acting out" our dream, insisting that Maliki's Shia sectarian government perform within the parameters of our dream to "unify" the state, insisting that Maliki is a sort of Iraqi George Washington seeking to benefit all for the greater good of all.

He is not that. He understands that his task is to consolidate Shia Arab power while using the United States to accomplish that task. To that end he will tell us whatever we want to be told. He will sacrifice however many of his brethren are necessary to maintain the illusion so long as the loss is not crippling to his effort. He will treat us as the naifs that we are. Our "mission" in Iraq will be over some day, but there will be other fields for our "missionary work." There are other dreams to dream in; Syria, Saudi Arabia, Egypt, Iran.......

"Politics" in Iraq

(January 18, 2005)

"But surely you can't negotiate with Muqtada al-Sadr or make a deal with him? You don't really believe, do you, that he could be brought into the new Iraqi government?"

An American journalist asked me these questions last summer in reaction to my having told him that al-Sadr's actions at Najaf were mainly an attempt to establish his credentials with the Interim Iraqi Government (IIG) as someone who would have to be taken seriously as a political player.

"Political" in this sense means the process of re-distribution of power in the new state now emerging in Iraq from the rubble of the old regime. This is "politics" in its most primitive form. This kind of politics is far older and probably far closer to the atavism of man's inner self than the bloodless constitutionalism that we are comfortable with at home. The Iraqi kind of politics has little to do with the stylized ritual of civic activism to which we are accustomed in the West, and everything to do with the reality of the Arab World where the real game of life-or-death politics and conspiracy is played behind a "Potemkin Village" facade of westernized forms. In America, we seem to be largely unaware of, or at the very least unconvinced of, the reality of the kind of politics that I had meant in talking to my reporter friend.

Carl von Clausewitz, the German philosopher of war is much referred to, sometimes quoted and little read. Among his most famous *dicta* is the now overworked remark that "War is nothing but the continuation of politics by other means." This is often thought to mean that Clausewitz believed that war represented a resort to violence as an alternative to "political," i.e. peaceful means of conflict resolution such as diplomacy, negotiation or an electoral process. In other words, it is often thought that war and politics were considered by him to be opposed principles or states of being and that the existence of one pre-supposes the absence of the other. This notion logically leads to an assumption that war exists in a kind of vacuum, insulated from the process of power sharing between or within states that we call politics. A close reading of "On War" in its entirety reveals that Clausewitz did not think that at all. In an appendix to his masterpiece, Clausewitz says clearly "war is simply *a continuation of political intercourse <u>with the addition of other means</u>.*"

This means that for Clausewitz war and politics are the same thing, and that between the two conditions only the means vary, not the process itself, and that the business of settling human quarrels is not limited to the two simple states represented by the words "War" and "Peace." Instead, the two conditions are variations on the same theme of competition among humans. From this one can see that human political relations vary across a great and diverse spectrum of conflict and confrontation. At one end of the spectrum there is "absolute peace," a theoretical condition in which all conflict has been resolved and the lions really do lie down with the lambs. At the other end of the spectrum is "absolute war," a condition in which all conflicts are referred to organized, unlimited violence for solution and in which the lions have finished off the lambs and are looking at each other speculatively and licking their "chops."

In Iraq we are acting as though we think the war against the insurgents is an end-in- itself, and not a process embedded in the political evolution of the new Iraqi state in which the various parties, including the Iraqi insurrectionists, are playing roles within the "system." We are behaving as though the destruction of the various existing insurgent forces will automatically bring the fighting to an end and result in the creation of a pro-Western, secular, liberal and open country that will "kick-start" a social revolution throughout the Arab World.

Actually we seem to expect not just a social revolution but also a cultural change so deep that the lions will not know that the lambs really represent dinner. What we are talking about are changes as deep as those brought on by the Protestant Reformation or the French Revolution in Europe.

We do not seem to be willing to accept the idea that war and politics in present day Iraq are basically a contest among the lions for the spoils of the "kill" that we Americans have left on the desert floor in Mesopotamia. Some of the lions wear business suits and shave themselves clean, others wear clerical garb, some belong to one "pride" or another, but they are all contestants for power, nothing else.

The country over which they are struggling is a monument to the vanity of Western governments. It was created as an "after thought" by the victorious Allied powers in the peace negotiations after World War One. Several factors contributed to the project of creating a country called "Iraq" where no similar country had ever existed. "Mesopotamia," as Iraq was classically known had always been a mere geographical expression describing the fertile land between the Tigris and Euphrates rivers. Over the centuries the various regimes that ruled the area (often these were external) divided the region into provinces, satrapies, wilayats, etc. None of these divisions of the land implied "nationhood," among the various peoples who now inhabit the modern country of Iraq. No, it took Western colonialism to create Iraq, as we know it.

The French allowed the British to do what they like with Mesopotamia because they wanted British acquiescence in what they planned for Syria and later Lebanon. The British needed access to Mesopotamian oil. They needed air bases on the imperial communications route to the "Raj" in India. The British also needed a place to "stash" Prince Feisal bin Hussein al-Hashemi, their ally in the world war against the Turks. They had attempted to give him Syria for a kingdom but Arab fractiousness and French objections had ended that idea. Mesopotamia would serve as a substitute.

So, the British Empire screwed the lid down on Mesopotamia, installed King Feisal, and hoped for the best. The country exploded in a mostly Shia tribal revolt shortly thereafter. After several years of fighting the British felt secure enough in what they had done to grant Iraq a rather liberal Western style constitution under the Hashemite (read foreign) monarch. This government ruled Iraq with a certain benevolence on a parliamentary basis until 1958. The government functioned much as does that of the Jordanian branch of the Hashemite family. They are restrained, civilized people, the Hashemites. Those who claim that Iraq has never known democracy seldom mention this experience of responsible and representative government. There was early evidence that such a government might not endure in Iraq. The unsuccessful 1944 revolt of generals of the Iraqi Army who hated a continuing British presence and who favored the German side in World War Two was a bad omen.

In the end, however, the opportunity and temptation provided by such a government for conspiracy and plotting among ethno-religious communities on the basis of Arab Nationalism and religious hostility proved too great. The monarchy was overthrown in 1958 with great cruelty and public disgrace. There followed a rapid succession of nationalist, communist, Baathist and other governments who waged both peace and war against and with the non-Arab and non-Muslim minorities (Kurds, Yazidis, Turcomans, etc).

The lid "screwed down" by imperial Britain lasted remarkably well long after they had gone, and it functioned largely on the basis of the British sponsored continuation of the millennium long domination of the area by the Sunni Arab community. The Sunni Arabs remained the real rulers of the country until the American invasion of 2003 and the Shia Arabs remained in the position of a despised "underclass" while the largely Sunni Kurds observed the process and resisted it when they dared. Oddly enough, the Baath Party served in Iraq as a political vehicle for the entry of Shia and Christian Iraqis into the "mainstream of Iraqi life. The Baath was founded by Christian Arabs and was designed by them so as to identify people as Arabs, not by religion, but by language and culture. This suited the purposes of the Iraqi Shia perfectly and many, many of them joined the Baath Party rising quite high in the government and armed forces. Indeed, the lieutenant general commanding the Republican Guards Armored Corps in the invasion of Kuwait in the first Gulf War was a Shia.

The present American and British occupation of Iraq has the specific intention of re-organizing the country on the basis of "one man, one vote." The declaration of this intention pried "the lid" off the "can of worms," of relations and understandings that had long kept the forces of chaos in check in Iraq. In the Middle East people understand that they must vote for candidates from their own ethno-religious community. To do anything else is a revolutionary choice, something that only a radical would do, perhaps a Baathist. To make that choice is to risk rejection by your own community.

In this context we can expect that the coming election will produce a Shia dominated government under the influence of the higher clergy and likely to be inclined toward Shia Iran in a massively Sunni part of the world.

"Freedom is on the march?" No, chaos and war are on the march.

Giving Peace a Chance
(June 29, 2006)

The old Beetles' song begged that we should "give peace a chance." The noise generated in the United States over the issue of "amnesty" for insurgent fighters in Iraq who may have killed or wounded American soldiers makes it sound as though a lot of us are not willing to give peace a chance.

Iraq's Prime Minister, al-Maliki has constructed an offer to the non-Jihadi insurgent groups which proposes their re-integration into Iraqi society. They have responded with a counter-offer that revolves around a two year time table for the withdrawal of coalition forces from Iraq. In return for that they offer a complete cease fire on the part of all guerrilla forces under their control. In my opinion an agreement like that would isolate the Jihadis and permit their extermination by coalition and Iraqi forces, some of which might be found among the parties on both sides of this dialogue.

Some people in the United States find this possibility for peace to be unacceptable because the insurgents whom al-Maliki is negotiating with have been fighting American soldiers. The reasoning is that those insurgents are criminals and perhaps murderers and that they must receive criminal justice for their crimes.

This is a truly stupid attitude. It is true that the propaganda that has supported the war effort had described the insurgents as uniformly Jihadist and terrorist. The same propaganda has described them as criminals. This may have been useful in shaping public opinion in the United States over the last three years, but it is no longer useful. The coalition now confronts the need to assist the al-Maliki government in bringing together enough of the disparate factions in Iraq to build itself a support base which will enforce and maintain a peace that will justify the sacrifices soldiers have made in the war.

The United States has rarely, if ever, taken the position that mere service in war against itself constituted criminal behavior. In a few instances after World War II individuals were held accountable and punished for their personal culpability in "crimes against humanity," "planning and waging aggressive war," etc., but this sanction was not applied to the men who served in the ranks. Indeed, very senior officers were held blameless for their participation in the struggle.

It is axiomatic that peace must be made with enemies, not friends. If Iraqi insurgents who have fought and perhaps killed Iraqi and coalition soldiers are excluded from the possibility of reconciliation and amnesty, then who will be left to make peace with?

The answer is simple. No one. That would mean that the war will go on and on and on. In that case it would prove impossible to withdraw coalition forces for a long time.

It should be obvious that the al-Maliki government would not have made this offer of amnesty and "national reconciliation" if it believed that it will be able to suppress the insurgencies by force of arms.

The coalition has spent a great deal of time and effort in the process of bringing into being a representative and constitutional government in Baghdad. That government knows that it must reconcile itself with its countrymen and none more so that the nationalist insurgents.

Are we really going to allow our domestic politics and lack of realism in public attitudes to interfere with the efforts of the sovereign government if Iraq for peace?

Two Book Reviews: Fiasco and Insurgency and Counterinsurgency in Iraq

(Middle East Policy Journal Winter 2006)

Fiasco, the American Military Adventure in Iraq, by Thomas E. Ricks. Penguin Press, 2006. 496 pages. $27.95.

A plethora of books now exist about Iraq, Afghanistan, and related themes such as the Bush administration's decision-making processes, intelligence failures and internal propaganda. Half a dozen are in the marketplace so far, with more appearing every week as reporters finish their writing projects.

These books are very useful for creating an informed electorate, and in some cases, they are so richly sourced that historians will find them to be important starting points for scholarly research. Fiasco is likely to serve that purpose. Thomas Ricks' wide acquaintance with military people and his long preoccupation with the psychology of warriors have made it possible for him to dig as deeply as anyone could into the war's meaning in terms of its impact on the "collective mind" of the American military and the terrible results of that mentality.

Fiasco is very rich in detail that supports its judgments. Ricks spent a lot of time in Iraq absorbing the feel of disaster. He has captured it well. Ricks painstakingly describes the ineptitude of the Coalition Provisional Authority (CPA). This ineptitude formed the background for the collective military mindset that brought about the catastrophe in Iraq. It is still occurring there and still prevails in the American armed forces. I suppose we must accept L. Paul Bremer's claim that it was his decision (and his alone) to disband the Iraqi security forces. He accepts responsibility for this egregious error, so why shouldn't we? The standard argument of the pro-Bremer group is that the Iraqi armed forces had ceased to exist and that therefore there were no security forces to disband or employ. What they mean by that is that there were no units to be found by the time the American forces captured Baghdad and that cantonments had been looted and abandoned across the country.

What this argument completely ignores is that armed forces are social groups, the functional equivalents of tribes. They are not just collections of weapons and men. In any reasonably coherent military force, the whole is greater than the sum of its parts. As Ricks' military interlocutors in Iraq saw clearly, the Iraqi forces still existed as bodies of trained and disciplined men even if they were dispersed. They could have been "weeded" at the top to remove politically unacceptable people. After that, large numbers of men and officers might have been recalled to the colors, where they could have been used to stabilize the country.

The authors of another of the books on Iraq discovered that only a small percentage of Iraqi military officers had ever been members of the Baath party. It had been a national army, not a party militia. The decision to disband, supposedly made by Bremer, was the most important decision made in occupied Iraq. It may well have been the moment at which the war in Iraq was lost. The abrupt dismissal of hundreds of thousands of Iraqi soldiers drove many of them into the various Sunni insurgent groups. It is no accident that the insurgents possess a strong capacity for the technical aspects of bomb making and the operational planning that enables them to survive and, indeed, to prosper as our enemies.

In spite of Ricks' obvious disdain for the CPA, which he likens to a "children's crusade," his central subject is really the poor job that the senior officers of the U.S. Army have done in Iraq. He has far fewer negative things to say about Marine leadership, seemingly because of the marines' greater flexibility and willingness to adapt. Ricks seems to find that the Army's generals have done poorly in Iraq, and the evidence supports his judgment. There are several armies contained within the larger framework of the U.S. Army. The largest by far is the combined-arms, armor-dominated, heavy structure built to fight the major wars faced by the United States in the aftermath of World War II. These forces were created and maintained for almost two generations for the purpose of fighting massive "force on force" battles of attrition in Europe and Korea. Throughout that period, it was clear that these forces would always fight outnumbered and that a dogged and inflexible defense would be necessary to achieve any sort of success. Rigid discipline, careful adherence to orders and an unquestioning attitude are critical in such fighting. In response, the heavy forces of the Army developed in that direction, as did the collective mentality of its officers. At the same time, there was also a "minor theme" in the Army that existed for the purpose of conducting guerrilla warfare, counterinsurgency, and the training of foreign troops in the field. U.S. Army Special Forces (the Green Berets) were the major actors in this role. Other groups that are not as well-known also developed.

In Vietnam these two different "armies" fought in the same country, but, in essence, they fought two different wars. The "heavies" fought the main-force divisions and regiments of the North Vietnamese Army out in the woods, where they seldom had anything to do with Vietnamese civilians. The "greenies" (Special Forces) and all the other "people's war" fighters fought the Viet Cong, tried to build the villages up and did a good job training local militias. When the war in Vietnam ended badly, the "heavy" army wanted nothing further to do with any of this and suppressed as much as possible anything that had to do with counterinsurgency. They actually destroyed the records in many cases. If it had not been for Congressional insistence on maintaining some capability against terrorism, the Green Berets would have ceased to exist.

As Ricks reports, the U.S. Army entered Iraq in 2003 with no doctrine concerning counterinsurgency, no plans for dealing with insurgency and lacking leadership enough to perceive the continuing guerrilla war as it developed. At the same time, the few Special Operations Forces that had survived successive Army purges had been largely transformed into counterterrorism commandos. As a result, the Heavy Army had to be asked to perform a task in nation building and counterinsurgency of which it was completely ignorant. The result lies before us, a sorry spectacle. Over the last three years, the "Heavy Army" has sought to learn how to fight such a war.

The Army's institutions of learning are now replete with "Institutes of Cultural Studies," "Urban Warfare Operations Laboratories" and the like, and every grenadier is expected to be respectful of Islam. As Ricks points out, this process of inventing the wheelbarrow is very slow. Along with all the other parts of the Army, the "greenies" are re-learning their proper trade. As a pedagogical exercise this will probably succeed for both groups, because, as the president has said, "It is going to be a long war."

Insurgency and Counter-Insurgency in Iraq, by Ahmed S. Hashim. Ithaca, NY: Cornell University Press, 2006. 482 pages. $29.95 hardcover, $14.95 paperback. Jeffrey Record, professor of strategy, Air War College (his views are entirely his own)

Ahmed S. Hashim's Insurgency and Counter-Insurgency in Iraq is the best book published to date on the Iraqi insurgency's "origins, motivations, and evolution and the U.S. policy and strategic and operational responses to it." Completed in November 2005 and released in March 2006, the book presciently anticipated the subsequent sharp escalation of sectarian violence in Iraq that threatens to saddle the United States with its greatest foreign-policy disaster since the Vietnam War.

Hashim, a professor at the Naval War College and an expert on both Middle Eastern strategic issues and irregular warfare, served three tours in Iraq between November 2003 and September 2005 as an advisor to the U.S. command in Baghdad. He is exceptionally well qualified to examine the performance of both sides in a war that will soon enter its fifth year and that constitutes a continuing and dramatic demonstration of the limits of American conventional military supremacy. Hashim contends that three American "structural defects — ideological rigidity born of certain predispositions, failure to implement reconstruction, and the organizational culture and mindset of the U.S. military — promoted the outbreak and perpetuation of the insurgency."

The neoconservatives, who provided the intellectual rationale for the U.S. preventive war against Iraq giddily, assumed that American forces would be greeted in Iraq as they had been in France in 1944; that the Sunni Arab community that had dominated governance in Mesopotamia for over three centuries would go quietly into the night of political marginalization; and that expert concern over the sectarian fragility of the Iraqi state was overblown. There followed the disastrous decisions to invade Iraq with a force too small to secure the country, to disband the Iraqi army (by not recalling it to paid duty), to deprive the reconstruction effort of sufficient money and essential Baathist professional expertise, and to fight a counterinsurgent war in a manner that benefited the insurgency itself.

Neither the neoconservatives nor the White House anticipated the possibility of an insurgency, much less the unfamiliar insurgency that did arise: a loose, decentralized coalition of some 20 or so resistance organizations (Hashim lists and discusses them in detail), some secular-nationalist, others jihadist, and all of them motivated to fight foreign occupation for reasons of "nationalism, honor, revenge and pride." The "prime goals of the insurgency are to eject the foreign presence in Iraq…and to overthrow the [political] order."

The Last Best Chance In Iraq:
New Plans of Action

Moderator: Daniel Benjamin
Panelists: Max Boot, Prof. Noah Feldman, Col. W. Pat Lang,
Salameh Nematt, Prof. Paul Pillar (March 7, 2007)

Daniel Benjamin:

Pat Lang understood this conflict very early on. He summed it up for me, saying, "When you drive the car over the cliff, your options narrow." I haven't heard anyone improve on that since.

We have 130,000 troops in Iraq. We have the chaos there that has been amply discussed. Although I would say the conventional wisdom is that we have no good options, and certainly very few that have many virtues to them, we are in this mess nonetheless. We need to come up with the best idea possible for going forward.

While it may be true that the options have narrowed, certainly there have been many different plans put forward. We are, of course, headed for the surge. That seems like a foregone conclusion right now. It is also being called by some "The McCain Doctrine," for reasons I cannot imagine. Other options are "double down" and "go long." There are the Gelb-Biden Partition Plan, the Galbraith Partition Plan, the Murtha Redeployment Plan, and the Levin Redeployment plan. Others, and I think this is more inchoate, have come up with humanitarian intervention to protect the innocents as they relocate in the ethnic cleansing. There are garrisons and cantonments, and I am sure that we are soon going to see the "Give War a Chance Plan" as one way of dealing with the Sunni insurgency.

This raises, I think, serious questions that we need to grapple with, which include: What plan will do the best to safeguard, so far as possible, American interests; to limit the killing which, as Noah Feldman has pointed out, is a moral obligation of ours, since we did get the Iraqis into this mess in a very real sense? What should we do to avoid a wider war, a regional war, a proxy war? There are many different interests at stake here in what is the most economically vital part of the world.

I'd like to ask the panelists to illuminate the particular virtues of these different plans, or to put forth ones of their own.

W. Patrick Lang:

There is positive value in proposing actual options for the future, even if they have narrowed considerably over the last few years. I start by saying that I do not think there is any doubt whatsoever that the president's intentions, as stated, (which are, of course, national policy) are the ones he intends to adhere to. Given that, I think there is going to be a tremendous struggle in Baghdad, and to a lesser extent in Anbar Province, over the next year. I personally think that, however much we wish our expeditionary force all the best opportunities they could have, we will still have this situation unresolved a year from now, and we will still have a large force in Iraq. I think that is what the future is very likely to be.

Nevertheless, I have felt for some time a personal responsibility to state what I think would be an alternative policy, to counter the argument "Well, you don't like our plan, what's your plan?"

I don't represent anybody, but I thought that I would offer such a plan. My position is that ongoing combat operations, and any future combat operations that are likely to ensue with regard to Iran or Syria, or anything of that sort, are not likely to be decisive in resolving the foreign policy issues in the United States' favor, much less the various other countries.

Although it is useful in a diplomatic sense to threaten people, either explicitly or implicitly as appropriate, and to keep a large military force around as a balancing weight in negotiations, I think that the best way to resolve this would be for the United States to emphatically, strongly, and persistently lead a round of negotiations with both the internal and external parties to this conflict in the greater Middle East. The United Sates should seek to engage each of them under our leadership, that is, the leadership of the president and whatever other foreign partners we could engage, in an attempt to reduce the number of conflicts-of-interest that are perceived to exist between us and the various players.

This would not be with the belief that you could create a paradise-on-Earth in which there would be no hatreds, no conflicts, and no killings, but rather to reduce the level of heat in these various conflicts to a level at which it would again resemble something we are more familiar with.

I am very much in favor of continuing the war against international jihadism. I think that the international jihadi movement, which people in this country like to call "al Qaeda," is a dedicated and irreconcilable enemy of the United States, and that they should be pursued to the ends of the Earth and destroyed because there is no way to make peace with them.

But with regard to regional peace in the Middle East, and all of the various problems and conflicts that threaten to break out into war at present there, I think we should do as I said. We should go around in a tough-minded, not accommodating, not "we're giving up to you" kind of spirit and seek to negotiate all of the different issues that exist between us and them, or between them and them, whoever the "them" is.

We cannot do that just on the basis of trying, for example, to negotiate with the Iranians over what it is they are doing in Iraq that we do not like. That would be just foolish in my opinion, because if we do that, the Iranians, who have the upper hand there, will have no particular reason to negotiate with us at all. But there are a lot of different issues that the Iranians have over which we could reach enough of an accommodation to reduce the level of heat and the possibility of war throughout the region.

Many will say that this is *realpolitik* with a vengeance. It certainly is. I am in favor of an aggressive waging of diplomacy, with the end in mind of preventing the outbreak of war. I have considerable personal experience with war, and I do not wish to see it break out in any more places. I think that avoiding war, if you could reach a reasonable accommodation with people, is a worthwhile goal in itself.

Daniel Benjamin:

Could we have the kind of diplomatic initiative that you suggest if it is not backed by force, since we seem to be a little out of luck in that regard? And second, could we actually contain the issue of the Iranian nuclear program within this round of diplomacy? That issue seems to be almost as big as what is going on in Iraq.

Pat Lang:

To the first point, I think that the United States, whatever our present difficulties are in Iraq, remains by far the strongest military power on Earth. By maintaining a force in being in the region while negotiations of this sort are conducted, backed up by the enormous, overwhelming power of American strategic and other forces, there is no difficulty in having the military weight to influence the outcome.

As for the Iranian nuclear program, I am unconvinced that the Iranians really wish above all else to possess nuclear weapons and the missiles to employ them. There are a number of Iranian issues having to do with their place in the international order in the Middle East, and involving their economy, all of which we play a role in with a good deal of enthusiasm. And so, I think that if we went to the Iranians on the basis of all of the different issues that involve us and them, with the aim of, for example, getting them to put their nuclear program under the full safeguards of the International Atomic Energy Agency, there would be some chance of their doing that. It is certainly worth the attempt.

A Hidden Danger: Lines of Supply in Iraq
(July 19, 2006)

American forces in Iraq are in danger of having their line of supply cut by guerrillas.

U.S. troops all over central and northern Iraq are supplied with fuel, food and ammunition by truck convoy from a supply base hundreds of miles away in Kuwait. All but a small amount of our soldiers' supplies come into the country over roads that pass through the Shia dominated south of Iraq.

Until now the Shia Arabs of Iraq have been told by their leaders to leave American forces alone, but an escalation of tensions between Iran and the U.S. could change that overnight. In addition to that the ever-increasing violence of the civil war in Iraq can change the alignment of forces there unexpectedly.

Southern Iraq is thoroughly infiltrated by Iranian special operations forces working with Shia militias. Hostilities between Iran and the United States or a change in attitude towards US Forces on the part of the Baghdad government could quickly make the supply roads into a "shooting gallery" 400 to 800 miles long. Civilian truck drivers would not persist in that situation. They would have to be much more heavily escorted by the U.S. military. It might then be necessary to "fight" the trucks through ambushes on the roads. This is a daunting possibility. Trucks loaded with supplies are defenseless against things like RPGs, small arms and IEDs. A long, linear target like a convoy of trucks is very hard to defend against irregulars operating in and around their own towns. The volume of "throughput" would probably be seriously lessened in such a situation. A reduction of supply rates would inevitably affect operational capability. This might lead to a downward spiral of potential against the insurgents and the militias. This would be very dangerous for our forces.

Are there alternatives to the present line of supply leading to Kuwait? There may be but they are not immediately apparent.

A line of supply consists of the route and the facilities at both ends. Our present line of supply now originates in Kuwait with its ports, stevedores, warehouses, etc. A new line of supply leading to Turkey or Jordan would have to have similar facilities. Turkey has not been very cooperative in this war and a supply line leading to Jordan would have to pass through Anbar Province, the very heart of the Sunni Arab insurgencies. Creating new facilities in these places would be possible but politically difficult and it would take time.

Few of the permanent requirements for uninterrupted re-supply can be satisfied out of the local economy. The economy lacks reserves of these supplies and there would not be anything like enough "left over" for our forces to subsist on.

What about air re-supply? It appears that only 5 to 10 percent of day-to-day military deliveries into Iraq are presently made by air. Inside Iraq, local deliveries by air probably amount to more. In a difficult situation the tonnages delivered could be increased but given the bulk in weight and volume of the needed supplies it seems unlikely that air re-supply could exceed 25 percent of daily requirements. This would not be enough to sustain the force.

Compounding the looming menace of the Kuwait based line of supply is the route followed by the cargo ships en route to Kuwait. Geography dictates that the ships all pass through the Strait of Hormuz and then proceed to the ports at the other end of the Gulf. Those who are familiar with the record of Iran's efforts against Kuwaiti shipping in the Iran-Iraq War will be concerned about this maritime vulnerability.

Potential adversaries along the line of supply include many, many combat experienced and well-schooled officers or former officers. We can be sure that they are acutely aware of this weakness in our situation.

What will happen in an American withdrawal of forces from Iraq?
(August 5, 2007)

The first question to be asked is whether or not the withdrawal will be under hostile pressure. The two kinds of withdrawal would be radically different.

* A withdrawal conducted under non-hostile conditions would very much resemble the manner in which US forces left the Canal Zone after the return of the territory to Panamanian sovereignty or the withdrawal of coalition forces from Saudi Arabia after the First Gulf War. For this kind of withdrawal to occur a general political settlement would have to have been reached or a complete pacification of the country would have to have been achieved. Under either of those conditions, it could be assumed for planning purposes that there would be no serious indigenous interference with the departure of American forces. This kind of withdrawal would be an exercise in logistical planning in which the force would be taken out in an "administrative" (non-combat) mode. Departure would be arranged on the basis of the most efficient use of transportation as well as its availability. Most units would be returned to their permanent posts across the world without their heavy equipment, (tanks, infantry fighting vehicles, artillery, etc.) because it is more efficient to send the troops home in passenger aircraft and the equipment in separate transportation (sea usually) in the care of drivers. A withdrawal of

this kind would take a long time. Large sized logistical capabilities would have to be kept in Iraq until the end of the departure to conduct the shipments. The removal of larger US Forces from Saudi Arabia after the First Gulf War took around a year and a half.

* A withdrawal under combat conditions would be very different and in the light of present political circumstances in Iraq seems more likely. During such a withdrawal there would be continuing combat operations designed to defend the force from enemies that are increasingly emboldened by American withdrawal and the prospect of "settling scores" with sectarian, political and ethnic adversaries. In that kind of departure, the force would have to be withdrawn in "slices" (*tranches* in French). The withdrawal from VN conducted by the Nixon Administration was of this kind. The phased departures of these "slices" would be designed to gradually "uncover" the regions of the country in a logical order as American forces move away from areas that are more easily abandoned. At the same time, the remaining forces in Iraq would have to retain a balanced combat capability that could continue to carry out force protection defensive actions as well as "spoiling" attacks against detected preparations for assaults against the ever-weakening US military presence in the country. Infantry, armor, artillery, and particularly aerial forces (both Army and Air Force) would be needed to protect the course of the withdrawal. The routes of withdrawal would have to be outposted and protected to keep them open while the withdrawal takes place. At the same time, the remaining force in Iraq would continue to be re-supplied over the same routes. There would likely be a lot of fighting in the course of the withdrawal. In VN, 20,000 US soldiers were killed during the several years of the withdrawal. This would be a "last chance" for the enemy forces to exact a price for the US presence in Iraq. They would be likely to take that opportunity. The logic of the present logistical situation would point to a withdrawal in phases (*tranches)* down the existing Main supply Route (MSR) to Kuwait where the forces could be received in prepared camps prior to departure by sea and air. The improved situation in Anbar Governorate might also make possible a smaller withdrawal to the west and into Jordan. A small percentage of the withdrawal would be conducted using air force heavy lift assets. The units withdrawn by air are likely to be air force.

A "residual" military presence in Iraq is another major issue.

In a withdrawal conducted under administrative conditions, it will be possible to position a "force" of trainers, suppliers, SOF jihadi hunters and force protection people wherever they are needed. The force protection element of this force might be a reinforced heavy brigade. Altogether the benign atmosphere presence might be 20,000.

In a "contested" withdrawal, the existence of these forces will be problematic from the beginning. A "residual" force with less than a reinforced heavy division and appropriate air support as the basis of its security would be a very risky venture over the long run. This force would number something in the area of 35,000 to 40,000 people. The logistical problems involved in supplying this force or any sized force overland would be enormous.

PART V

Short Stories from the Post-Civil War Period

Col. Lang has written a Civil War espionage trilogy, focused on Confederate spies, foreign mercenaries, and the role of intelligence in the conduct of the War. The trilogy includes some of the most vivid accounts of the Wilderness Campaign. In the essays in this section, the author picks up some of the key characters from the trilogy and follows them around the world in the post-Civil War decades. It begins with a short story that is a prequel to the trilogy. Each of the stories stand on their own but are greatly enriched if read along with the three volumes that comprise the Strike the Tent novels.

Sharpsburg

(Prequel to The Strike the Tent Trilogy)

"This must be a ruse. Surely it is a ruse?"

George McClellan's question was strangely melancholic. He had been like that of late.

Handsome Joe Hooker looked at the little man standing across the farmhouse kitchen table from him.

The "Young Napoleon" was six inches shorter and ten years younger.

Hooker despised him. He had always despised him. The dapper, self-assured manner, the instant success that followed McClellan everywhere, all of this contributed to the dislike that Hooker felt. Now, Hooker was an army corps commander under McClellan. *Oh, well, h*e thought, *everything has its price.*

The farmer's family cowered in the cellar, herded there by civil but unsmiling men in blue, men with muskets and bayonets, strange men from lands far to the North.

"It sounds like Lee," Hooker said levelly. "You know it does."

Brigadier General John Gibbon had the Rebel papers in his hand. He had said nothing while reading. "General Order 191," he said now. "I think it is a true copy of his direction to them all. The assistant adjutant general's authentication looks correct. Venable signed it. I wonder whose copy this is." He looked at McClellan. "I think it is genuine," he said. Gibbon had long been a friend to the army commander. They had been cadets at the academy together.

McClellan looked doubtful. "You think he is really that spread out?" he asked, "with Longstreet on South Mountain, and Jackson at Harper's Ferry?" McClellan turned and pointed theatrically at the looming green ridge very near in the west. "How many miles is Lee from us here?"

Gibbon looked at the map lying on the kitchen table. "Ten miles maybe and far enough from the rest of them so that we can beat them in detail if we move fast enough. According to this order, Jackson is at least twenty miles away doing God knows what."

Hooker spat out a window in disgust. He raged invisibly over McClellan. *The little bastard can't stop acting...*

The sizeable village of Middletown lay just to the east on the macadam road. The field where an infantry private found the order wrapped around two cigars was back there, near the village.

The cigars had disappeared. Someone in the kitchen had them.

The farmhouse yard was full of sweating men and horses. Staff officers, cavalry escorts, an ambulance, it looked like an anthill. The sun was very bright. South Mountain looked like a wall.

They are watching us now. I wonder who is up there, who among my old friends? I could use a drink, Hooker thought. *Have to give him a push, get him to do something.* "Who has the cigars?" he demanded.

"Why?" McClellan asked.

"I want one, no sense in letting them go to waste."

A sergeant stepped forward to offer him the cigars.

Hooker took one.

The sergeant produced a match and lit the general's cigar. The smoke drifted across the room. The sergeant stood there with the other cigar in his hand.

"That is yours," Hooker said. "Thanks for the smoke. What are you going to do, Mac?" he asked. He looked at Gibbon. *For Christ's sake, say something,* he thought.

McClellan seemed to wake from a dream. "I know what to do," he cried and waved the order at Gibbon. "Here is a paper with which if I cannot whip Bobbie Lee, I will be willing to go home."

Ah, Hooker thought, *at last...*

McClellan telegraphed President Lincoln: "I have the whole rebel force in front of me, but I am confident, and no time shall be lost. I think Lee has made a gross mistake, and that he will be severely punished for it. I have all the plans of the rebels, and will catch them in their own trap if my men are equal to the emergency... Will send you trophies."

Eighteen hours later he began to move the Army of the Potomac forward. On South Mountain, Longstreet, D.H. Hill, Lafayette McLaws, and Robert Rodes watched the vast blue host approach across the green plain.

White cumulus clouds floated toward the mountain.

In Turner's Gap at the top of the ridge, D.H. Hill rubbed his stomach ulcer and watched them come. He was comfortable sitting on a stump by the side of the road. He wondered how long it would be before the Yankees reached him. "Well, so be it,' he said to his staff. "So be it."

The blue army began to climb the mountain.

In the next hours, the noise of battle became so loud in Boonsboro west of South Mountain that Lee was certain "Pete" Longstreet's men on South Mountain faced the whole of the Army of the Potomac. Listening from the front porch of the courthouse, he knew that eventually McClellan would take the mountain passes. With that judgment, he knew what must be done. He had brought his men into Maryland to seek a decisive fight with a big Union army, any big Union army would do. What was needed was a victory that would be enough to lure the British and the French down off "the fence" to break the blockade and enforce mediation in the quarrel.

Many in Richmond, and indeed in his own army, did not think the pursuit of such a decisive battle was wise. They argued that the South was inherently weaker than the North and that the loss of precious and irreplaceable manpower should not be risked in such a combat. Lee did not agree and he had carried the argument with the only man who mattered, President Jefferson F. Davis. Nevertheless, he knew that in the day of climactic battle he would be much weaker than McClellan.

The campaigning year had begun early in the spring.

Jackson was then engaged in a series of running battles the length and breadth of the Shenandoah Valley and into the Allegheny Mountains to the west.

McClellan had invaded the Virginia peninsula system to the east of Richmond at nearly the same time. He came by sea with the host that he had been training and organizing since the Union defeat at Manassas the previous year. With this army he marched toward Richmond sweeping all before him.

At Lee's urging, President Davis summoned Jackson, requiring him to bring his strong force of mountaineers and Shenandoah Valley men to Richmond as rapidly as possible.

Then, providence intervened and the Confederate commander at Richmond, Joseph E. Johnston, was struck down while fighting in the outskirts of the city.

Lee was given command of the combined army. In a week of murderous combat McClellan was driven back, away from the capital. He then began a long retreat to the sea and the safety of the U.S. forts and ships.

Having taken the measure of McClellan, Lee turned his back on him and marched away to the northwest where he met and defeated another large Union army at Manassas. He drove that army into the Washington defenses and marched away again to the northwest. He crossed the Potomac into Maryland.

McClellan's returned army was soon somewhere to the east moving north, groping to find him.

Six months of marching and fighting had greatly weakened Lee's force. Casualties, straggling and loneliness had taken their toll. His army believed that it was fighting the second American Revolution, a renewal of the struggle for local government and popular sovereignty. For many in the army, an invasion of the North did not serve such purposes. Letters from home were often strongly against such an invasion. Some suggested that such "aggression" might imperil the soul.

For all these reasons, Lee reckoned that he would give battle with many fewer men than McClellan. Nevertheless, he knew McClellan well and had a low opinion of his strength of will. He had remarked recently that he "hoped to continue against McClellan for some time."

He decided to withdraw from South Mountain, move south and make his stand near the town of Sharpsburg, Maryland just north of the Potomac. He would wait for McClellan there on the low, ascending ridges just north of the little town.

Jackson was still at Harper's Ferry on the Potomac. The enemy garrison there had surrendered easily, and somewhat unaccountably. Jackson needed time to parole thousands of prisoners. Fortunately, McClellan could be counted on to dither for a day or two. There should be enough time for Jackson to arrive at Sharpsburg. There might then be enough men to make a defensive battle plausibly possible.

There was a grave difficulty in this plan. His engineers had learned that the bridge over the Potomac between Sharpsburg and Virginia had been destroyed. That meant that he would stand against McClellan with an unfordable river at his back. The nearest crossing was a ford a long way off down the river.

I might have half their numbers, he thought. *We might have that many if everyone comes up in time. At first, I will have 25,000, perhaps. McClellan will have three times that many... On the other hand, it is McClellan. I remember him in Mexico when he worked for me...*

A rider came in from the left flank on South Mountain.

"We have about two hours or so," Lee said after reading the note the man brought. He looked at the group of "gallopers" waiting to carry his orders.

They sat under the big trees around the courthouse square. The men in brown watched him and listened to the sound of the guns. Their horses were unbridled and feeding on the lawn, uncaring and indifferent in this historic moment.

"Major Taylor."

"Sir?" Taylor sat on the porch rail waiting.

"We must tell them all along the top of the mountain that they are to depart before becoming fully engaged and make their way to our new position at Sharpsburg. Suggest routes. Tell them I will expect them by dawn. Pick the strongest riders to go to Jackson. He is farthest away..."

Up on South Mountain near the right end of the Confederate line,

Kemper's Brigade looked down at the Union Army infantry who had tried all day to drive them from the crest and from Crampton's Gap.

There were immeasurable numbers of them. They stood in blue lines twenty ranks deep. Their artillery was "in battery" behind them, perhaps a hundred guns. Shells came over the top of the ridge every few minutes. The projectiles could be seen *en route* from the cannons. They passed over, accompanied soon thereafter by the sound of their going. Soon the report of the guns would arrive. There was a dreamlike quality in this sequence.

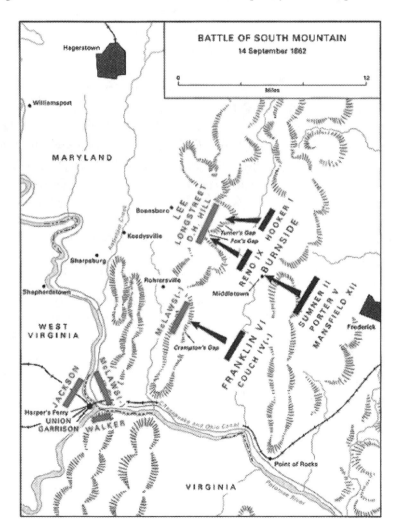

The blue infantry tried four times to capture the gap that day. They were driven back each time. Their dead and wounded covered the slope. Some crawled toward the bottom. There were wounded in the ditches beside the road that ran down the slope on the way to Middletown. If they did not seem mortally hurt, someone in the brown ranks on top of the hill inevitably shot them again. It was the only prudent thing to do.

Farther to the north two more roads ran up to passes and then down to towns to the west, towns like Boonsboro. Most of the Confederate force was up there, north of Kemper's Brigade.

The blue waves had beaten against the rest of the mountain with no better luck but Kemper's men knew this could not continue.

Behind the right flank of the mountain and a dozen mile away to the south, Lafayette McLaws' small division still stood on Maryland Heights looking almost straight down into Harper's Ferry. In this position they had sealed one of the sides of Stonewall Jackson's trap for the 15,000 U.S soldiers in the town. The federal commander had surrendered them all, but Mclaws remained in place with his artillery looking down on the town. With so many Yankee prisoners in the town, the possibility of revolt was worrisome until they could all be disarmed and paroled. Mclaws' "back" would be exposed to any Union force that succeeded in forcing its way through Crampton's Gap. The gap must be held until McLaws moved away.

In the gap was Kemper's Brigade.

There, the 17th Virginia Infantry Regiment held the center of the line. Like everyone else in the army they had fought and marched for hundreds of miles since spring. Their numbers shrunk as the long route marches and the attrition of death and wounds had their effect. There were sixty officers and men present for duty on South Mountain when the Union assaults began.

At three o'clock in the afternoon, Captain Claude Devereux stood in his company's line. He had ten men. "H" Company, of the 17th Virginia at full strength would have had one hundred officers and men. At Manassas six weeks before, he had counted forty. Now, there were so few, his brother Jake, his old friend Fred Kennedy, Moses Samuels the watchmaker who lived on Washington Street, his lieutenant Bill Fowle, and a few more, neighbors all. On the back side of the mountain the regiment's trains waited. With the wagons was another friend from home, Bill White, the regiment's head teamster.

The Yankees started up the slope again. Devereux knew that this effort would bring an end.

A bugle sounded "recall." A drumbeat "withdraw."

Sergeant Frederick Kennedy contemplated a well mounted blue officer below. His sandy blond hair and mustache made a contrast with the weather and sun darkened skin of his face. He saw Captain Devereux walk to the rear to find out what was happening. *We are leaving,* he thought. He had decided to kill the mounted officer. Now, he must act quickly.

Private John Quick went to stand beside him. "Best be swift, Sarn't. We'll be goin' soon." The Irish giant peered down the hill. "Shoot at the horse's chest. The bullet will raise up…"

Kennedy braced his Enfield against a tree. The brim of his floppy hat blocked his view. He dropped it on the ground. The sweaty white of his forehead and his pale blue eyes were starkly contrasted with the tan of his lower face. He took a breath, let half out and concentrated on the alignment of his sights against the brown horse's chest.

Lieutenant Fowle saw Devereux waving for them to come. "Come on boys," he yelled. "Let's git!"

Kennedy's rifle jumped in his arms.

"Good!" Quick laughed. "One less and you missed the horse…"

They ran for the top of the ridge where Devereux waited.

Longstreet's "wing' of the army marched all night going down the farm roads that led south.

Farmers hid in their houses with the shutters closed, afraid of the passing columns. These were not Southern people.

They crossed Antietam Creek at five in the morning. Longstreet was waiting for them by the bridge. They walked up the track into the little town. Kemper's men filed off to the south. As the sun rose, they "fell out" and collapsed in their blankets and rubber groundsheets.

Claude Devereux was shaken awake several hours later by Snake Davis, one of his company cooks. The day was bright but cool.

"We found the supply wagons, cap'n. We got breakfas' today, good breakfas'. We got biscuits and bacon and such…."

Devereux looked around.

"We dug a slit trench over by the road there, Mistuh Claude."

"Thanks. I'll be back in a minute. Save me a couple of biscuits."

"Jinrul Jackson come in fum Hahpuh's Ferry while you was sleepin'. His cook, Jim, had a lot of that nice Yankee Army coffee."

They waited all day for McClellan on the 16th. More and more of Stonewall's soldiers arrived over Boteler's Ford. By nightfall everyone had arrived, everyone but Ambrose Hill and the "Light Division." The odds had improved. They were not good, but better.

"Where are they?" Devereux muttered, walking up and down in the farm road in which the regiment had been placed.

Brigadier General James Kemper watched him pace. "Devereux, calm down. They will be here tomorrow. We know Ambrose. He always arrives when needed." Kemper stroked his bushy beard. "How is your lovely mother? I won't ask of your father, a thorny subject."

Devereux remembered that lawyer Kemper had much of the bank's business in the Richmond area. "Let's start digging," he said. "Let's wake them up, all three hundred men of your 'brigade.' Let's dig behind this fence here." He put his hand on the top rail.

"With what?" Kemper asked. "Our fingernails? We have no tools. None, and Uncle Bob doesn't want it. He wants us ready to 'maneuver.' What is it with these West Point people?"

"Jim, let's get them up, and go over to those barns and take tools." Devereux pointed to farms along the road a few hundred yards south. "Let's dig! To hell with the West Pointers! There will be thousands of Yankees climbing up those ledges between us and the creek tomorrow. Let's dig!"

Kemper thought. "Get them up, Claude. We won't live through tomorrow, but you are right. Get them up."

⁂

McClellan attacked at dawn on the 17th. He attacked *en echelon* from right to left, from north to south, by army corps. Joe Hookers', 1st Corps began the dance. Then Mansfield's corps, then Sumner's, etc.

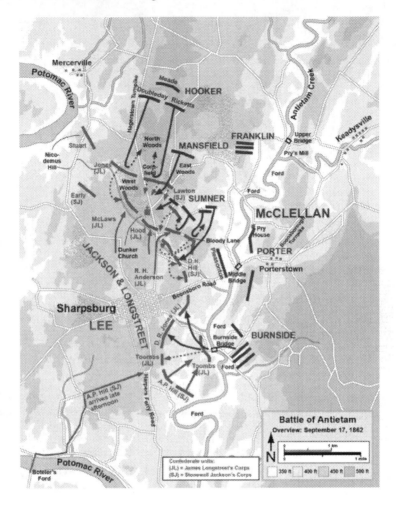

Men died in droves. They stood and fought each other eye to eye in the corn and along the country roads. The "Iron Brigade" from the upper midwest, the Louisiana "Pelicans," the madmen from east Texas, they screamed and fought with rifles, artillery and bayonets as the fight came down the line toward Kemper's Brigade.

Devereux heard it come. In the mid-afternoon, it centered on the bridge a quarter of a mile down the ledges from his position. The noise grew and grew. He could hear the rebel yell until an hour before sundown and he knew that the Georgians who held the bridge from the hill above still prevailed. Then, that ended and Yankee "huzzahs" were everywhere below.

The first blue men came over the terrain mask near dusk. There were Zouaves in the lead. The 17th Virginia shot them to bits. The colors went down and more men in baggy red trousers picked them up. They, too, went down. The Zouaves stopped coming but more and more blue men came on behind them, coming over the edge of the ledge and into view.

When they got to fifty yards range, Devereux waved his men back. The brigade was falling back. He looked over his shoulder at the hard surfaced farm road. He saw a red shirt.

There were men in brown coming on behind Ambrose Hill's red shirt.

Yankee bullets whined in the air.

Kemper was at the road. He waved Hill forward. "Come on! Come on!" he yelled.

Devereux turned to watch.

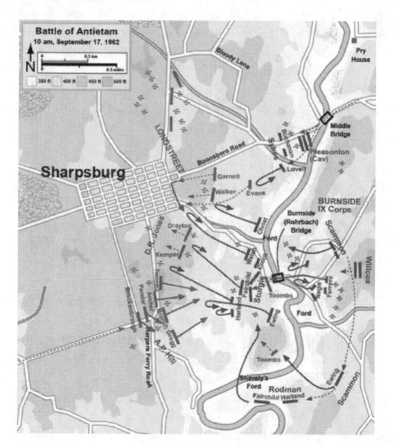

The bullet took him in the knee. It drilled through the joint from right to left ripping out cartilage and tendons and chipping the ends of the major bones. It made a hole through his knee that a ram rod could have been put through. It didn't hurt at all at first. It felt like a blow with the flat of a shovel against the side of his knee. The leg buckled under him and he fell heavily in the shadow of the rail fence beside which he had stood. The rocks his company had piled there sheltered him from the fight. He reached for the lowest rail and tried to pull himself to his feet. He felt the bones grate and sank back into the dust. The leg began to throb. He could see the flow of his blood into the dirt, but looking at the leg he saw that he still had a knee. Even in the moment of his wounding, he knew that what hit him must have been a pistol or carbine bullet. A lead slug from a rifled musket would have flattened against the big bones and smashed the joint to bits.

Hill's men passed him at a dead run, hurdling the fence and screaming their rage at the blue infantry.

Devereux rolled onto his side to watch them go. The Union line of battle hesitated for a moment and then broke for the rear leaving his line of sight below the lip of the nearest shelf.

The noise of gunfire and the sound of men in battle remained close by.

His brother, Jake, knelt beside him. "My, God, Claude, what have you done to yourself now?" His brother had been a classics student at Charlottesville before secession. Now he was an infantry sergeant, and well known for a wry sense of humor.

Devereux tried to see the humor in his situation. This was difficult. "Well," he finally said as Jake cut his trousers away to look at the wound, "Looks like Pat and I are going to have even more in common…"

His other brother, Patrick Henry Devereux had been crippled in a riding accident and walked with a permanently stiff left leg.

"Not funny," Jake replied, "not funny. You are going to lose the leg. They'll take it off above the knee."

Private Johnnie Quick arrived. The old soldier had served in several wars, most notably perhaps, in the Crimea. "I dunno" he said, "looks worse than it may be… Small holes goin' in and comin' out. We should put a tourniquet on that. Don't want you to bleed out, do we, sor? I'll use yer belt," he said without waiting for an answer.

Jake and Quick carried the captain off the field and into the village of Sharpsburg. They carried him along with an arm around each of their necks. His wounded leg stuck out in front. They made a splint from pieces of broken fence rail.

Claude felt more and more faint. He did not know how long he would be conscious. There were no townspeople to be seen. "Why is that?" he wondered aloud.

Artillery shells burst in the street close by as an answer to the question.

The noise of the fight persisted but even a little distance took the edge off the clamor of the battlefield.

They found a field hospital set up in a livery stable. Three surgeons were working inside. They were busy at the usual work of amputation of damaged extremities. There was a lot of pain, a lot of hurt in the sounds coming from the stable. There were pieces of people lying in the shadow of the building. Flies buzzed happily around them.

Jake went inside to talk to someone useful. He watched for a minute or two and then walked to a young man gory to the elbows who was wearing a rubber apron covered with both fresh and dried blood. He seemed to be in charge. The dense blond hair on the backs of his forearms had bits of drying tissue trapped in the fur.

"Doctor, "Jake said in a loud, firm voice.

The man looked at him, looked for wounds. "Who are you?" he demanded impatiently. "I am occupied, as you can see…"

Jake knew that his answer would decide the outcome for his brother. "Sir, I am Sergeant Joachim Murat Devereux of the 17th Virginia. My brother, Captain Claude Crozet Devereux lies gravely wounded in the leg outside. I would ask you to look at him."

The doctor stared at him, then turned and started back to his work. Halfway to the old door on saw horses that served as an operating table, he changed his mind and returned to Jake.

"The banker Devereux family of Alexandria?"

"Yes, sir."

The doctor wiped his drying hand on the apron and held it out. "I am Hunter McGuire. I am the Second Corps Surgeon. I know your father. He lent us the money we needed four years ago for work on the farm, my father's farm… Show me your brother."

"The easy thing would be to take it off," McGuire finally said after examining the knee. "It is ruined enough that it will never be strong. It will always hurt you badly." He was on his knees beside Claude in the dusty street. "I suppose you want to keep it?"

"Yes."

"Well, someone will have to go with you all the way to Richmond or Lynchburg. Richmond would be best. Otherwise, somebody will cut it off when you are unconscious or some such thing."

John Quick held up a paw.

"Are you a nurse?" Dr. McQuire asked.

"Close enough, sor." Quick growled.

"Did you splint this?" McQuire asked.

The answer was yes.

"All right. You did well. It might as well stay this way until you reach a good surgeon." He sent Jake into the charnel house for writing materials. He wrote a note to a particular man at Richmond's Chimborazo Hospital. "I presume that you have money?" he asked Jake.

"Not an issue," Jake replied.

McGuire nodded at the expected answer. "Get a wagon. Get a couple of quarts of brandy or whiskey." He looked at Quick.

"Put it on the leg?"

"Yes, and you can give him a drink now and then, but not too much. Take him to the railhead at Front Royal and then to Richmond as fast as you can. Time is important. I believe that the man to whom the note is addressed can repair this somewhat."

They nodded at him. Claude was now in a lot of pain and groaning aloud.

Quick took the note.

"He has a thousand dollars in US and Confederate money in his wallet. You do, don't you," Jake asked his brother.

"It is not bleeding much now," Mcquire said. He had loosened the tourniquet. "Try not to put that back on if you can avoid it..."

Quick nodded. "Yes, sor, the gangrene, I know."

"Good. On your way, then, I must return to my butchery. Good luck" he said to Claude and walked away.

They broke into a saloon that was under the provost marshal's closure and threatened to shoot the guard inside if they would not take a bribe to give them the brandy. A Sharpsburg merchant was more easily dealt with. He looked at the money and offered to drive them to Front Royal himself so that he could bring his team and rig back.

Five days later Claude Devereux was in Chimborazo Hospital. The surgeon saved his leg after much argument.

John Quick returned to the regiment. He found them, those who were left, in a tent camp outside Berryville. Stragglers and wounded had begun to return.

Jake Devereux was commissioned a lieutenant in "H" Company a month after Sharpsburg.

The secret service came for Claude in October and sent him to France on their business. He was carried onto the ship in Wilmington, North Carolina.

La Brigade. 1870 – Paris

Tiger, tiger burning bright
In the forest of the night
What immortal hand or eye
Has framed thy fearful symmetry?

Blake

Colonel Jean-Marie Balthazar d'Orgueil stood at his office window in the Navy Ministry watching the street below. He had stood at another window nine years before when he was summoned to the *Quai* d'Orsay to be told of a mission to America.

The city seemed surprisingly calm in defiance of the disastrous news arriving daily from the east where the Germans were everywhere victorious and advancing on Paris.

Colonel d'Orgueil had been assigned to administrative duties since his return from America in 1866. As part of his secret mission in America he had at first observed the Civil War from within the Southern Army and had later actually joined their ranks. Towards the end of the struggle, he had been captured and had spent six months as a prisoner. He had married a war widow in Virginia and when released had collected his wife and children before returning to France.

When home he found that his return was met with mixed attitudes, often in the same man. His achievements as a leader of a combat infantry battalion were admired but his unwillingness to accept the guidance of the French military attaché at Washington was not. He found he was mocked occasionally by seniors who addressed him as "John Balthazar" the name he had used in America. In fact, they were awestruck by what he had done as a combat commander and by the quality of his work at the ministry. He had been transferred to the French Marines against his will, but he yet prospered and in 1869 he was promoted to colonel. And now in 1870 with the death of the Second Empire at hand, he awaited the attention of the navy minister.

"Ah, Colonel Balthazar, come in." The minister looked down at papers before him. "Excuse me I meant to say Colonel d'Orgueil"

"No matter minister, no matter. How can I help you?"

"You know we are defeated by the damned Germans?"

"Of course, I know."

"We had three brigades of marines fighting under army control. They were defeated as well, several times in fact."

Balthazar stared at him. He was thinking of his Confederate infantry battalion destroyed at Cedar Creek.

"And?"

"I have sent instructions to the remnants to fall back on the city to certain places where they are to report to you to be formed into a *brigade de marche* to take part in whatever defense we can manage."

"Do you have this in writing? I do not wish to be court-martialed if I survive."

The minister handed the fancy piece of paper across the desk.

Balthazar read. He looked up. "I can have whatever I want from what is left here in men and supplies?"

The minister waved a hand expressively.

"Well then, minister. I advise you to flee with the government when they go. That will be soon." With that he turned and walked out of the room with his precious scrap of paper.

⚜

He rummaged around the ministry gathering up "old sweats" from the colonial wars whom he thought had one more big fight left in them, much like him.

They set up gathering points and waited for the defeated to arrive. He looked at the old sergeants and the much passed over officers who had been waiting for retirement since they had no future hope of promotion. Would they stay with him to fight?

The defeated began to trickle in. At first there were just small groups and then an entire company marched to the assembly point. He confirmed the commander in his position. He picked out a lieutenant and made him adjutant of his *brigade de marche*. "Don't do anything crazy without asking me," he told him.

As the men gathered, he told them that he would not "piss them away."

They would fight as long as they could and then withdraw to the southwest of Paris and wait for a change of fortune.

With that and his name they turned their faces to the enemy and started digging.

He told Victoria Devereux d'Orgueil that she must leave the city with their children.

"You plan to die here?" she asked.

"No, but I cannot concentrate on my work if you are here."

He picked three of his old sergeants to send with his family. "Take them to my home place, Soturac on the Lot River. I have a house there and we are in funds at the local bank. Stay with them and protect them and I will see that you will be well provided for."

"If you live," one said.

He nodded.

A day later one returned to tell him that just outside the city they had encountered a Bavarian infantry regiment moving to take its place in the encirclement of Paris. The commander was a south German nobleman who read the note that Balthazar had given this sergeant. The officer approached the carriage to assure Victoria that the lady of a brother officer could safely go on her way. With that he told the driver of her carriage to proceed.

In the end Balthazar had close to one thousand officers and men. They held a section of line against the German Army throughout the long months of siege and endured the endless whistling of German artillery shells passing overhead on their flight into the city. Throughout the siege he continued to train his marines. By the time the siege ended they were a first-class fighting force. The Treaty of Frankfurt with its incredible humiliations brought the withdrawal of German forces, now the forces of Imperial Germany from the lines around Paris and the election of Adolphe Thiers as the first president of the Third French Republic, a country which had lost Alsace and much of Lorraine in the treaty of peace. The government located itself at Versailles west of Paris, fearful of the Paris mob and the 250,000 amateur soldiers of the National Guard who represented that mob. President Thiers began to assemble regular French forces between Paris and Versailles, among them Balthazar's *brigade de marche.*

As had been expected, sensing an opportunity the forces of the Left rose in rebellion in Paris. Marxists, socialists, anarchists, anticlericals and radical feminists formed a political entity which aimed to create a new form of government for all of France. They called this new form The Commune of Paris. They attacked the banks, burned public buildings and took 100 hostages, among them the Archbishop of Paris whom they later shot.

Having consolidated their position in the city, the Communards decided to move on Versailles to capture President Thiers. Army command had been given by Thiers to Marshal MacMahon.

The forces of the National Guard advanced on Versailles without reconnaissance, cavalry to screen their flanks or significant artillery support. They were met at the *Pont de Neuilly* by French Army forces and were resoundingly defeated and driven back into Paris. In truth they broke and fled like rabbits. Balthazar's marines, attached to an army division distinguished themselves by their steadiness in this decisive battle.

As an indication of how savage the restoration of order was going to be, the policy was that National Guard prisoners who had previously been members of the armed forces or who were bearing arms when captured were shot on the spot.

⌒⎯⋙⎯

In May, 1871 Thiers ordered Marshal MacMahon to capture Paris. With 120,000 regular troops the French Army broke through the National Guard defenses and proceeded to over-run the metropolis quarter by quarter dispensing "justice" as they went. This process is remembered in French minds as *"La Semaine Sanglante."* or "The Bloody Week."

Balthazar's task in this was to methodically clear a strip of city that extended through the heart of Commune controlled territory. There was a lot of killing although this was somewhat reduced by the steadily increasing tendency of the National Guard to throw away their weapons if they saw the game was over.

In the midst of this a prisoner was brought into Balthazar's temporary command post in the lobby of a hotel. That was unusual. The practice was for the officers to make life and death decisions outside and a firing squad was waiting in a courtyard.

"And who are you, sir" Balthazar asked the well-dressed young man.

"Georges Clemenceau'" was the answer.

This sounded vaguely familiar. Balthazar looked at the piece of paper that his adjutant had handed him.

The lieutenant looked hungry.

"You were the mayor of this part of the city in the Commune government?"

"Yes, but I resigned a few days ago"

"Why"

"They are too radical for my taste."

The lieutenant laughed aloud.

"You lived in New York City," Balthazar said after looking again at the paper.

"New York and Connecticut. I taught French and history in a girl's school in Hartford."

Balthazar smiled at him. "I lived in America also. My wife is American."

The lieutenant looked concerned. Such interviews, when they occurred, were short and pro forma.

"But I was an officer in the Confederate Army," Balthazar said. "So, we are both rebels…"

Clemenceau did not see the humor of that.

"Tell you what, Clemenceau. I am not in the mood just now to kill someone like you. You like politics?"

"Yes, very much."

"All right. If you promise to leave politics for five years, I will release you. Otherwise, the lieutenant will escort you to the courtyard. What do you choose?"

"Thank you."

"Good, Lieutenant, find Sergeant Desmarais. While he is doing that, let's have a glass of this admirable Armagnac from the hotel bar."

Some minutes later Sergeant Desmarais appeared, and Balthazar instructed him. "This is Mr., sorry what was it again?"

"Clemenceau."

"I want you to take him out to the farthest reaches of our present perimeter and release him. He is to walk straight away. If he hesitates or even looks back, shoot him. Understood? Go now before I change my mind."

"Sir, that was capricious," the lieutenant said.

"Yes, indeed. It was that."

Some days later the butchery ended, and the Third Republic was firmly established. MacMahon was the next president of France.

Victoria returned from the Lot and a grateful nation decided that Jean-Marie Balthazar d'Orgueil should be promoted to major general of marines and awarded the Legion of Honor yet again.

At the ceremony the Minister of War announced that Balthazar would be appointed to the post of military attaché in Cairo at the court of Ismail Pasha, the Khedive of Egypt.

Victoria looked concerned until told that she could have any house she wanted and unlimited staff.

The "grateful nation" wanted Balthazar out of the country for a while and he was glad to go.

Ruqqiya: An American soldier in Egypt

(a romance)

"If only I were that warrior.
If only my dream might come true!
An army of brave men with me as their leader
And victory and the applause of all Memphis!

And to you, my sweet Aida,
To return crowned with laurels,
To tell you: for you I have fought,
For you I have conquered!

"Heavenly Aida, divine form,
Mystical garland of light and flowers,
You are queen of my thoughts,
You are the splendor of my life.

I want to give you back your beautiful sky,
The sweet breezes of your native land,
To place a royal garland on your hair,
To raise you a throne next to the sun."

Giuseppe Verdi

The Khedive Ismail Pasha
Cairo - 1875

It was a lovely evening. The oppressive heat of a Cairo summer was now a dreadful memory. November in Egypt was always the beginning of a season of entertainments, balls and arrivals of foreign tourists. The ladies who arrived with European tour groups sought adventure and often found it.

Yuzbashi George White strode purposefully towards Shepheard's Hotel. Afternoon Tea on the verandah of this grand establishment was a special reward for a hard day's work. This was a ritual he had come to need in his daily routine. A cup of Turkish coffee, a piece of *baklava*, a few moments calm after a day of coping with the chaos of Egyptian Army headquarters, these were things to be relished. He tried to make the time free every afternoon, but events often intervened to rob him of these hoped for occasions.

His blue uniform tunic and red trousers made him a striking figure. The two trefoils of gold braid at his cuffs marked him as a captain of the Khedive Ismail's Army. A red *tarboush* rode jauntily on his head, cocked to one side in the manner favored by the Egyptian cavalry. He had been an officer of this arm for three years, but now he was employed by General Staff in the capital.

The wide street was crowded with horse drawn transport: carriages, farm wagons, mounted policemen, all the hurrying business of the large city. A line of donkeys trudged by him, loaded with burlap wrapped cargo and tied together in a long line. A *gellabah* clad *fellah* led them through the traffic, shouting, gesticulating, and beating them occasionally to urge them forward. There was a general miasma of horse smells, compounded with the buzzing of flies, filled the space around White. Even in this quite European quarter of the city the faint aroma of sewage tinged the air. Buildings reminiscent of Paris under Napoleon III lined the avenue.

Shepheard's imposing façade loomed before him. He trotted up the steps, nodded to a doorman as he passed, and settled into a wicker chair on the hotel's wide verandah. His food and drink arrived. The first sip of a cup of the heady brew was always the best. He had just replaced his cup in its little saucer when a splendid carriage passing in the street attracted his attention. A finely matched pair of greys drew this barouche. The body of the carriage was so lacquered as to reflect a deep inner blackness. A painted crest was on the door. He saw the khedival arms in half the design. Two ladies sat facing each other chatting. He heard the lilt of Parisian French. The vehicle passed and he returned to his dessert.

A woman's voice cried "Lisette! Lisette!" from the street.

Looking up, he saw a small white dog investigating something in the gutter in front of the hotel's steps.

The barouche was halted just down the street and a door was open. One of the women was descending.

Another column of donkeys was gathering behind the carriage, impeded in their intended forward march.

Captain White picked up a piece of *baklava* and walked down the steps "Lisette! Come here sweetie" he said holding out the treat. "This is much better than that rubbish, much better."

Lisette looked up at him, and at the *baklava*. She sniffed suspiciously, then wagged her tail and came for the sweet.

When she had finished, White picked her up and while holding her realized that someone was standing at his elbow.

In Wordsworth's words, "she was a phantom of delight." Everything about her cried out for George White's adoration. Dressed in a prudent version of French fashion of the season, she stood as high as George's chin. White linen became her. It accentuated her pale but healthy complexion, shaded by a broad brimmed hat to protect the lovely skin from the Egyptian sun. Her eyes were blue. Her hair was chestnut. She was dazzling.

Her liveried driver stood close by, far enough, but not too far.

"Merci, capitaine, vous avez sauvé ma belle petite Lisette…"
She waited for a response.

White tried not to stare. Her accent in French was very good. He had learned French from Madame Clotilde Devereux, an upper class *Parisienne,* and knew what it should sound like. This was the real thing, but underneath the flawless diction was something else.

"*Un grand plaisir, madame,*" he began, fishing for an answer.
After inspecting him for a few seconds, she said, "Ah you are one of the Americans my uncle employs…"
He then knew that he was speaking to a lady of the khedival family and that the accent underneath the French was Turkish, or more accurately Osmanli, the dialect of the Ottoman upper classes.
"And it is, miss, not madame. Thank you again." With that she walked back to the carriage carrying her little dog…
The coachman held the door but did not touch her,

Her lady companion held out a hand to assist on the step of the barouche. Captain White stood, fez in hand, and watched them roll away.
At a corner a block away, she looked back at him and his heart stood still.
Somehow Cairo seemed a more beautiful place. His world had changed forever.
The waiter brought him fresh coffee. George beckoned to the *maître d'hôtel.*
The black jacketed man had been standing in a corner of the verandah watching. He stood next to the table, attentive and looking interested.
"Do you know of the lady with whom I spoke?
"Ah, the Princess Ruqqiya, the khedive's ward. Yes, she comes occasionally for Tea, with other ladies, of course."
"She seems European."

The headwaiter smiled. "Yes, sir, she would. She lived at Istanbul for a long time and I believe she was educated in a ladies' school there and in France."

George paid, rose and departed.

The hotel staff stood together to whisper of what had happened.

⁓✻⁓

Later that week, Captain George White was summoned to the office of *Ferik Pasha* Charles Stone, the Chief of Staff of the Egyptian Army. Stone was a handsome man who had graduated from West Point in the mid-1840s, had served very well in Mexico as an engineer officer under Lee and whose US Army career had fallen to bits in the Civil War after his defeat at Ball's Bluff, Virginia in 1862. The Congress of the Unites States under the control of the radical Republicans were displeased with Lincoln's perceived failure to destroy the Southern secession and had formed a "Joint Committee on the Conduct of the War" for the purpose of "helping" the president run the war. Stone was a conservative Democrat who did not pretend to share the hatred of the radicals toward the South and that was his undoing. The Lincoln Administration abandoned him to the illegal cruelty of the radicals. They accused him of treasonous conspiracy with the enemy. He was imprisoned for a year and then released, never to be employed again in any position worthy of his abilities. After the war he was employed as a civilian engineer but never lost his taste for military life. When the Khedive Ismail approached the US Government seeking officers for his service with whom he could replace Britishers and Frenchmen then training his army, Stone was a natural choice, a man of high ability who had been poorly treated. William Tecumseh Sherman, then commander of the US Army proposed the service to him and to another fifty former officers of both the US and Confederate services. All were men whom he and President Grant esteemed. Stone proposed to the khedive that a general staff be formed, a body that would coordinate the standards and activities of the army. This idea was accepted, and he remained in Cairo at the head of that body while some others like WW Loring became commanders in the field, explorers, heads of schools and staff officers to senior Egyptians.

"Sit down, White." Stone Pasha looked at the dossier before him. "I had some correspondence with Colonel Marco Aurelio Farinelli. He is at Fort Vancouver now in Washington Territory... He sends his regards, his best regards. I suppose I could call you 'Georgio Rinaldi.' Farinelli reminds me that this is the name under which you served in the Regular US Army, first as a sergeant, and then as a lieutenant after Farinelli and your many friends and evident admirers in Washington found a vacancy for you in… 1869?"

Stone was an imposing man. He radiated strength and intellect. The dark blue tunic with gold bullion epaulets contributed to that impression. He was not a tall man but seated behind a massive desk he seemed so.

"Yes, sir, I had been in the Volunteers until Marco, and I escaped together from our captors. We made our way to the James River where we were rescued by the navy. He found a place for me under that Italian name. I served with him until the end of the war both at the Cavalry Bureau in Washington and then as an officer in the regiment he was given. I was a lieutenant by then. Colonel Farinelli stayed in the army after the war and took me with him to the Northwest."

"I suppose most people eventually decided you were Black? You do look like an Italian or a Greek. I can understand that the impersonation would last quite a while. It took me a couple of years to understand. The blue eyes and brown hair are convincing. How much Black are you?"

This was becoming uncomfortable for White. He shifted very slightly in his chair wondering what was going to happen. Would he be sent home? If so, to what end would he be condemned? Would his brother Bill find a job for him? Did he want that? What would his white Devereux cousins say if he arrived on their doorstep?

"Just a trace, really, just a trace, my parents could easily pass for white and did so at times when outside Virginia."

"They traveled?"

"Yes, my father was butler and my mother the head cook in the household of his half-brother, Charles Devereux in Alexandria, Virginia. They were both free long before the war… The Devereux were, are, Catholic and my parents were well treated by their… kin."

Stone had been looking at his desk. Now he looked up. "You all lived in one house in this town? Did not people in the town guess or know?"

"There were several houses near each other, all family properties, but, yes, we lived together. Oh, Alexandrians knew, but it was not spoken of, ever. The Devereux wanted us near them, but they also wished to be considered white. My cousin, Claude, killed an old friend in a duel because the man insisted on speaking of it in public."

Stone shook his head. "Southerners have always been a mystery to me. You left home to join the United States Colored Troops?"

White nodded. This conversation was making him miserable, but he understood that it had to take place. It was surprising that it had not happened before. "Yes general, it was a bitter thing. All the rest of them were Confederate through and through. Well, I am not sure about my parents, but they stuck with the family throughout. My mother is still the cook. Father passed just after the war. It was easier to go to the West Coast with Colonel Farinelli."

"You can't go home?"

"I don't know. I really do not. The Northwest is a green and lovely place. I had some peace there, peace from the memory of the home I left and, in some sense, betrayed…" He looked up.

Stone did not seem to have heard.

"There were 'difficulties with the Modocs, Nez Perce, Shoshone, Arapaho and all the rest, but it was active service and to tell the truth I relished it."

"You are an educated man." Stone was trying to absorb the totality of what he was learning and attempting to integrate the idea of one of his best officers being someone so different from what he had thought.

"Madame Clotilde Devereux educated my brothers and me at home and we had the use of the considerable family library. She would bring us books we wanted to read. We were free, so it was not illegal to educate us, but most would not have, a wonderful woman, a second mother."

Stone looked at the back of his own hands. "I suggest that you allow me to write to the US War Department that Lieutenant Georgio…" He looked at the papers "Rinaldi, Rinaldi, is the same man as George White. This will be useful to you if you ever go back." He saw the doubt. "There are many George Whites."

The captain nodded. "Thank you, sir. Do I still have a job?"

Stone looked surprised. "Of course, you do. You have done wonderful work in the last years with the cavalry in the western desert. Loring thinks very well of you." Stone smiled. "Yes, Loring Pasha, late Major General, Confederate Army thinks well of you and recommends you for advancement. We left all that behind us… You are to be promoted to *binbashi*, to major. I thought you knew that. A prince of the khedive's house will be here momentarily to do the honors. "Ah, by the way, I hear from the 'watchers' that you have met Princess Ruqqiya. She is a charming girl, and the apple of her guardian's eye, the very model of his vision of the future. Just be careful George, careful. Understand?"

"Sir."

"Mrs. Stone would like you to come to dinner on Saturday if you are available…"

Binbashi White bowed slightly.

⚡

White waited every afternoon on the verandah of Shepheard's. The staff eventually came to understand what he was waiting for. An air of condescending pity set in.

And then one day her barouche halted at the steps and Ruqqiya walked to him with her companion.

He stood and bowed his head slightly.

"I came to see you, again," she said. She looked incredible in peach tinted silk. Her beautiful cheeks were slightly flushed.

Egyptian upper-class women of the day were not particularly retiring. They were in the process of emerging from such limits, but there were still limits.

"May we join you?"

He indicated a chair facing him.

She sat with her "friend" at the next table.

"Ah, a major now, congratulations," she said, dimpling prettily. "I understand that you have earned this…"

They talked for half an hour while the waiters, the scene, her older companion, and the world faded from view. Her eyes became more and more fixed on his. She ignored the *helwiyaat* on the linen covered table.

"You will come to my uncle's reception next week?"

"Will I be invited?"

She translated that for the older woman. They smiled as did the waiters. She glanced at them and the smiles disappeared.

When she had gone, the headwaiter stood at George's table with his head slightly bowed. "*Ya beg*, how may we serve you?" he asked.

George did not realize that his future had been decided but the waiters knew.

⚡

The reception

White was splendid in blue and gold. His new uniform had come from the best Italian tailor in the country. He still felt awkward in his role as a major but was approaching a state of reconciliation with his newfound dignity. He had ridden to the Khedival palace and left the horse with a majordomo in a courtyard along with the customary *bakshish* needed to insure the man's attention to the animal's welfare.

The ballroom was immense. The style was distinctly French. The flocked wallpaper, the beautiful draperies, all of it.

He looked around at the collection of Ottoman-Egyptians, European businessmen and the diplomatic community. After a bit, his eyes were drawn to a familiar face. He looked at the woman, lovely in blue silk and finally he knew...

He walked across the room, waited for her attention, and then said "Victoria."

She was startled. "Do I know you, sir?" she asked in English. He looked very strange at first.

"George White," he said in a conversational tone seeking to disguise his excitement behind a soldier's face. "How can you be here?"

"I married a French volunteer in our army."

"Is he here?"

"Yes, he is standing just behind you. He is never far from me at things like this."

George turned to find himself two feet from a major general of French marine infantry wearing a military attaché's *aiguilette*.

"Jean-Marie Baltazar d'Orgueille," the smiling mustachioed man said. "You know my wife?

"George White."

The Frenchman looked startled but recovered well. "Ah, yes. I was known as John Balthazar in America. Your brother, Joseph, died under my command at Cedar Creek.

"He is my cousin by marriage" Victoria murmured.

"How can you be here?" George asked in puzzlement.

"Ah, yes, when I went home after... after the emperor's government decided not to let me return to my Algerian Riflemen and put me to work with the Colonial Infantry, the Navy Ministry's troops. But he shrugged with a smile, "They gave me a brigade and my Confederate rank.

"What happened in the German war," George asked.

"Ah, we did well, and even better against the Communards in Paris. A sad thing… So I was judged "loyal." He laughed and then frowned. "You must be the American who has caught Ruqqiya's eye."

Victoria had listened to all this, comparing this George White to the youth she had known in Alexandria. She looked around the big room. "She is not here yet. We have a few moments with you, George."

"How did my brother die?"

Lieutenant Colonel John Balthazar, CSA, was suddenly in sight. The Frenchman looked in pain.

Victoria reached for his hand. "Not now, George," she said. "Not now. The battalion was destroyed, and the survivors captured. Not now."

"So much cavalry." Balthazar murmured. They ran straight over us. Thousands." He seemed elsewhere.

Victoria looked over husband's shoulder. "Here she is, the lovely Louise."

George spoke. "You know her by that name?"

"She prefers it …"

Before George could turn, Balthazar grasped his forearm. "Remember, she is not as we are. All the Ottoman aristocrats want us to think them European, but they are not. She plays by her people's rules. Be careful. Come see us.".

White nodded and then walked to his beloved's side. Her face lit as she watched him approach.

⸙

They were married several months later in a Muslim contract followed by a ceremony that mimicked Christian ritual except that the bride wore a blue velvet Ottoman wedding costume heavy with silver embroidered bullion. George had professed Islam as a prelude to the marriage, but no one expected him to take the formal step seriously. Ruqqiye was all that George had hoped for. That she was not a virgin meant little to him at the time. She was soon pregnant. This was not surprising in a relationship as intense as theirs.

General and Madame Balthazar invited the newlyweds to dinner. They arrived behind a pair of matched greys in a carriage with the khedival arms on its lacquered doors. The meal was convivial, a blend of Parisian dishes and the best Virginia cooking. Ruqqiya exclaimed in delight when she tasted the courses. She was particularly pleased with the peanut soup although she had been warned of the ham in it. She merely shrugged at that and asked for seconds.

Later, when she and Victoria had left the men to cigars and brandy while they retired to Victoria's little parlor, she informed the hostess that she was three months *enceinte*. When congratulated she remarked that her guardian, the khedive was pleased and that a medical team from Italy had been summoned to help with her pregnancy and delivery. "I have not kept a baby this long before<" she said casually. "There are women in the city who are skilled in such things. It feels very strange. I will endure this for George, but only once."

When George and "Louise" had departed gaily waving from the open carriage, Balthazar heard his wife's account of the women's talk. "I am Catholic," she said. "My people, in Virginia do not accept the killing of unwanted children."

"Joseph's brother will be very unhappy when he realizes the extent of her 'experience,' very unhappy."

"And she will not stop," Victoria whispered.

"No," the general said. "There will be lovers. Not discretely as in France, no, indiscreetly as badges of success."

And so it was,

＊＊＊

Ruqqiye endured her pregnancy. The medical team from Europe helped her to deliver a healthy girl who was named Aysha in memory of the prophet's most beloved wife.

George White returned to his duties, duties that took him to every part of the Khedive's domain. In particular, his absence in the Abyssinia War was protracted. A number of American officers were blamed for failure there, a failure which had been brought on by the ineptitude and laziness of the native Egyptian officers but for whom the Americans made convenient scapegoats. In particular, Loring Pasha, a great friend and benefactor of George, was singled out for blame. Somehow White did not share in the general criticism. Instead, he was praised and promoted to *kaymakam*. This would have been lieutenant colonel in a Western Army. At the time it did not occur to him to ask why.

It was only at the visit of former US President Grant to Cairo that White began to learn the truth of his wife's behavior in his absences or perhaps also during his periods of work in Cairo.

At the gala dinner for General Grant at the palace, White watched with growing interest and apprehension as men gathered in small groups in corners sniggering and sneaking looks at him and his wife. With his suspicion aroused he began\ to observe closely her behavior and especially her absences from their home without much reason given.

He grew cold in his feelings toward her and finally accused her. She stared at him, beautiful as ever. "What did you think would happen?" she asked. "Do you not have other lovers?" When he answered, she shook her pretty head and left the room.

A month later she announced that she had the khedive's permission to live in Istanbul where she had a house, and would do so. "You are free to join me there" she said without much evident enthusiasm. "The Europeans are certain to depose my uncle for his debts and their desire for the canal and I do not wish to be here then. I plan to place our daughter in a French school."

They had been married four years.

⟜⁓⁓⟊⁓⟊⟊⁓⟊⟿

"And now she is gone," *kaymakam* White told John Balthazar in his private office at the French embassy. I wish to leave as well, but do not want to live in Istanbul … I do not know what to do."

"This was all sadly foretold," John Balthazar said. "Do you wish to continue soldiering?"

"I know nothing else… I have the name of the school in Paris," White said holding out a slip of paper. "I had enough thought to ask for that. The name means nothing to me."

"Ah, Victoria and I know the headmistress well. We will look after the girl.

I think I can obtain for you a commission in the *infanterie de la marine,* our marines. I am leaving Egypt very soon to take charge of appointments and promotions at the Navy Ministry You are a very experienced and valuable officer, and the Navy Ministry owes me a lot."

"To do what," George asked.

"To help us 'civilize' Tonkin" the general replied.

"I accept."

Clotilde Jarai

In 1880 as the prospect of European invasion loomed, Qaymaqam George White resigned his commission in the Khedive Ismail's Egyptian army and traveled to Paris to meet with his patron, Major General Jean-Marie Balthazar d'Orgueil who had been known in America as John Balthazar and also to visit his daughter at the boarding school to which George's wife had sent her when she left him the previous year en route to her new home in Istanbul. Before he left Cairo, George went to a mosque and with an imam as witness renounced Ruqqaya as his wife in the traditional Muslim way. Before he resigned, he sent her the document as official correspondence.

After some discussion with the Navy Ministry in Paris, a decision was made on Balthazar's recommendation and in light of White's long experience in training American Indian scouts and Bedouin levies that he would be given a lieutenant colonel's rank in the French Marines if he would serve in the emerging colony of French Indochina while doing the same work. To legally facilitate this arrangement General "Balthazar" claimed that Madame Clotilde Devereux, White's spiritual mother in Virginia had adopted him. She was a French national and that ruse sufficed. The fact that she had taught him and his brothers who were technically free Negroes of very diluted African descent to speak excellent French was a great help in the discussions that led to his appointment. Balthazar introduced him to an excellent tailor and soon he looked the part of a French officer of marines.

He took ship from Le Havre bound for Cochin China by way of Suez and the Indian Ocean. After looking around his suite, complete with fine furniture and a full bar he thought absentmindedly that Ruqqaya would love the opulence. He laughed aloud at the foolishness of that thought, straightened his blue tunic in the mirror, carefully closed the beautiful mahogany door behind him and went to the first-class lounge in search of woman.

He arrived at Saigon a month later, the ship having visited a number of ports along the way. He landed at Vung Tau and was struck by the green beauty of the landscape, the handful of French built buildings, the humidity and a crowd of Europeans on the beach enjoying the seaside.

Saigon itself was a small city being transformed by the colonial government into a far eastern version of Paris. Streets were being straightened and widened. A cathedral was under construction in a central plaza. There were modern hotels and apartment blocks. He checked into the largest and found that his arrival had been awaited. Messages were waiting. The governor of Cochin China wished to see him.

Le Myre de Vilers was his name. He was a civilian, the first such to hold this post, but he had been a naval officer. He was said to be a busy man, and much absorbed with economic development of the colony.

At the palace George was hustled up marble stairs by Vietnamese staff. The building was immense, and the governor's office was the size of a tennis court.

"We don't see many Americans out here" de Vilers said looking up from the sheaf of papers on his desk.

"I am a French citizen," Gorge replied evenly in French.

"Yes, yes, I can read, colonel. You must have powerful friends. The description of you that I have received is incredible, incredible. Well, so be it. We badly need someone like you to create militias of the non-Vietnamese tribal groups that surround this city. We have finally managed to comprehend their animosity toward the Vietnamese." He laughed and shook his head. "It took us forty or fifty years to understand that. They will be useful in controlling the colony and in our expansion of the territory we actually control. I am building railroads and I need to have them protected. We do not have enough European troops. Can you help with this?"

White now saw that he had the upper hand in this discussion. "I don't see why not. This is quite like my previous work."

"How long do you expect to stay in Indochina?" de Vilers asked.

"I have no plans to leave."

"All right. Good. Bring me a budget and select a place where you can establish yourself and your operation.'

With that the conversation ended and de Vilers showed him to the door.

After some searching White found a girls' school that had long been tolerated by the native aristocracy of Saigon. It had declined in popularity since the French occupation and was bankrupt. The compound had walls and assorted buildings within them. One would serve him as residence. With that achieved and the governor's money in hand he set out to make the acquaintance of the tribal peoples.

He went out with patrols from the marines, zouaves and Foreign Legion to visit the scattered villages and shanty towns. He found scholars in Saigon who were studying the tribals now beginning to be called *montagnards*.

They taught him that the tribes could be grouped by type. There were two groupings.

Tribes like the S'tieng and Mnong Gar were short, thin people with quite dark skin who filed their teeth to points, chewed betel nut to stain them and had no concepts of distance, time or number. They also had no military tradition and were easily abused by the Vietnamese. They made wooden crossbows for the purpose of hunting monkeys and other small game.

The second group resembled Tahitians or Maori in New Zealand. They were taller and better muscled than the first group. They were quite warlike and fought Vietnamese domination with all available force.

Tribes like the Bahnar, Sedang and Jarai belonged to this group. White decided that he would recruit among these. He also decided that he would keep his *montagnard* units free of more than one tribal identity. He knew from long experience that tribesmen from different groups would not mix well.

He spent a lot of time visiting with village elders while seeking their cooperation. In the course of that he ate a lot of rather repulsive food. The selling point in these recruiting trips always seemed to be that the tribesmen would be armed with modern weapons and that the French would be their allies against the Vietnamese.

Soon there was a steady procession of small tribal units living in his Saigon compound for a month for training in arms. On the streets of the city these men quickly learned that the Vietnamese had more to fear from them than the other way round. That was exhilarating for them.

George was surprised that these men always wanted to learn to speak understandable French. He hired a missionary Catholic priest to teach the language. His name was Raymond Dupont. He was from Gascony.

Teams graduated and went forth to be attached to French forces. They easily satisfied George's expectations. There were no complaints from the governor and his budgets were approved without comment.

This work went forward well. He and the priest, who was not a representative of a religious order, but rather of the Missionary Board in Paris, became well acquainted, perhaps even friends.

George White could always find female company but as the months passed he felt an emptiness in his heart if not in his bed. He was lonely.

One day in 1882 Father Dupont asked if he would like to accompany him and a group from the missionary society in a medical treatment visit to a newly established Mnong Gar village a day's travel from Saigon. The tribesmen were steadily moving closer to the city in response to the colonial government's construction of roads.

George could not think of a reason to decline. The village was one he had not explored. He accepted on condition that a squad of his "troops" would guard the site while they were there.

On the day appointed George and his little group of Bahnar warriors met the religious folk at an intersection on the edge of the city. His men would walk while he would ride his big black gelding.

The missionaries rode in three carriages and what must have been a wagon full of supplies followed behind. In the carriages were nuns, priests, doctors and a young woman driving for three European nuns. The girl was interesting. She wore Western clothing but looked like George's notion of what a Tahitian might look like. She was quite pretty and he was very attentive to pretty women.

The little caravan moved off down the hard surfaced road between rice paddies filled with Vietnamese peasants' intent on their work.

George's Bahnar lined the road on either side to lead the way. He rode down the road between the two files. He could hear the conversations behind him. After a few miles, he began to think of other times and places. Through his revery he heard the name "Clotilde." That startled him into full consciousness.

He rode back to the first carriage, touched the bill of his kepi and asked, "Who is Clotilde?"

The "Tahitian" looked up at him from her concentration on the horses. "I am. Clotilde Jarai, why?" she asked.

"One of my mothers at home was named Clotilde. Clotilde Devereux."

"Where was home?"

"Virginia in the United States."

"You fought for the South in the great war? You are the right age." That last was in English, another surprise.

He flinched. It may have been visible. His secret feeling that he had betrayed his family by not fighting alongside them remained strong. "Why Clotilde" he asked.

"Father Dupont adopted me… He named me for his mother. There seem to be at least two mothers involved."

The French and Vietnamese nuns listened with interest.

He rode back to his place with his Bahnar.

<hr>

At a break on the road, he asked Father Dupont about Clotilde.

"We found her in a Jarai village when she was three or four years old. Her mother was Jarai and her father was evidently a Chinese peddler. Her mother abandoned her and the people in the village rejected her as a mixed blood. She was running around naked, living on garbage and scraps and the men were already starting to molest her. They were happy to be rid of her. Our Sisters have raised her. They have hoped she might have a vocation and stay with them, but she does not seem to want that."

White watched her tend to her horses. She was watching him as well without seeming to stare. "And the English that she knows?"

"We have a nun from Guernsey. She is learning from her, Clotilde is a very ambitious young woman."

"How old is she?"

"Probably twenty-five?"

<hr>

The Mnong Gar village was an awful muddy mess. Animal dung was everywhere. The huts were poorly built, and the place stank.

The Mnong were afflicted with the usual skin diseases, broken bones and something that looked a lot like pneumonia.

White's Bahnar stood apart, unwilling to mix with these small, dark people and feeling quite superior.

After some time, Clotilde left the group to sit apart on a fallen log.

George saw the invitation and asked to join her.

In the next hour of conversation something magical happened. They both knew that life had suddenly changed.

Father Dupont who had observed them asked White if his intentions were honorable.

"Yes, yes, somehow, they are. I have your permission to court her?

In the next months the love affair blossomed and deepened. They assumed almost from the beginning that they would marry. When she learned of his previous marriage in Egypt, she told him that he must return to Christianity. Father Dupont heard his confession, and they were married in the new cathedral by the bishop of Saigon himself. The wedding of a foreign-born senior officer of marines to an obvious daughter of *la mission civilizatrice* was irresistible for the notables of the colony. The governor was there. He kissed the bride and later danced with her at the reception. The garrison commander was there as well, full of jollity and good red wine.

At the celebratory luncheon, the governor whispered to George," Don't let them send you to Tonkin. That will be a murder game." Stay here, please. Stay here with her … Your *montagnards* love you. And now you have married one of them. She loves you. Stay here. How old are you?"

"Forty-five."

"You have fought enough."

She adored her new home. It was the former headmistress's house in George's compound. She got rid of most of his furnishings, while filling the house with teak and mahogany pieces of local manufacture that would someday be thought great works of domestic art.

She bore George two children, a boy and a girl, Claude and Marie.

His work in developing tribal militias to support the expansion of French rule was ever more successful. Perhaps it was too successful. Imperialist France was intent on dominating all the other parts of what it called *Indochine:* Tonkin, Annam, Cambodia, and Laos.

George was willing to train Europeans in his methods but unwilling to leave Saigon permanently himself. He had a happy life with Clotilde and a growing family to care for. Nevertheless, pressure grew steadily as time passed for him to move his main training center to Hanoi in Tonkin.

He was beginning to think seriously of retiring to France when an escape route miraculously appeared on his doorstep in the shape of an American consular officer who had travelled from Hong Kong to meet with him.

"Quite a setup you have here, colonel, very nice, very nice." The consul was a sandy haired little man who looked to be about thirty-five.

Looking at him over the rim of a teacup in which his wife had brought them refreshment, George was sure that Clotilde was included in the "very nice, very nice." Inspecting the man closely, George was surprised that they had not better tailors in Hong Kong.

"Always wanted to come down here to see what France is doing. Very impressive indeed."

George waited, knowing that this creature would eventually get to the point.

Papers appeared from a large satchel. There were a lot of papers.

The creature spoke. "The US Government has been looking for a foreign adviser. At the recommendation of many important people in Paris, the French government has agreed that you be assigned in Washington as a military attaché and to advise our government with regard to Indian Affairs. We evidently considered others, including British officers, but in the end you were selected."

The Whites looked blankly at him, surprised into silence.

The consul began to lose confidence, afraid that he might have to return to report failure to the consul general. "The French say they will promote you," he stammered. The Army will give you a house at Fort Myer. That is near Washington I suppose. I have pictures …"

Clotilde came close to see. The photos were of a big, brick, three story house with a wraparound porch. She put a hand on her husband's shoulder.

"Indian Affairs?"

The consul seemed fascinated by the cream-colored hand. "Yes; Indian Scouts for the Army. They have troubles with them. Treaty relations with the tribes, Indian schools, Reservation agents. All of that."

"And Paris has agreed?"

"Yes, someone named d'Orgueil seems to have carried a lot of weight in the talks and there is the fact that you are American …"

"French."

"Yes, yes, French now."

"How would we arrive at Washington?" Clotilde sat down to listen for the answer.

"A suite on the 'Empress of China' from Hong Kong to San Francisco, then a Pullman Car compartment to Chicago and finally the Baltimore and Ohio to Washington." He was reading notes from the satchel.

"British ship?"

"Canadian. It will go on to Vancouver after San Francisco."

"You know I have family near Washington?"

"They say they look forward to your return."

"You have been thorough. You know I am part Negro, one sixteenth to be precise?"

The consul looked through the papers searching for something. "The US Army says that in light of your exact ancestry, previous service in The War and as an officer thereafter, even though as someone name Rinaldi, the small amount of Negro blood that you have is irrelevant. The army has previously declared you to be white, as well as White." He thought that funny from the look on his homely face.

George did not think it funny. He looked at his wife.

She nodded.

"Yes," he told the consul.

They left a month later just after George was promoted. They were given diplomatic passports. Clotilde had her furniture packed and shipped to Washington consigned to the post commander at Fort Myer.

On the Embarcadero at San Francisco, the customs man looked at their passports, excused himself, and disappeared, returning with his chief.

"Colonel White," the chief said, "I have a letter from the army headquarters here that told me to expect you and madame." He bowed slightly in her direction. "You have rooms at the Palace Hotel where your rail tickets are waiting. It is a fine place. If you will sit in my office for a bit, we will arrange transportation.

⸎

The four-day trip to Chicago passed in relative comfort. Their compartment was furnished well and the children were fascinated by the everchanging scenery. There was a dining car but after having been stared at a few times, Clotilde began to take her meals in private. From Chicago the remainder of the trip was less than a day.

They arrived at Washington to find a lieutenant waiting for them with an army carriage and driver. A telegram from Chicago had brought help in taking them to their new home. Standing with the officer on the platform was a man from the French embassy. The lieutenant had a note from "JM Devereux" addressed to "Colonel White" welcoming George and family and expressing a hope to receive them in Alexandria at George's "earliest convenience."

⸎

Within a few days George and his extended family were gathered in the parlor of the big Devereux family home on Prince Street in Alexandria, Virginia.

The present head of the family, Joachim Murat Devereux, (Jake to his friends) sat by Clotilde White holding her hand. She bore the same name as his deceased beloved mother and he wanted her to feel at home. Of the three Devereux brothers he was the only one to have survived the great war of the 1860s and he was now the head of the family's merchant bank, "Devereux and Wheatley."

George White sat on the other side of his wife. The two White children could be heard in the kitchens being cared for by the help.

Bill White, George's full brother sat across the room. Like George, he was of mixed race, and a cousin to the Devereux family, their fathers having been half-brothers. In the present family business, he was Jake's closest friend and counselor.

George's father had been butler in this same house and his mother, Betsy, the head cook. The Devereux brothers and the Whites had been raised together in this house. The mothers of the two sets of boys had loved them dearly.

Isaac Smoot and his wife, Hope, sat by the big black marble fireplace. Smoot had been the comrade of the Confederate fighters in the room, had lost a hand at Spotsylvania and had married the widow of Claude Devereux, the eldest Devereux.

Closest to the door was the only non-family person in the room. He had come on official business, having been told that George would be present. This was the sheriff of Alexandria.

Offered a glass of the family's best liquor, he sipped from the cut glass tumbler in his hand, listened to the newly reunited family explore each other in reminiscence and steeled himself to say what had to be said. He put down the glass and cleared his throat.

They all looked at him.

"Colonel White. I am certainly happy to make your acquaintance. I hope to know you better … but there is a problem."

"What is that?" George asked.

"In Virginia, a white man may not be married to a colored woman. This is the law"

"But I am not white," George replied. "Everyone in this town knows that. The older ones remember that I left home to join the 2nd US Colored Troops Cavalry after a tremendous row out in the kitchen with my parents. And in any event, we now live on federal property where Virginia's law does not apply."

"The army says you are white. We asked. I am here to make sure you continue to live there so that there will not be trouble."

The soldier in blue who had driven them from Ft. Myer could be heard outside a window comforting and soothing the team of horses.

Faces hardened around the room.

The sheriff rose and crossed the room to Clotilde. He bowed slightly.

Looking up at him, she saw the pain and held out her hand palm down.

He took it and bringing his lips to a precise one inch from her skin, said "Your servant, ma'am."

Jake Devereux escorted him out.

And thus, George White came home at last.

The Hog's Snout (An alternative history)

President Walter Herron Taylor was the sixth chief executive of the Confederate States of America and halfway through the single six-year term allowed under his country's constitution. He was fifty-six years old and looked healthy as the proverbial horse. Dressed in a black suit, he sat at ease in the parlor of the Confederate White House in Richmond, Virginia. He was a beautiful man growing gracefully white haired but still slender. He looked comfortable in a simple chair. He had emerged from behind a big, dark colored wooden desk to sit with the reporter.

The New York Times man who had been given an interview eyed him appraisingly. "Would you tell sir, something of your early life," he asked.

"I was born in Norfolk in 1838. My people were merchants. The family had been here since the early days of the Virginia colony. I decided to attend the military institute at Lexington and studied there for a while until my father died and I was called home. I worked for a bank and read law until war came. I was in the Norfolk militia and joined a volunteer company in Tidewater after secession."

"As an officer?"

"They did me that honor… Yes. Shortly thereafter one of my numerous relations suggested to General Lee that I might be useful to him as an adjutant and member of his headquarters staff."

"You were not the only officer on the staff."

"No. No. There were quite a few of us; Charles Venable, Charles Marshall, Colonel John Fairfax, you know of him. He was the eleventh Baron Cameron. Born here among us, but he was a picturesque man, always quoting the King James Bible and a great source of good whiskey. Then there was the usual collection of 'galloper' officer couriers et cetera."

"But you were close to him? I mean Lee…"

Taylor thought about that for moment. "Yes, and the longer the war dragged on the more he was like a father to me, but I suppose that would be true of us all. Is there something in particular you wanted to talk about?"

"I am the military editor of the Times. I would like to know what happened at the North Anna. Grant's plans to end the war were progressing well until then. But suddenly things started to come apart. Ben Butler was pushed back at Drewry's Bluff south of Richmond on the 12th of May and that strange defeat in the Shenandoah Valley happened on the 15th at New Market, but still, observers thought that after Spotsylvania Court House it was just a matter of time until we reached Richmond and then there would be a total downfall of your… government." The reporter looked in the portfolio he had brought and found a photograph. He handed it to Taylor.

"Ah, yes," the president said. "Grant and his staff relaxing at Massaponax Church on the way to our renewed encounter at the North Anna, they look confident, sure that we were finished. We thought the same thing. We thought we were doomed. The only thing holding us together by the time we arrived at our new position on that river was our loyalty to 'the tycoon' himself."

"Lee?"

Taylor smiled. "That's what we called him, and he pretended not to know. He tried hard to be a tolerant man, but he was a volcano inside. It showed on the battlefield, and he had a terrible temper. When it got the better of him we would all go hide as best we could." The president seemed suddenly to remember that he was talking to his old enemies through this man. The smile left him and he waited.

"The North Anna?"

Taylor nodded. "Do you like the wallpaper?" he asked after a minute. "My wife tells me that it is French, flocked in that fuzzy red material, and that it was here when Jefferson Davis sat in this chair. Yes, I heard you, the North Anna. We call it the 'Hog's Snout.' We were chewed to pieces by your people by the time we arrived on the North Anna River. The Wilderness, and Spotsylvania had taken an awful toll. I was in charge of calculating our strength every day and we were at about half strength from what we were when Grant crossed the Rapidan two, three weeks before. He just kept coming and coming at us. We had lost all manner of animals in the artillery and trains. Edward Johnson's division had been pretty much captured or killed in the Mule Shoe at Spotsylvania. Supply had broken down again and there was nothing to eat except what we took off your men's bodies. We killed your people and killed them and killed them but there were always more. We beat Grant to the North Anna and could cover the Virginia Central rail line and the Telegraph Road where it crossed the rail line, but we had no idea what we would do when Grant arrived in strength from Spotsylvania. We were right desperate.

The newsman saw that Taylor was looking at him in a way that made him uneasy.

"And then reinforcements arrived, Pickett's Division came up from south of Richmond. They had just whipped Ben Butler and were full of themselves, and Breckinridge reached us from The Valley. Both of them had been done pretty hard in the previous weeks but the men were somehow still full of fight. There were a lot of Virginians. This was our home place…"

The reporter nodded in seeming understanding.

"So, Grant came in from the northwest and tried to force a crossing of the river at Jericho Mill upstream from most of us.

(The North Anna at Jericho Mills)

Wilcox's Division drove them back, but Grant kept moving southeast toward us. The river was actually quite an obstacle then. These days with all these new kinds of horseless transport, maybe not…

And then, something unexpected happened. The army's Chief of Engineers, Major General Martin Smith, a Yankee by birth, but one of us, talked to the boss and they devised an ingenious scheme with which to trap Grant and his handmaiden, George Meade. Smith was a very clever fellow. He and General Lee had the foresight to build a corduroy road to Spotsylvania west and parallel to the Brock Road in the winter before. They reasoned that such a road would be needed to stay ahead of Grant if he tried to march south on the Brock Road through the Wilderness. That is how we got to Spotsylvania before Grant. After Spotsylvania those two decided that the topography of the North Anna area was a good place to lay a grand trap.

On the north side of the river a move to the Telegraph Road by Grant would have to cross the river twice on ground not served by roads or bridges. Such a move would take time and a great deal of field engineering work to achieve in any circumstance, especially a crisis circumstance. Because of this our planners decided to set up a position in which an inverted "V" would be created with available units positioned in a wedge, the point of the wedge resting on the south bank of the North Anna just where the greatest scarcity of lateral roads existed on the north bank. The opportune arrival of Pickett and Breckinridge allowed them to be positioned as the army's reserve within the wedge.

"And you were privy to all these arrangements? You would actually have known this?"

Taylor sighed. "Ah, yes, I and all the other officers of the staff in the field. The hope was that Grant would move to the east of the Telegraph Road through the roads well north of the river, and that is what he did."

"What did he do then?"

"Well, you know the answer. Why you are asking me is almost a mystery, not quite a mystery, but almost. Nevertheless, I will answer the question. The Second US Army corps was sent to the southeast of the North Anna with evident orders to keep pressing down the Telegraph Road to the south, toward Richmond. The city was at that moment but fifteen miles away. Our side believed that Grant had no clear idea of our wedge-shaped disposition. We were correct. He had sent

Sheridan and the bulk of the Union cavalry on a massive raid into the Richmond area. These scouting troops were unavailable to spy out our locations. They had not yet returned to the main battlefield. It was understandable that he was effectively blind, but his dispatch of Second Corps isolated them on one side of our wedge, isolated by the bends in the river and the likelihood of an attack by our troops in the "nose" of the wedge into the Union flank if the rest of them tried to move east to rescue Second Corps from an assault on them.

"The result was a disaster for us, and the United States," said the newsman. I was with Second Corps as a correspondent and was captured and imprisoned at Libby."

"Welcome back to the capital," President Taylor said straight-faced. "I hope your rooms are more satisfactory this time…"

The grey haired, portly visitor grew red in the face. "May we continue? We have never learned exactly what your plan was except by the effect, and I understand that you, personally, drafted the orders."

"Well, sir, we have not had a close relationship since those unhappy days, but, to answer, we knew we had only a short time until Grant realized his error and withdrew Second Corps to safety. General Lee decided to attack Second Corps east of the river with all available force using both Breckinridge and Pickett as well as Harry Heth's division and to do that in a massed column of attack by brigades."

"When was this planned to happen?"

"In the pre-dawn on the 24th of May, when were you captured?"

"I was taken by Heth's men that afternoon. There must have been great difficulty in putting all this together and getting men into position with troops who had recently lost many leaders, and a lot of friends."

"Yes, that is true, but the main worry was that it seemed Lee was about to be seriously ill. He had dysentery, bad dysentery, and this dysentery was as bad as he had suffered at Gettysburg. He also had chest pains. This angina was a symptom of the illness that later killed him. He no longer had the advice and moral support of General Longstreet who was wounded at Spotsylvania. If he could not command through his illness, we would fail, but somehow, he did command."

"And?"

"At five in the morning our lead brigade struck the front line of Second Corps and found that there were a lot of surrenders. They pushed through the trenches. The following units went through the hole, and we found that the shoulders of the penetration were equally soft. We had not understood the extent to which losses in the campaign had weakened the Second Corps, and indeed all of Grant's force. Resistance folded up as our people got farther and farther into the rear. Your troops began to move away in disorganized masses and the corps commander's capture with most of his staff around noon pretty much ended Second Corps resistance."

"And then?"

"General Lee ordered a general advance when Hancock appeared as a prisoner at our headquarters. Pressure from south of the river by troops on our left and on the rest of Grant's army on their now open flank caused them to start withdrawing to the northwest and pressed by Hampton's cavalry they continued to fall back until they were across the Rapidan once again. As you know, Grant, in his confidence, had changed his supply base to the coastal river ports. When compelled to fall back, his lack of a base to the northwest was a major embarrassment."

"Hampton?"

"Yes, Major General Wade Hampton, now governor of South Carolina, he took over when you killed Stuart at Yellow Tavern."

The newsman grimaced. "Yes. Grant was relieved of command in August. McClellan was elected president in November, and he accepted the offer of mediation by Britain, France and the Vatican. Pius the Ninth was always a friend of yours and a negotiated settlement was done that gave you independence, for now…"

"Are you sure you work for a newspaper?" Taylor asked. "Your government accepted our independence because your citizenry would no longer consent to the unspeakable losses suffered for little accomplishment. I guess you ran out of the poor people needed to fight your war against us, people who could not buy exemption from service."

"What of slavery?"

"Our constitution reserves changes in the institution to the states. Increased use of farm machinery is steadily making slave labor more expensive than machines. Three states have abolished slavery on a compensated basis and Negroes are steadily leaving us for the North…"

"Any chance of reunion?"

"Not in the lifetime of my generation, but who knows what might happen in the future. My secretary will show you out. Don't overstay your welcome in Richmond…"

The End

Note: In real history Lee grew so ill that the plan could not be executed.

PART VI

Middle East Strategy

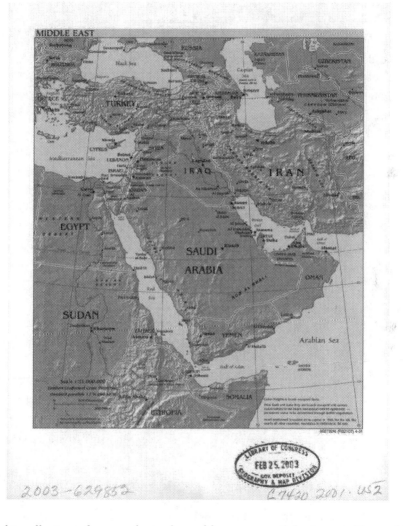

2003-629853

LIBRARY OF CONGRESS
FEB 25 2003
GEOGRAPHY A MAP DIVISION
GOV. DEPOSIT

C 7430 2001 . U52

In this collection of essays, the author addresses some of the intractable troubles that have beset the Middle East region historically and in recent decades. He offers a series of policy proposals for how to manage and ultimately solve some of these difficulties to bring about a future of greater hope.

197

A Concert of the Greater Middle East
(November 13, 2006)

In the aftermath of the Napoleonic Wars Europe was a political shamble. Decades of what Clausewitz thought to be "total war" had ruined the economies and "status quo ante" social systems of the many European states. To overcome the instability of the continent and the likelihood that this would lead to further disastrous warfare, the Great Powers of the time met at Vienna after 1815 to create a system of balanced agreements which would bring into equilibrium the interests of all the possible adversaries on the European scene. This system preserved European peace for many years until it came to pieces in August 1914. The system has been known to history as the "Concert of Europe." What is now needed is a "Concert of the Greater Middle East."

In the "Islamic Culture Continent" extending from Morocco to Indonesia and from Central Asia to the Indian Ocean, the states, factions, and sects of the region tremble on the edge of the chasm of massive military conflict.

- Iraq is torn by Sunni insurgencies both secular and jihadi and is "governed by" a controlling Shiite majority which is itself the prize being struggled over by competing Shiite militia armies.
- Iran pursues a dangerous nuclear program which threatens all its neighbors (including Israel) with the possibility of war and hegemonic domination while meddling deeply in the political destruction of Iraq.
- The Kurdish "nation" now possesses a homeland in northern Iraq which is threatened in the long run by Turkish animosity and suspicion.
- Syria exists in a precarious state balanced between American hostility and the policy pressures of its Iranian senior ally. The long term stability of its government is threatened by sanctions and political covert action.
- Lebanon is transitioning toward a political expression of Lebanese Shia majority numbers. This could lead to civil war. Lebanese Christian allies of the United States and Israel do not want to give up the unwarranted power in the country that their small numbers no longer justify.

These and many other factors threaten war in the region both inside and among these countries, war which could easily spread to their sponsors in the world community.

This situation is so dire and fraught with the possibility of major war that a regional conference of ALL the actors is justified, indeed is imperative. This conference should be designed to bring into equilibrium the interests of the state and non-state "players" whose real or imagined grievances and needs threaten the peace of mankind. Just as the Great Powers of 1815 sponsored the Congress of Vienna to forge an understanding of what had to be done to achieve a lasting peace among those who hesitated on the brink of war, the present Great Powers; the United States, Russia, China, France, and Britain must call for a definitive international round of negotiations to settle ALL outstanding disputes among the peoples of the Greater Middle East. Would such a series of conferences meet under the auspices of the United Nations? The present structure of international law makes that unavoidable, but the attitudes and direct and continuous participation of the Great Powers will be a pre-requisite for success.

What might the set of agreements and policies making up the "Concert of the Greater Middle East" look like? From an American perspective they may look like this:

- A "Grand Bargain" with Iran in which Iranian and Shia aspiration to be treated for the first time in history as equal in importance in the Islamic World with the Sunnis and in which the position of Iran as a major power in the Greater Middle East is accepted by the United States. In return the United States should demand of Iran that it place its nuclear and missile programs under full international controls and that it both restrain the Shia government of Iraq from de-stabilizing excesses and desist from the Iranian support to international jihadi terrorism for which it is well known.
- A "Bargain Among Allies" made between The United States and Turkey with regard to a Kurdish Homeland in what is now northern Iraq. The terms – Kurdistan will make all its oil export and refining deals with the Turks. – Kurdistan will abandon irredentist claims in the Turkish Republic and will take an active role in the suppression of armed PKK activity in Turkey. – Kurdistan will support the rights and position of the Turcoman minority in areas accessible to it, and in particular, in Kirkuk. – The United States will maintain an air

base and substantial ground garrison in Kurdistan to enforce all the above. (This will be necessary in any case to provide a military "reserve" needed to support the safety of the United States diplomatic presence in Iraq)

- Lebanon and Syria to be brought to a mutual and legal recognition of their distinct national identities in which Syria undertakes to refrain from political activities of ANY KIND in Lebanon and in which Syria accepts that violation of this undertaking opens it LEGALLY to armed international intervention in its internal affairs. In return Syria would be absolved from the unending American hostility to the existence of the present regime on Damascus.

- Israel must be a full participant in all conferences and meetings involved in this process. In return, Israel will undertake to make Palestine (the state) a vital and thriving economy.

- In the Sunni Arab areas of Iraq, the United States should learn to differentiate among those who fight; - against Shia domination in Iraq, - those nationalists and Baathists who fight for their condemned leader, - Sunni Bedouin tribesmen under the tribal Sheiks, - "Alawi" style nationalist Shia, - and local or international jihadi types. What the US and the international community must learn to do is "divide and conquer." The variety of people in the Middle East is no different than anywhere else. The need to "neuter" Islamic jihadis is overwhelming. Muslims and Arabs hate the idea that outsiders can see the "daylight" between them and make use of it, but the fact is that there are enough mutually hostile factions in the "Sunni Triangle" that those who are useful in the struggle for stability in the region and the world can be made allies in the fight against jihadism. The needs of mankind outweigh the psychology of anti-colonialism and a choice should be made among present adversaries and those who are chosen as potential allies should be supported against the true enemy. It is likely that the Bedouin tribes would become allies against the fanatics.

- US Forces in Iraq (outside Kurdistan) should be scaled back in their activities to a mission which concentrates on training the forces of governments friendly to the USA and securing our citizens and embassy.

Is there a practical alternative to a "Congress of Geneva" (or wherever the grand meeting is first held? Yes. The alternative is war and chaos.

A Survey of the Situation in the Middle East

ADDRESS AT THE MILLER CENTER, UNIVERSITY OF VIRGINIA (November 1, 2010)

Speaker: W. Patrick Lang
Date: November 1, 2010

Description:

COLONEL W. PATRICK LANG is a retired senior officer of the U.S. Military Intelligence and U.S. Army Special Forces, who trained as a Middle East specialist and served there for many years. He was the first professor of Arabic at the U.S. Military Academy at West Point and served as the Defense Intelligence Officer for the Middle East, South Asia, and terrorism. Colonel Lang is currently a television news analyst.

Moderator: Welcome to the Miller Center forum, I'm George Gilliam. Our guest today is Colonel Patrick Lang. Pat Lang was literally born into the Army. He entered the world in Ft. Devens, Massachusetts. He was educated at VMI with graduate work at the University of Utah, the Armed Forces Staff College and the U.S. Army War College. Col. Lang served in the regular Army as a commissioned officer until 1988. His postings included serving as the senior military officer in our embassy in North Yemen and then in Saudi Arabia. He taught at West Point, where he created all the instructional programs in the Arabic language and Middle East studies. Upon his retirement, Col. Lang joined the senior executive service of the U.S. Civil Service. His Civil Service jobs included serving in the Defense Intelligence Agency as the Defense Intelligence Officer for the Middle East, South Asia, and terrorism, and as that agency's Human Intelligence Officer for Collection. Col. Lang has also written three books and has contributed to many other books and journals. He's a regular on all the network news programs, as well as those in Australia, Germany, Canada, and England. And he presently serves as a member of the Board of Directors of the Harry F. Guggenheim Foundation. Please welcome our friend, Pat Lang. [Applause] [Full house]

Lang: Thank you, George, I appreciate it. It's always a pleasure to be back here. I've been here a number of times now. I'm sure it's nothing like a record, but I'm going to work on that record in whatever remaining time I have.

We don't have a lot of time here today, and George and I have talked about what I should talk about. The prospect I face is giving you yet another drink from a fire hose, in that no one would ever possibly expect that you would remember everything I am going to talk about. But at least you'll have something to argue about when you go home. So, what I'm going to try to do is give you my analytic opinion of what the future holds in several key areas of conflict and geographical areas across the Middle East, in one part of the area that I used to work on so much.

Now, analytic opinion is something that comes up from time to time as to what that is. As a matter of fact, I think that Mr. Juan Williams had a run in with that concept not too long ago. In my opinion, having been the boss of a whole lot of analysts ... I think that analysis is really opinion applied to a given set of facts. So, anybody who tries to separate opinion from those facts is not really doing anything other than just chronicling what went on. So, I'm going to give you my opinion about all this. And I want you to remember that it is all my opinion, and I certainly don't expect you to agree with me.

I would like to start with the present situation that is ongoing with regard to the negotiations between Israel and the Palestinian Authority. I have contemplated this a lot, in the hope that I have nurtured for many years, that this dispute could be settled, because I am almost a commuter to the Holy land, from various items of business, involvement in the Catholic church among other things. And, if people would stop hurting each other there, I might go live there for the remaining part of my life, but it doesn't seem very likely.

A couple of years ago when I was here, I remember telling the people that the problem of settling the peace between these two peoples is that there really isn't sufficient good will on either side to enable a peace to be reached in fact. If there was enough good will, the issues could be signed by taking one piece of paper and drawing an outline of the borders on it. Taking the other and drawing up a list of the conditions; everybody could sign and we'd be off to the races. But in fact, that doesn't happen because the two sides nurture a kind of bitterness against each other which seems to be almost impossible to overcome. And that's a shame because I can remember times during my life, when things were much, much better between these people than they are now.

After the Oslo Accords, when Ehud Barak was Prime Minister, and the Palestinian Authority was doing its best to develop the West Bank, things were much, much better. I could get out to Ben Gurion airport in Tel Aviv in about 25 minutes, instead of the usual 2 ½ hours now, under intensive questioning by Israeli security, which is an experience that if you have not had it, you should have it at least once to see what it's like.

Things have broken down steadily ever since in this process. And I think that the problem is that the two sides are not reconciled to the idea of each other. There's only one piece of territory there, and deep in their hearts, both groups want it altogether for themselves. And so on one side, you get a kind of slippery tactical maneuvering on the side of the Palestinians, which often takes place, hoping for better days and greater opportunities; on the other hand, you get a position on the side of the Israelis, especially in the present, in this existing government, which seems to be making clear, that what they really want, and have always really wanted, since the time of Begin's signing at the White House, is really an autonomous area for the Palestinians within the Israeli state.

You can really see that, because – and they're quite willing for us to call it a state if we like, and to have the Palestinians call it a state—so long as they understand that this is a completely demilitarized state, without a police force that has any significant amount of armaments; which does not control its own borders, and which has no real control over its economy. If those conditions are okay, well, then you can call it a state. If the Palestinians are willing to sign on that basis, they could probably have a state next week.

Now – they're not willing to sign on those terms. In fact, deep in their hearts, they believe that someday they're going to have a *real* country. So, I think that probably this situation is not coming to a real solution in the near future. But we can always hope for the best – what choice do we have?

Another significant problem in regard to this is that the present Israeli government, and indeed a lot of Israelis, is so focused on Iranian nuclear program right now, that they're not terribly interested in the Palestinian issue. In fact, they have tried to negotiate with the U.S. government a couple of times so far, over what it is they might get in return for signing some kind of piece of paper or another with the Palestinians, and a lot of it has to do with what our intentions are with regard to Iran. This is a big problem for the United States. The President does not really wish to see us go to war over Iran again. There've been enough wars for the last ten years – wars we really can't afford—and he certainly doesn't want to see any more wars of that kind in the near future.

But the situation is quite plain, and I continue to have a lot of people insist on talking to me about these things—that many, many Israelis, and a good many of them in the government, are quite convinced that the Iranian government is made up entirely of a collection of madmen, who would, if given any sort of nuclear capability, would almost inevitably attack Israel with that. And from an Israeli point of view, this is a daunting prospect if you believe that. Because the Israelis only have only two counter-value targets that are of any real value. Now, I came from the part of the intelligence community that dealt with guys who carry rusty bolt action rifles that rode around on funny horses, but I still know a little something about this. And the fact of the matter is that if you can put one nuclear weapon on Tel Aviv and another one on Haifa, you'd break the back of Israel. There really would be no state. So, it's understandable that the Israelis would be extremely sensitive about such a thing. But at the same time, you hear this fear expressed in terms of the kind of thing that Dick Cheney used to say about terrorism: that if there was even a 1% chance, then that was intolerable. And on that basis, you begin to wonder what's really going to happen with regard to Iran.

Now, tomorrow we have an election. Has anybody noticed that (laughter). I'm looking forward to voting in the hope that they all just shut up! (laughter) It seems very likely that the Republican Party is going to hold at least one House of Congress, and according to the latest polls, maybe even both Houses. The Republican Party has made itself very clear that it has every intention of backing the more extreme types of postures towards Iran. And if you have President Obama having to deal with a Congress that is leaning heavily in that direction, and he has many, many other problems—and we can go down a list of those problems—the Republicans are going to be pushing steadily for him to take a very hard line toward Iran. I feel sure that that's the case. I don't have any doubt about that at all. And, as I've discussed with a number of my friends in Israel and other places, the chance that the Israelis are going to wait forever for the United States to be able to assure them—in a way that they would accept—that Iran is not really a danger to them, seems pretty remote. And the prospect becomes stronger that sometime in the next year or so that they will lose patience with us, and run some sort of strike package themselves, against what they consider to be the most key Iranian nuclear facilities, in Natanz or someplace like that.

There are a lot of very big problems for the United States in that. First or all, if you think that this will be anything like the strike against the Iraqi nuclear plant at Osirak many years ago, it would be NOTHING like that, in fact. The Iranian nuclear program is much, much bigger. Unlike the one building they had at Osirak, this stuff is almost all underground, spread all over the place. Target knowledge of this is extremely imperfect, and the Israeli air force, however admirable it is in capability and quality, is really not big enough for the job. I mean, they could mount a sizeable strike against Natanz, overfly Iraq probably—they know perfectly well that we're not going to shoot them down. Instructions – this has already been discussed in command channels of the U.S. Armed Forces; everybody knows. The command in Iraq actually already asked, "what if the Israelis overfly us, what are we supposed to do?" Because remember: the U.S. is, by treaty, responsible for the protection of Iraqi air space. Well, the answer was, "You know we're not going to shoot them down." The Israelis also know we're not going to shoot them down either. So that means they're going to have to go all the way deep into Iran, come all the way back out against Iranian opposition, and they're steadily acquiring more and more anti-aircraft stuff from the Russians among other people. And to go that far, you're going to have to have a lot of tanker aircraft, and they really don't have enough tanker aircraft to do this well. What it amounts to is that they can do one large strike with conventional weapons against one or two Iranian – significant Iranian nuclear facilities.

And then what happens? And then the roof falls in, because what'll happen is that everybody in the Middle East—actually in the world—will probably say that the United States is complicit in this effort, and in fact, would we not be?

Once that happens, I have a very hard time believing the United States would abandon Israel to its fate, because this action would have opened the doors to a really disastrous possibility, because there already is an existing nuclear power with a developed delivery capability in the Islamic world. There already is one, and it's called Pakistan. And the Pakistanis have a large number of nuclear weapons, they've done a lot of work on their delivery means, mostly air breathing fighters; they've got a significant number of tankers, and anybody who thinks that the Pakistani Air Force and Armed Forces would not react to an attack on Iran because they're Shia, and the Pakistanis are Sunni, just doesn't know anything about what this is all really about.

Because under attack from an outside infidel, in this case a Zionist power, it doesn't seem very likely to me that the Pakistanis would do anything but side with the Iranians. And all you need is a few dozen fanatics in the Pakistani Air Force to do something like decide to deliver weapons on the

Eastern coast of the Mediterranean, so who knows in what direction such a developing combat situation could go? Right? In any event, we certainly would have to be the people cleaning this mess up.

Now, this raises the issue of our forces in Afghanistan. I presume that by next year, next summer, our forces in Iraq would be down to a very few. But we'll still be in danger and we'll still have a lot of forces in Afghanistan. Now we had a demonstration recently, in fact, that if the Pakistanis are displeased with us, the Pakistan army, the security services, and various groups of fanatics can lean all over our supply lines. They start down on the Indian Ocean, in the port of Karachi and other ports, and then are trucked up to the interior, to the Khyber Pass -- sounds romantic doesn't it, the Khyber Pass-- or across Baluchistan to Quetta and then into Afghanistan. This makes our force extremely vulnerable.

The old saw in the military business is that amateurs talk about strategy and tactics, and professionals talk about logistics. I'm a professional, and I will always talk about logistics. I spent a lot of years in the Army as a Special Forces officer before I wandered off into the world of intelligence – actually, I got too old to run up and down hills is what really happened (laughter). So, I'm very aware of how vulnerable a conventional force is to an interruption of its supply lines. Especially when they're that long and extended, as in Afghanistan. I mean, Afghanistan has no seacoast, right? All these supply lines either run out through Pakistan, through all this potentially hostile territory or they run up through the former Soviet Union, through another mass of Muslims there north of the border in Turkmenistan, Uzbekistan, where it connects with the Russian railway system. So, you could supply the force in Afghanistan by air, at a very minimal starvation level, but anybody who knows military history, knows that an effort to supply a large ground force using air transportation has never worked very well over a long period of time. So, the Pakistanis, in my opinion, have the capabilities to make us extremely uncomfortable in Afghanistan, and they probably would do so in this kind of situation.

You have to wonder. David Petraeus is an extremely intelligent man; I think we've all observed him enough to believe that to be true. He's politically astute, he's jammed into a corner there because in the great review of Afghanistan that followed Obama coming into office, Gen Petraeus and a number of other people coming from various think tanks in Washington prevailed in the argument that instead of having a small footprint in Afghanistan that concentrated on counter-terrorism stuff against people who are really our enemies, that we should instead go in for counterinsurgency or COIN, for which Petraeus has become a main advocate. And this has become essentially armed nation building.

The problem with that is that there never really has been a nation in Afghanistan. This is a big place; it has a number of different nations in it, nations that speak mutually unintelligible languages, honest to God, and even inside the same ethnic groups, some of the dialects are mutually unintelligible. But they make lovely carpets, and the food is terrific. So these people have been through, for a long period of time, in which their country was created essentially as a way of drawing the lines around a blank spot in Central Asia, in the hope of isolating all the trouble makers there, really.

When the Russian Empire, and the British Empire were face to face in the 19th Century, that's essentially what they did. And both of those groups, the Russians and the British, regarded any effort to unify these people excessively as something of a threat in itself. And nobody ever succeeded in doing that. There was a period of about 30 or 40 years in the beginning of the 20th century, when there were kings in Afghanistan. They got a lot of foreign aid, actually; there are a lot of roads there that go all around that were built by the US Agency for International Development in the 1950s and 60s; there were huge agricultural projects from us – that area around near Marja, where the Marines have been fighting for six or seven months, was created as an agricultural area by US AID. An agronomist from the United States; the Russians were around in there doing the same thing of things. It's as though, they can't hold on to this kind of unity, because things all began to fall apart, it all fell to bits, and the Russians invaded the place, the Communists took over, and then we sponsored a war to run the Russians, the communists out of the place – I confess to having been a participant in that. Through this, things got worse and worse, and more and more disintegrated until they were back to where they were before there had ever been a King in Afghanistan. And so now, we face the prospect where all these different disparate groups, of tribes, and villages, ethnicities, political factions and so on, all at daggers drawn with each other, and President Karzai is in Kabul, essentially as Mayor of Kabul, that's what he essentially is, Mayor of Kabul. And we're operating around in the rest of the country.

There's a further complication here. That is, our narrative of what's going on in Afghanistan is different from that of all the regional participants. We see, at least we say we see, this as an extension of the war against the extremist Islamic zealots that attacked us on 9/11. Okay, that worked for the initial invasion of the place because we got rid of those people. The problem is, the

Indians, and the Pakistanis, and the Russians, they don't see it that way. The Pakistanis in particular are the important people, because like the British in India before them, and this is what used to be Northwest British India, right? In fact, the Pakistani attitude is that their principal adversary is India. As long as they have an ongoing confrontation with India, the Kashmir frontier to the Northeast has kept much of their forces occupied, until we dragged them away last year, and put them to fighting in Waziristan on the Western frontier.

Now for the Pakistani Army – if you're a Pakistani Army General Staff Officer, I've had several of them tell me this. If there is a foreign power in Afghanistan to the west, which potentially could unify ethnic elements within Pakistan, in a disruptive way to the Pakistani government, that is a deadly existential threat. So, for the Pakistani Army, and that's really Pakistan, the Pak army and the Joint Intelligence Service, if there is a foreign power that is seeking to dominate and mobilize the Afghans in any way, then that is a major, major threat. And for that reason, from the Pakistan point of view, what you have in Afghanistan now is a proxy war between them, the Pakistanis, and they're backing all these Pushtuns in the southeastern part of the country. They also have a lot of Pushtuns. And on the other side you have India, which has been the traditional supporter of what we used to call the Northern Alliance—you know all the Uzbeks and Tajiks, people like that up in the north. And President Karzai, I hope it's not a great secret to anyone here, has a very close relationship to the Indian government. So, from the point of view of Pakistan, what we have done is to sponsor a kind of coalition in Afghanistan, which is threatening to Pakistan's existence. This explains, I think, at least in part, a good deal of their lack of cooperation with us, and in fact, the other thing they worry about, the Pakistanis, is their sovereignty.

Now, Americans don't tend to think much anymore about our sovereignty; you know, we sort of had it ironed out of us, with a giant iron, so that we're all kind of pressed flat. Maybe not all of us (laughter). But these people over there, who are kind of successor states to colonial empires, for them, the issue of sovereignty is enormous. It has to do with their identity, personal pride, this kind of thing. And now what we are doing, in our attempts to create Afghanistan in the COIN process, is we're running all these drone bombing machines across the border into Pakistan, and bombing parts of Pakistan hither and yon, without coordinating this with the Pakistanis. And I see today in the Washington Post, this thing about Yemen. In Yemen, the CIA – sorry folks, whoever you are out there. I love the CIA, I have a lot of CIA friends – is pressing in fact to have these special operations forces that belong to the

Army and the Navy, turned over to them and be authorized to do more and more Predator attacks in Yemen!

And this is interesting; we're going in what I would think to be, an unproductive direction. Now we had this thing happen the other day in which these two bombs were sent out of Yemen on the UPS. I lived in Yemen once for about three years, by the way, a long time ago. Although, President Saleh, the guy who is president now, was president then too (laughter), and has been ever since. He's a very crafty little guy; in fact, it is now been said all over the place, that the reason why we found these bombs was because the Saudi Arabians and the United Arab Emirates elite lightning-fast intelligence services learned about this and warned us so that these planes could be searched. But, I've hung around all these places for a long time, and I'm here to tell you that the Saudi Arabians would have a hard time finding a crossword puzzle in the New York Times (laughter). And the UAE has a pretty good police force, because the British trained them and ran it for a long time but I don't think they could do this. My guess would be, and hey, I don't know anything, this is my opinion, but my guess would be that President Saleh, my old buddy in Yemen, has a hell of a good intelligence service. Because even the strange little place that Yemen is, Yemen was a prize of the Cold War. Everybody struggled over the Yemen; I was there struggling over Yemen. So, Saleh's police force, over the last 40 years, has been variously trained by the KGB, the East Germany Stasi, the CIA, the British MI-6 and the French SDECE, though I guess today it has some other name. They were trained by all these people: trained, mentored, equipped, all this stuff. So, they're pretty good, they're really pretty good. If he wants to use them against you, you're going to have big trouble, and lately he has -- Though Yemen is a funny place, they have four or five little wars going on all the time, everywhere. It's very entertaining, like an Evelyn Waugh novel, Scoop, or one of those things. And they usually have two or three tribal wars going on against the government just because that's what they do.

And right now, what they have is this thing with Al Qaeda in the Arabian Peninsula. And these guys are really dangerous to somebody like President Saleh of Yemen. Because they don't believe in anything, except salvation—as they define it. Anybody who's like that is really a dangerous person in fact. So, they don't believe in countries, they don't believe in nationalism, they don't believe in Presidents, they certainly don't believe in Kings. They believe in "God" as they define God, and the rules to be followed in following God. So, they don't like Saleh at all, and would like to get rid both of him, and the Yemeni state. So, he's been very intent on cooperating with the United States against these characters. There's probably only 200-300 of them, but even if there's only 5 of them, if you're in the wrong place, this is the end of the road. So, he's been cooperating a lot, and I would bet, any amount of my own money, that in fact, the Yemenis were the source of the information regarding this, and we have persuaded these other people to cover for Saleh in this matter. Because, most Yemeni people, being as difficult and problematic as they are by natural inclination; they live up in the mountain crags, and everybody's armed to the teeth—it's really something—they tend to favor the rebels. They are also quite religious, even though some are Sunni, and some are Shia, so they're not all that unsympathetic to Al Qaeda in the Arabia Peninsula. This is a little secret that we're not supposed to discuss. So President Saleh, even though he's not a democrat, small D, still has to rule by the consensus of the Yemeni people. Therefore, the idea that we would have to go out and cover for him by having the Saudis claim, "Hey, we told them." I find that to be absolutely plausible and I think that's what happened there.

Now, this all sounds extremely depressing, I know. But, you know, Judy Miller, who used to work for the New York Times, I run into her from time to time, and she says, "Oh Pat, here you are again, old gloomy Gus," and then walks off in disgust. Well, she's right. But the thing about the Middle East, and it's wonderful from my point of view, is that if you're kind of negative and don't expect too much, you're hardly ever wrong. (laughter).

But on the other hand, there are a lot of people in Washington who really do see this quite clearly. Do you all know what an NIE is? The National Intelligence Estimate is the "ground truth of the American government" hammered out on the anvil of the Lord, in the intelligence community. Then, once these things are approved, people stand up at meetings and wave them and point to them and say, "See here, it says here that Saleh is a fink, see...." And then everybody has to agree that Saleh is a fink. Luckily, I'm not in his clutches, here.

There are two of those that have been ongoing, have been for the last six to eight months. One is on Iraq, and the other is on Iran, and they can't get them published, because, having learned their lesson in October 2002, with the infamous Iraq NIE, and all the untruths that it contained, that was produced under *enormous* pressure. I don't care what the 9/11 Commission said – it was produced under enormous pressure. Analysts in the intelligence community are just refusing to sign up this time for a lot of baloney. I regard that as a highly encouraging sign of the times, as well as the fact that President

Obama is showing a very healthy sort of skepticism over the fact that the generals want more and more and more all the time, and don't want to admit that they're wrong about anything.

Now all these negative things are in the pictures, but there are also all these positive things as well. So, I will stop there. I've been told by a very, very wise person – my wife – to never send them away empty handed, so I'll stop there. That's why I mentioned that positive stuff at the end. (applause)

Q: Pat, I'd like to start the questions by having you start by talking a little bit more about the really variegated nature of the Islamic religion and the Muslims. As I understand it, there is no hierarchy; it is very, very difficult to find anything other than small groups of Muslims to really respect the same theology. How in the world do we strike a deal with all the various Muslim groups who believe that secular governments are illegitimate? Why do they want to deal with us, and how do we get them to the table?

L: The answer is, you don't. You find the ones that you want; that you want to work with and that will work with you. To be a bit more expansive about this: the Islamic world. There was this famous scholar; I hope he's famous still, at the University of Chicago about 40 years ago, named Marshall Hodgson, anybody heard of him? No? He wrote this three-volume book called *The Venture of Islam*, and if you want to read that, get all the way through it, understand it, you can come give this lecture next time. It would be no problem, whatever. It is great stuff.

Hodgson defined--and had some interesting terms that he used. One was Islam, which is the religion itself, like Catholicism. And then there is Islamdom – like Christendom—all the area that is significantly and deeply affected by the religion. The third one is "Islamicate civilization" in other words, that civilization and body of customs and things that are deeply imbued and affected to one extent or another by the Islamic religion.

Now obviously this varies a whole lot amongst groups of people, and areas, and states across the Islamic world. Some of these places were very deeply involved as parts of the Ottoman Empire, before the First World War, and almost all the countries we have now in this region were created in the aftermath of World War I and the dissolution of the Ottoman Empire. Basically, the Europeans drew a bunch of lines on the map—however they felt like doing it—and that's the source of a lot of problems in these places because they include all sorts of groups that don't really go together very well. So there is a large component of European civilization and law involved in some of these countries. Egypt would be a good example, Lebanon, Syria, are examples of countries that are heavily acculturated to the West. But don't get the idea that I am saying, "completely," but somewhat.

And then you have other parts of the Islamic world, like Saudi Arabia, where the regime is committed by alliance with the Wahabi sect of Sunni Islam to *excluding* Western influence, to the largest extent possible, Western law and all that kind of stuff. So, there is great variation. Sometimes you find that variation in the hearts of individuals as well. There are individual people, and I have lived amongst Muslims for a long, long time, and it is very hard to know what the mixture is in the heart of a man or a woman on any given occasion; it depends on the pressures acting upon them as to what comes to the fore.

In regard to the religion itself, I think what George mentioned is very important to talk about, that is the fact, as he said, that Islam is essentially a religion of laymen. There are parallels in some parts of Christianity, I know, people will think of it. But there is no clergy in Islam. The people who we call clergy amongst the Muslims are actually religious scholars; they're scholars in the religious sciences. Because for the greatest part, Islam is a religion of law; the orthodox parts of the faith conceive of God Almighty as the great divine creator, unimaginable in power and form and substance, and down here, you have us, pathetic rat-like creatures. And in between, you have to decide how it is you're going to do what that Being wants us to do; after all, what other purpose could you have in life except to do what He wants you to do.

So, they have all these religious sciences that have to do with the analysis of scripture—the Koran, and Hadith, the customs of the early community and the Prophet, have to do with case law by analogy, in some parts of Islam, by individual effort to understand it—that's mostly among the Shia—and amongst these groups of people, it is decided what Islam is. Since there is no hierarchy, even in Shia Islam, there is no hierarchy, no Bishops, no Pope, what you have essentially is *consensus* among groups of Muslims. But of course, if you're a Grand Ayatollah, you're convinced that it is only the Grand Ayatollahs that have the right to have an opinion. But Muslims in general believe that they all have a right to an opinion, because after all, there is no clergy.

So, groups of Muslims either following the teaching of some group of scholars, or amongst themselves come to an opinion about what Islam is. Since Islam has universalist claims, each of these groups believes that its belief concerning Islam and Islamic law, is the only real one, and the other people are not really Muslims to some extent or another. Sometimes the variations are not so big that there's a complete rupture. A lot of misunderstandings come from this. I've talked to a lot of Congressmen – I'm not going to name any names, he's running for Governor in Washington State—and one told me, "You're all wrong about this, you think these people are capable of violence and destruction and all this kind of stuff." And I said, "It's true, I do, among other things." He said, "Well, I've had Syrian, Lebanese and Palestinian ladies in Chanel dresses who smell like flowers come to my office and explain to me that Islam is a religion of love and peace. So, you're wrong." I said, "They're not lying. For them, that's what Islam is, for whatever beliefs they have about this. On the other hand, if you've got 2,000 guys with AK-47s and a big grudge, who believe that Osama Bin Laden and Ayman al-Zawahiri are correct in saying that it is the duty of every Muslim to wage violent Jihad on an unending basis against the infidel, and against corrupt Muslims, that's real Islam too for those guys. And if you run into those guys, don't think that you're going to be able to talk to them about how God is Love. Because they're just going to shoot you and discuss it afterwards, (Laughter), and ask "Who was this crazy person?"

You have to understand that there are all these different kinds of Islamic groups and they hate the idea that Islam is divided in this way. They will deny it endlessly because that is contrary to the principles of their belief. Because, after all, God Is One, right? God Is One, that's the most basic principle of Islam. Well, if God Is One, then how could God's community be all divided like this into a bunch of different opinions? Therefore, it must be true in fact that some of these people are right – us, obviously, and the other people are wrong. It has to be that way.

To give you an example about this, let's say that that this group of people that fill up this row over here decided that this third man from the end here is a great religious scholar, and he understands really what Islam is. The rest of you believe that this gentleman with the white beard over here is the real guy, and he understands the real truth. For you, these guys and all the rest of you folks are apostates, outside the community of Islam and subject to punishment as they should receive. But for *them,* you're in the same position, and if they get the chance, they're going to do you. And that's the basic nature of this fractionated situation that you see. So, people who go around trying to say that Muslims in general are a threat are just crazy, because in fact, Muslims are a thousand, or ten-thousand different things, depending on which consensus group they belong to in understanding what Islam is. I have just glossed over the whole Sufi thing here – we can do another two hours of that if you like.

Q: Thank you for your honesty and for being here. The question I have for you and that I have asked a previous speaker; given the knowledge that most people will say Israel's ability to affect bombing the Iranian nuclear plants is nearly impossible, etc., etc., would you agree to this statement that Israelis frankly don't care, and are willing to take action regardless of the effect on Israel, in order not to allow Iran to have the nuclear bomb?

L: I think you put your finger on something important there. I tried to touch on that. I think they are collectively, not universally but collectively working themselves into a kind of almost hysteria over this—a condition in which they feel they have no choice but to attack the Iranians or to be put back into the situation that European Jewry was in during the 1930s or something like that. So, in the end I think it is quite possible that they might do something that is quite irrational. If you talk to most U.S. strategic thinkers, most of them think, like Trita Parsi, the Iranian-American scholar, who I believe you all had in a debate; they all believe like he does that in the 30-some years since the Iranian revolution that these groups have changed and evolved so that they have stake in personal and selfish interest that they will not want to see destroyed in the inevitable response by the United States and Israel to an attack on the Israeli state with a nuclear weapon. They know very well that we will simply destroy Iran – they know that, and they don't want that. Even if they are clergymen, a lot of them – see, I said it! [clergy]. It's amazing; it's hard to get away from that. Even if they are very religious people like that, in fact they still know and believe that they have a duty to safeguard the people of God on earth, in this case, the Iranian Islamic Republic, all these Muslims. So, to do something like that, that would destroy, set the thing up for destruction, I don't think they would do that.

It's the general belief in U.S. circles that if this evolves to the point that the Iranians eventually have a nuclear weapons capability that some sort of MAD, mutually assured destruction thing will come into being. That is, if the Israelis don't trigger the whole thing, which they may well do, because of exactly the kind of thing that you are talking about. I don't know; my crystal ball is a little cloudy on that subject.

Q: You told us what you thought would happen were Israel to try to launch an attack against Iran, what do you think would happen if Iran were to launch a nuclear attack against Israel? Because it seems to me that Tehran would not be a place that you would want to be touring following that attack.

L: Yes, that's what I just said. I think that's absolutely right. First of all, deliverable Iranian capability is several years off, but it seems to me that although their largest effort is intended to create an electric power generation system, because Iran is not the richest oil state in the world, and they want to export most of their oil production to gain foreign exchange. The Shah's government had the same policy, actually. So, surely, they know, and there can't be a lot of doubt that if they attacked Israel with a nuclear weapon that in fact the resulting counter-attack from the United States would be absolutely devastating. There should be *no doubt* in anybody's mind about that, because if there is doubt, then the situation is really bad.

Q. Good morning, Colonel. Thank you for your insights. Another question on Iran. Would you comment on the strength of the domestic opposition to the Iranian regime, and would a hard-line U.S. posture toward, which as you said, may be coming, would that help or hinder the various opposition efforts?

L: It is a favorite thought in the circles surrounding the American Enterprise Institute in Washington that if enough pressure is put on the Iranian people in terms of economics and things like that, that eventually they will revolt against the Iranian government and the Revolutionary Guard, and everything will be great. I kind of doubt it myself. It takes an awful lot of courage to go up against formidable opponents like the Iranian Revolutionary Guard and overthrow them. It takes a lot of courage, and I just don't see that happening. Another thought that people have is, if you have that first strike and then another strike, the state crumbles and then we can just pick up the pieces. Well, maybe so, but you're going to need a hell of a big basket to do that. It's going to be a hell of a big job. It's not likely that they're going to rise up and overthrow the government. I have not seen the overthrow of governments *generally* in the Islamic world. They don't seem to go into that.

Q: This is a Navy question (laughter). The drones that you mention seem to be so successful and seem to be the ideal weapon against the enemy that you've described—the people up in the mountains and so on, the ones that are plotting and planning--not only for the surveillance, but for the pinpointing of the weapons. If, for some reason all the ground troops are withdrawn from these areas in the Middle East could we still operate those from the sea?

L: I don't think everyone will be withdrawn. Let's say, take Iraq and Afghanistan both as examples. What I would imagine is going to happen here is we're going to get down to a smallish presence in both countries eventually, and a lot of the people in that presence are going to be intelligence people, of various kinds. And they'll be there to know what's going on in the local government and keep generating target data on the ground to be meshed with stuff from overhead to be able to create target packages for these drones and things of that kind. The actual firing platforms for the missiles, or the aircraft, it doesn't really matter because if you've got a Cruise missile and you're going to launch it off a ship, the drone aircraft it is just as easy to fly them from Nevada or someplace where some guy in a bunker wearing a flight suit with his joystick flies these things in.

The problem with these things is not they are not effective; it's that the footprint of these things is always bigger than you'd like it to be. And in the case of Pakistan that the Pakistani military *deeply* resents is that we're operating over their airspace and killing their citizens without their acquiescence. They deeply resent that.

That's a big political problem that is different from a military problem, although military and political issues can never really be separated.

Q: Col. Lang, I'd like to make a couple of comments. There is an old Arabic, Muslim saying, translated roughly would say, "I can fight with my brother, and my brother and I will fight against my cousin, but my brother and I and my cousin will fight against the strangers," which explains a lot about the various sects and their animosity toward one another, and animosity in general.

L: That's a kind of codification of what I was just saying.

Q: Right.

Q: As for the Palestinians, this would take forever, but nothing was clearer than the so-called Oslo accord that called for a two-state solution. But, at that time, if you recall, Israel's population in the West Bank was less than 200,000 including Jerusalem, and today, it is well over half-a-million. That's between 1993 and today; that precludes ... and it's growing, because the Israeli government continues to allow the building of settlements. And you have an Israeli foreign Minister, Foreign Minister, now, who calls for the expulsion of *all ALL* Palestinians from both Israel proper and the West Bank. Just a comment on those, please.

L: Soon he'll be calling for their expulsion from New Jersey. No, you have a very valid point there, and I brought that up. And it doesn't really seem to me--well, I run a blog, that my wife has very cleverly called Sic Semper Tyrannis, you probably know that from somewhere, right?

Various people write to that. And I have a number of people who write there who are fervent defenders of Zionist positions, and some of them even make sense. One of these guys explained to me—and I think it's the truth— that in fact the present Israel government is not serious about seeking a two-state solution if the State is anything more than a State in name. And the basis for what they're really doing is they are going to create the situation they want in the West Bank, and then get this arrangement blessed by some kind of international accord if the Palestinians will only accept it.

I mean, in a cruel, hard kind of way, that would make a lot of sense economically from Israel's point of view, because you would have this large population there that could be used for labor, agriculture, light industry, construction… and that's what they always did until the Intifada business started up – people went back and forth across the border all the time, you know that. And a lot of them would like to go back to that position.

The problem with that is that there is *no way the Palestinians are going to accept that*! And so, I don't know what the solution is. A further fantasy aspect is the idea that some of them have that if you make a deal with Mahmoud Abbas, who has given up obviously about everything, the Palestinian people will decide that Hamas, down in Gaza, are a nuisance and a danger to their health and will abandon them. I would have to see that to understand that. Because several years ago, Hamas actually won an election – we chose to ignore it, but they did win an election, and people's hearts have not been warmed to the Israelis by things like Operation Cast Lead and things like that. So, I think there's an awful lot of fantasy going on in both sides here. By the way, my favorite Arabic saying is, the dog barks, but the caravan marches on.

Q: Sir, thank you for your presentation. Since you raised the possibility that Pakistan could retaliate against Israel, for a strike on Iran, I was wondering if you could characterize Pakistan command and control and safeguards over their nuclear weapons and then give your probability that they would conduct a sanctioned or unsanctioned retaliation against Israel.

L: I can't answer that, by which I mean I'm not a member of the Pakistani air force general staff. That requires an active decision on their part. But in terms of there being a decision to be able to organize and to generate enough sorties to be able to make such a strike with a chance of getting two aircraft through, if I were the Israelis, I would be a hell of a lot more worried about them than I would be about the Iranians any time in the near future because Pakistan is an extremely unstable country, and I think they could generate such a strike.

Q: Good morning, Colonel. Thank you for your time. It's been most enlightening. There are two areas in the volatile mixture in the Middle East that you haven't commented on.

L: Oh, there are many.

Q: Right, but two in particular; one being Lebanon, with the increased, at least from what we read in the paper, potential for Hezbollah taking another shot at Israel, and then the situation with the Mubarak regime in Egypt that is facing another election. And there was an interesting editorial in the Post a couple of days ago that basically was encouraging the present administration to take a harder line on what appears to be back stepping on the part of Mubarak.

L: That was the Washington Post lead editorial?

Q: Yes, that's right.

L: I read that, and I have a basic position about Islamists—not Muslims, right? Islamists, in that Islamist parties, wherever they are, in my opinion, regardless of whether or not they shave, or wear nice suits, or were educated in Paris, it doesn't make a difference to me. As far as I can see, they all basically have two main goals: one is to get elected and never have another election; and secondly to establish a Shariah law state. Because that's basically what they want to do. That's what they're all about, you know.

Even a place like Turkey. We have this supposedly mild-mannered Islamist-originated party in charge. Those guys have gone around and systematically purged the senior ranks of the Turkish Army of all these Gemalist secular officers and sent them into retirement so that the Army doesn't just rise up and throw them out, as the Army did once when I lived in Turkey. They do the same thing everywhere. They're bound and determined to create, as close as they can manage, a theocratic state along the lines of whatever brand of Islam they personally adhere to.

What was the other one? Lebanon. The problem is that we don't actually understand, in a lot of ways how Middle Easterners think about negotiations. When they talk about a two-track approach to negotiations, one can be rocketing you with 122-millimeter artillery rockets on your frontier settlements, while at the same time seeking to have peace talks with you; and they think that those two things are not really separable, that the rockets are just in fact a negotiating tool. So, this situation is a lot more complicated than you would think. I spent a great deal of time in Lebanon because I used to work for a company that was Lebanese owned, Sunni Lebanese owned, and I travelled all around. And the fact of the matter is that the Hezbollah is seen—and once against the narrative is seen from a different point of view by the Americans from the people over there—from our point of view, Hezbollah is on the State Department terrorist list because they shoot rockets into Israel, and went to war against Israel in 2006, and that kind of stuff. From the point of view of the Lebanese, Hezbollah is a kind of social movement for the downtrodden who are manfully standing up against the unwillingness of the Israeli neighbor to make peace. That's their kind of narrative of the situation. It's not really possible to reconcile those two solutions at the same time, as long as the Americans don't really understand who these people really are.

And this is an ongoing problem, you know, I have been doing this now, I kind of regret getting out of the Infantry, 45 years ago, and things then were much simpler then for me. Because ever since then I have been going in to see Generals and Admirals, and Chiefs of Station, or government Ministers, and things like this, and I will tell them about all the differences amongst all these people, political, economic, cultural, religious differences, and eventually you'll see these guys kind of glaze over, and after a while they'll say to you, "You mean you don't think that everybody is not basically the same?" And that kind of ends the conversation because they'll pat you on the head and say, "You're a nice boy, go back to your cave." That happened specifically, with the beginning of the first Gulf War, when Iraq invaded Kuwait, and I was lucky with my band of ruffians in the DIA to call that one—and it is pretty well documented that we did that—so we went around for the week preceding the invasion, telling everyone that the Iraqis were going to do that, and we were told over and over again all over Washington, "They won't do that, it doesn't make any sense; we wouldn't do anything like that..." (laughter).

This is an unending problem, unending. I had that happen to me at a meeting at VMI a couple of years ago. One of my classmates, sitting across the table from me said, "Do you really think people are not really the same everywhere?" I wanted to hide under the table.

Q: Col. Lang. Thank you for a terrific tour d'horizon of this part of the world. I just want to go back to one of the first gulps that I got from your fire hose, and take us back to the West Bank. I did have the notable displeasure of traveling through Ben Gurion airport as recently as last July...

L: a brother!

Q: Yeah, it was very interesting that one of the things that I observed in Ramallah and Nablus were posters and graffiti that were extremely favorable to the Turkish Prime Minister, the mildly Islamist Prime Minister in Turkey.

L: I'm not surprised.

Q: You opened the door on Turkey, so perhaps we can finish with you discussing the role of Turkey and its new regional muscle flexing in the area, particularly and notably in the aftermath of the May 31st food supply efforts for Gaza, and the role that Turkey is now playing in the equations that you're talking about. Thank you.

L: I think this Turkish government is trying to establish a completely new identity for Turkey, and identity that is much more Muslim, much more observant of the faith, and has a foreign policy that is much more dictated by Islam, and I think they're taking the thing in that direction. And there's a continual process, as I said, of their culling out secularist officers of the Turkish Armed Forces—who used to be all of the officers of the Turkish Armed Forces. I served with the Turkish Army once, among all these other things, and on the anniversary of Gemal Ataturk's death, I was living in Ismir on the West Coast and they would blow the big horn to announce he's died now, and these 100-foot-high banners would come down the sides of buildings with them standing there. And fishermen in the harbor would stop fishing and stand at attention while the horns blew. And this is for a guy who really enjoyed doing things like eating ham sandwiches in a public place during Ramadan, you know. He *really* was that way, you know; he was an enemy of Islam. Now they're going in the absolutely opposite direction. Your question brings to mind for me that my wife and I, and another guy from our Church group made a trip through the West Bank two years ago. We went, from Jerusalem we drove up to Jenin, which is almost at the top, and the farther you went up in there the more Hezbollah flags you saw, in a country which is altogether Sunni. The Hezbollah is very distinctive, and the further you got, the meaner and tougher the interaction got between the Palestinian workmen and the Israeli troops at roadblocks and things like this. So that whole area there is a seething mass of discontent in my opinion.

I decided that despite all the time that I spent in Israel and Palestine over the years, that I would never go back this time, because the relationship that is developing between the two groups—on the one hand a subtle but resigned hostility on the part of the Palestinians, and a kind of Colonial overlord mentality on the part of the Israelis, is a powder keg that is bound to come to no good end. I've seen them do things like, I was riding around in a car with my wife and this other guy, and some Israeli traffic cop stopped us on the outskirts of Jerusalem, and they got my driver out of the car, and because they'd seen him giving alms to some guy on the street, they went through this guy's papers and they found that his chauffeur's license was expired by a week. So, they arrested him and took him away, and left us sitting in this car on the street.

You never would have seen that a few years ago, I never saw anything like that a few years ago. There's an intensity of hostility here, and bitterness building up here, and we're not—it doesn't look to me like we're going to be able to solve this. It's just really unfortunate.

[music] [applause]

Moderator: Pat Lang is in real life a much more uplifting, fun guy than he gives the impression of, being here. Thank you, Pat Lang.

Is there a Profound Change Coming in the United States Foreign Policy in the Middle East?
(May 17, 2007)

Is there a profound change coming in United States foreign policy in the Middle East? Recent developments in Washington in the "manning" of key positions as well as shifts in attitudes towards long standing problems point to the possibility of massive change.

For many decades the US pursued a policy in the region which aimed to; protect Israel, insure the availability of oil and gas supplies and to exclude Soviet power from a significant role in the affairs of the regional states.

The fall of the Soviet Union removed that impetus from traditional American policy. The inconclusive outcome of the Gulf War of 1991 left the region in a state of political instability and tension. The rise of international Jihadism under the leadership of Al-Qa'ida added to the perceived threat posed by Muslim extremism. At the same time the Arab/Israeli impasse proved to be impervious to the many attempts made by the parties and other interested states to come to an outcome satisfactory to all concerned. The Madrid, and Oslo agreements created a nascent Palestinian governing authority that temporarily improved Palestinian life at a cost in corruption that was staggering. In the end that experiment in self-government came to nothing.

With all these disappointments in diplomatic and development efforts, the stage was set in 2000 for a basic change in US foreign policy with regard to the Middle East.

The Bush Administration brought that change. It came into office with well-developed ideas as to what the Middle East should "look like." The departments of the executive branch of the US Government became advocates of revolutionary social, economic and political change in the Middle Eastern region. The region had a long history of under-development, business and government corruption and inter-communal warfare and oppression. Basic freedoms were given "lip service" in many countries and an unending hostility to the West was thought to be a religious duty by extremist minorities.

The Bush Administration groped for solutions to these difficulties but an opportunity for decisive action only came with 9/11. The Al-Qa'ida attacks in the United States caused a military reaction that had as its goals both the destruction of hostile regimes and the "take-off" of thorough change in the societies that had nurtured those who had attacked the United States and had preserved the status quo in a troubled region for many years.

The United States led military coalitions into Afghanistan and Iraq in the attempt to enable Bush Administration policy. At the same time massive public relations programs were launched in the Islamic world for the purpose of influencing the thinking of the people. The United States sought to push the governments of the region towards democratic reform. The results, thus far, have been disappointing. Five years later, the wars in Iraq and Afghanistan are troubling in their lack of progress. Thousands of casualties, vast expenditures of money, a massive loss of influence and leverage have all occurred with no end in sight.

At the same time, the regional national and non-state "players" of the Middle East have not been "moved" by the exercise of both "hard" and "soft" power. The persistent problems of the last century have now been "joined" by new ones:

Iran continues to develop its nuclear capabilities in defiance of international sanctions and pressure. Iran continues to support international takfiri and other Muslim extremist terrorism. Iran continues to "meddle" in Iraqi affairs. Why does it do these things? The question is open to various answers but in some sense an Iranian search for a greater role in the world and specifically in its region of the world is a likely answer.

Syria continues to pursue policies which are contrary to American goals in Lebanon, Israel and Iraq. At the same time Syria continues to declare its desire to reach a "modus vivendi" with the United States.

The Sunni States of the region increasingly support Sunni insurgent groups in Iraq in spite of their clear interest in maintaining friendly relations with the United States.

Turkey is increasingly "uncomfortable" with its role as a NATO partner of the United States whose particular interests are "challenged" by Kurdish aspirations for national self-realization. The Kurds rely on US protection for their hope of autonomy.

Internal players in Iraq include; a variety of Shia Arab parties and militias with varying degrees of connection to Iran, a "galaxy" of Sunni Arab and secular Shia insurgent groups fight on for nationalist or Islamic causes of their own imagining, a government seemingly unable (as Senator McConnell recently said) to accomplish anything but the advancement of narrow interests.

In response to these difficulties, a new discourse has arisen within the executive branch of the United States Government and the Republican Party in Congress.

In the Department of Defense, Office of the Director of National Intelligence, CIA, State Department, and Central Command new voices are being heard among senior people who seek to influence policy away from the very hard line 'fight it out to the end" orthodoxy of the last six years and to move policy in the direction of a persistent program of negotiations with all the regional players, a program backed with force and determined to reach solutions designed to lower tensions enough to restore the peace in the region as a basis for long term evolutionary rather than revolutionary change.

Who are some of the "suspects" in the group more interested in negotiations than targeting?

Bob Gates, The Joint Chiefs of Staff, Michael Hayden, William Fallon, John Warner, Mitch McConnell, Arlen Specter. The list is much longer, but why name them? They will obviously deny it if asked. Does it include Douglas Lute? He is said to have opposed the most recent troop strength increases in Iraq. Time will tell.

What is it that this "rival" foreign policy group wants to accomplish? They want to bring President Bush to accept the idea that the best outcomes for the United States in the Middle East can be brought about by a mixed policy of fighting and bargaining.

There are some signs that this idea is taking hold. Most prominent among them is the new-found willingness of the United States to meet with the Iranian government over the issue of the fate of Iraq. In the first meeting in Egypt, there was a minimal contact but now there is to be a second meeting in Turkey. It appears that this is a process, a work in progress. At the same time, it is clear the hardline search for alternatives to the "slow" acceptance of regional governments towards Western style governance has been largely abandoned. For a time, democracy advocates in the Bush Administration expressed a willingness to accept the succession of Islamist governments in the Middle East if they would pledge support for democracy. That tendency in American policy seems to have ended.

It is now evident that forces in favor of yet another major change in US policy in the Middle East are active in Washington. The coming months will give us a clearer idea of their chance of success.

Bargaining is not Appeasement
(June 2, 2007)

There is an honorable and prudent "road" out of Iraq for the United States. We need to make a deal with Iran over the future of Iraq and US/Iranian relations. That deal should be followed by others with all the major internal and external players in this situation.

The recent meeting with Iran in Baghdad points to the "on ramp" leading to that road. The Iranian government offered at that meeting to help create a tri-partite group to deal with Iraqi security issues. The elected government of Iraq sponsored the meeting by having it held in Prime Minister Maliki's offices. We helped create that government. The Iranians favor that government. They should. It is dominated by their Shia co-religionists. That government will inevitably be friendly to Iran in the future. Iran is a major regional country, and it borders Iraq. It has three times the population of Iraq. Iran is always going to be very influential in Iraq. We need to accept that fact and make a deal with Iran that will cause that country to desist from the vast mischief that it has wrought there and elsewhere in the world.

A willingness to bargain, to use diplomacy as a serious instrument of our policy, is not a sign of weakness. Too often, this administration has acted as though it is weak to want to resolve issues without fighting. That should stop.

Administration spokesmen often say that in bargaining with the Iranians we would be in a position of weakness. That is not true. The Iranians are not stupid. Neither are they ignorant nor unworldly. The religiously zealous nature of the Iranian government does not prevent them from following the logic of deterrence. They can count the number of ships in our navy. They know the massive size of our nuclear and conventional potential.

Iran has an extensive agenda of policy and strategic issues with the United States. Iraq is but one of them. The Iranian state carries the burden of over a millennium of widespread Shia humiliation and subjugation at the hands of the much stronger and more numerous Sunni Muslims. Now, Iran is a great state on the regional scene. Iran seeks validation of the importance of its role in the world. Iran seeks an end to US impediments to its "place in the sun." Iran seeks to be acknowledged by the Sunni as equals. Iran seeks acceptance of what is says is an industrial nuclear program.

Since the Iranian Islamic Revolution, the Mullah state has behaved badly. It has sought to spread violent revolution across the Middle East. It has sponsored both Shia and Sunni terrorist groups. It has sought to de-stabilize governments, more or less friendly to the United States. It has maintained a seemingly deliberate ambiguity about its nuclear program. Much mischief can come from that stubborn ambiguity,

What can be done about this mixed record? How much of their bad behavior are the Iranians willing to give up to obtain US agreement to the more acceptable things in their own agenda or things that the United States might suggest?

How much would the Iranians be willing to agree to? We will not know unless the bargaining is attempted. How much can the Iranians be trusted? It is not a question of trust. They should be told "off-line" that if they break their word, there will be retaliation that from their point of view will be catastrophic. The United States must be prepared to do that to preserve the peace.

In the crucial matter of the Iranian nuclear and missile programs, any agreement with the Iranians must include submitting their program to fully transparent IAEA controls. The coming Iranian nuclear and missile threat is mainly about the danger to our ally, Israel. Tel Aviv and Haifa could be "held at risk" by a relatively small Iranian capability. If the Iranians want a deal with the US, they must be prepared to eliminate that threat.

Can a deal with Iran improve the situation in Iraq? It is often said that none of the external players in Iraq have that power. I doubt that this is true. Imagine an Iraq situation in which Iran actively seeks to assist in stabilizing the country. Imagine.

Lately we hear a lot about Sunni and secular Shia insurgents who now are willing to negotiate local "arrangements" with coalition commanders. LTG Odierno spoke of that this week in Washington. Are we to believe that this willingness to make a local peace is un-related to the possibility of a larger scale "arrangement" between the US and Iran?

Iran is not Nazi Germany. We are not living in the 1930s. Let us bargain with our adversaries.

Middle East Policy Council Capitol Hill Session: "Iraq, Iran, Israel, and the Eclipse of US Influence—What Role of America Now?

(January 19, 2007)

W. PATRICK LANG: Former Defense Intelligence Officer, Middle East.

I have been given the task today, which is always a fearful one of commenting on the effects on American power and policy overseas of its relationship with Israel. In the state of the take-no-prisoners kind of debate that goes on now in Washington and New York, I expect that the proper sort of savagery will occur during the question-and-answer period.

A famous American once said that the American Constitution was not a suicide pact, and that was quite true in the circumstance. I think you can paraphrase that today and say that we should hope that the U.S.-Israeli de facto alliance is not a suicide pact. In the last six years or so, in the period of the present administration here and the Sharon and Olmert governments in Israel, our attitudes have approached a kind of state in which we have plunged our hands into the boiling water everywhere and apparently contemplated plunging our hands into more pots of boiling water. And there is a general underlying attitude that is very difficult to deal with because it is one of a sort of endless belligerence. It is an attitude in which the idea seems to be that to negotiate with people is a sissified, weak sort of thing to do, unless you are negotiating with them to dictate the terms of surrender.

You sense this all the time, whether or not it is explicitly stated. One does not say this kind of thing openly in press conferences, but if you're asked, for example, "Why don't we talk to the Syrians," the answer is, "They know what we want." This is not exactly a call to the kind of back-and-forth process of negotiating an outcome with an adversary — or even somebody you just disagree with — that would lead to a process in which the answer would emerge from the process itself, the process of discussion.

There are places in the world where people do believe that negotiations are properly restricted to gracefully setting the terms of surrender. But that has not usually been our procedure in the United States, and it has not always been the procedure with the Israelis either. There have been other times when things were approached in a more open way, but this seems to be very much the case right now. There are real problems with this. I go to a good many foreign-policy seminars around this town and other places, and there's usually among the American participants a kind of unspoken assumption that whatever it is we really resolve to do, we can do. We are strong enough really to do anything. We possess the means, the population, the matériel, the money; and if we really set our minds to do something, we can achieve anything.

That isn't really true. It's a kind of illusion that proceeds from the fact that we are so very rich, strong, and numerous. It was just mentioned a moment ago that people who favor the Iranians might well take decisive action against us in Iraq if we struck Iran in a big way, maybe in any way. A lot of people assume that we could easily reopen the Strait of Hormuz and that our army is such in Iraq that we could defend ourselves. But it has now been endlessly, and I suppose boringly, said by many commentators, including myself, that our supply situation in Iraq is extremely precarious. Our forces are located in the central and northern parts of the country. And both internally, between our operating locations, and across the long, long supply route south to Kuwait, where our supply lines terminate, these lines of supply — revittled continuously by large fleets of trucks under minimal military escort — are extremely vulnerable to guerrilla action in all the villages and towns in southern Iraq, which are overwhelmingly Shia.

For people to assume that, because we are stronger and have more tanks and aircraft, that we are not vulnerable to people who are determined to take action against us, is not correct at all. I spent a long time in the army and Special Forces, where we knew a thing or two about guerrilla warfare. One man with one RPG launcher or two men with two AK-47s can sufficiently disrupt — put enough friction, as Clausewitz would have said, into the system and impede the process of resupply by X amount. If you multiply that by 1,000 men making 1,000 attacks, you end up spending all your time trying to keep your supply lines open; and, if you could do that, you'd be very lucky.

People ask, what about air power? The awful truth about this is that the U.S. Air Force knows very well that it now supplies 20 percent of the logistical needs of the U.S. forces in Iraq. It could conceivably do 35 percent — maybe — but not enough to keep the force supplied. We shouldn't be deluded into thinking that we can do just anything we like in the world. There are ways that people — little people in their great numbers who are determined to do something about you — can hurt you very, very badly.

That's one of the reasons you can't simply go around seeking to bully people all the time. You have to try to resolve your differences with them so that you don't get into situations such as the one I just sketched out.

Everybody here knows that over the last six years or so, for example, the Syrians have tried repeatedly to get the attention of the Bush administration to talk behind closed doors, in an attempt to resolve various issues that lie between us and them. They've gotten nowhere because we have relied upon this attitude of belligerence: take no prisoners, you know what we want you to do, and we're right. We're doing exactly the same thing with the Iranians. Whether or not Iran will ever be a great power, I have no way of knowing, but we and the Israelis largely tend to reinforce each other in this kind of attitude of eternal belligerence.

A good example is the war between Hizbollah and the Israelis in Lebanon last summer. Anybody who knows anything about what really goes on around here knows there was a good deal of prior discussion between the Israeli government and the United States, who agreed that if there were an opportunity to teach Hizbollah a lesson, it ought to be done. This ran into an inadvertent gesture on the part of Hizbollah and caused a tremendous explosion. The Israelis then assumed, based on their technology and superior skill in the military arts and the Westernized nature of their economy, et cetera, that they could crush Hizbollah and dictate the political result in Lebanon in a way that would be favorable to both the United States and to them. There is a good deal of effort right now to rewrite history about last summer's war, but anybody who really thinks that the Israelis didn't fail in their endeavor there just isn't paying attention or is easily persuadable by propaganda of one kind or another. They did fail. They failed terribly. And as a result of that failure, their reliance on brute force rather than real negotiations with various groups, including Hizbollahis, greatly strengthened the position of Hizbollah, and the Iranians standing behind them in Lebanese politics.

Are there any of us who don't know that it's true that their position was strengthened in this regard? I don't see any indication so far that the Israelis have given up their intention in the long run of smashing Hizbollah, so I would imagine that somewhere down the road, after they think it over and decide that they didn't lose, they're going to have another go at it. I don't believe for a minute that the United States is not at least tacitly encouraging that kind of thinking. It's typical of what we're doing everywhere. But there isn't any reason to think that the Israelis will do very much better the next time around.

What will be the further political catastrophe wrought upon all of us by something like that, as well as by the kind of Iranian adventure that might take place? On a hopeful note, I too believe in the concert of the Middle East.

I'm going to try anyway. I wrote an article some time ago in the National Interest Online entitled, "Toward a Concert of the Greater Middle East," in which I suggested it would be possible, using our force as a weight in diplomacy and using everything else we've got, to go around to the external actors and the internal actors in Iraq and throughout the region and in a series of negotiations, seriously try to resolve a lot of the perceived conflicts of interest among the various groups that see themselves as contestants. If you persisted at that in the way that people did in Europe after the Napoleonic Wars and tried hard and didn't give up, you might see compromise.

Compromise, imagine!

If you really did that, you might succeed in getting the temperature low enough in the region so that these things don't keep exploding into fighting. Everybody talks about the fact that there is a civil war in Islam between the progressives and the reactionaries. There are, of course, these conflicts, but the most dangerous of these is the ancient rivalry between the Sunni and the Shia, and we are beginning to encourage it by the actions of the American government. We should stop doing that. We should go around trying to help people resolve their differences enough so that they don't kill each other. That ought to be the goal of our policy instead of just saying to everybody that we know what you should do and let's see you do it.

Deterrence

(August 1, 2006)

In political-military affairs and in the Middle East in particular, your image is often at least as important as reality. Countries need to have armed forces that are feared. If their armed forces are not feared, then potential enemies will not hesitate to make aggressive moves against them.

The Israel Defense Force (IDF) has always had a fearsome reputation. They have won all their wars against Arab armies. The actual fighting in these wars has been brief, and the outcomes have seemed clear.

Like the US Armed Forces, the IDF has not done as well against Arab guerrillas. Our messy, prolonged struggle in Iraq is a lot like their messy, prolonged struggle against Arab guerrillas in Lebanon. That struggle lasted 18 years.

Now, the IDF is fighting Arab guerrillas again in Lebanon. In the last weeks, the IDF has followed a strategy of minimal ground combat and maximum air and artillery bombardment. This strategy appears to have accomplished little. A dug-in, hardened, fanatic and well-equipped army fighting on its own ground cannot be "rooted out" with fire-power alone.

This cannot be done "on the cheap." Only infantry and armored forces can do the job, one hilltop village at a time. And once the area has been cleared, more infantry and armored forces will have to occupy the ground to keep the enemy from re-occupying the area.

The IDF did not want to do that job. Israel is a small country. It has a small population made up of the descendants of immigrants from across the world. Israel does not believe that it can afford to lose its children fighting Arab zealots in the stony hills of south Lebanon. Because of this, Israel is very cautious in the way it approaches "pitched" battle. For this reason, Israel has tried to find a way to fight that does not involve pitched battles.

This gives the Shia Muslim Lebanese Hizbullah guerrillas a marked advantage. They are indifferent to losses and are evidently quite willing to "slug it out" with IDF infantry and armor.

The IDF is a conscripted army with most of its strength in its reserve forces. These are made up of family men, part time civilian soldiers who once served a few years in the full-time IDF forces. Forces like these are inherently under-trained. IDF reserve soldiers are supposed to be available for unit training one month a year. Skills like artillery gunnery are hard to maintain in that kind of system with that amount of available time. It is a fair question to ask how well these reserve units are going to perform against Hizbullah. Full time units like the Golani Brigade have had a difficult experience against this enemy.

Several weeks ago it seemed that countries like Saudi Arabia, Jordan and Egypt were going to refuse support to Hizbullah. That tendency has now reversed in the face of outrage from the populations of those countries. There was never doubt that Syria and Iran were inclined to support the Shia guerrillas.

Israel's performance in this war has not been impressive. The air and artillery fire has not had a measurable effect on Hizbullah rocket fire into Israel. The ground force "incursions" have seemed awkward and timid. It is another fair question to ask how much damage that poor performance has done to the deterrence which the fear of Israeli and American forces has exerted until now.

Israel has now announced that it is going to "campaign" to the Litani

River line and then wait to be "relieved" by an international intervention force. If there is not a cease fire in place, that force may never arrive, but what is almost certain to arrive is an ever- growing number of international Islamic "volunteers" come to fight with Hizbullah. This will not be pleasant.

Why should this matter to the United States?

We have 130,000 troops now at war in Shia dominated Iraq. As I wrote recently, the US supply line runs through Shia country to Kuwait. Hizbullah is a Shia movement.

Let us hope that IDF performance is all that it should be in the coming weeks.

"Defense" Can Win!

(August 28, 2006)

By fighting Israel to a standstill, the village guerrilla militias of the Hizbullah appear to have caused a revolution in military methods that will take some time to fully understand. In spite of all efforts to disguise the facts, the Hizbullah guerrillas fought the Israel Defense Force (IDF) to a "draw" in the recent month-long war in Lebanon.

The IDF is one of the most modern, heavily equipped ground and air forces in the world. It relies on mobile armored firepower and jet aircraft to dominate the battlefields of the Middle East and it has a long record of relatively easy success against all previous opponents. Over the decades of its existence, it has moved steadily away from tactics that involve ordering walking infantrymen to attack people who had previously constructed bunkers and other defensive positions.

The reason for that is simple. Israel, as we all know, is a small country with a small population. It cannot afford to lose soldiers. Their absence in large numbers from the gene pool and the economy is not something that Israel can endure for very long. All historical experience in combat indicates that the "side" that is standing up and moving when "contact" is made and the shooting starts is the side that will lose the most men in any particular engagement. It may also be that the moving, attacking side decisively wins the contest in any given battle, but in doing so it is certain to lose more people than the defensive side if all other things are equal. Israel traditionally has been imbued with the spirit of the "Blitzkrieg" (Lightning War), believing that short wars involving massive applications of lethal technology and lots of airpower will inevitably lead to lower Israeli casualties.

For this reason, armored fighting vehicles like the tank have seemed an ideal solution for the Israeli problem of casualty avoidance. The tank has been thought of by the Israelis, as a means of providing armor protected moving foxholes, each carrying in relative safety a small group of foot soldiers and a very large gun for dealing with threats rather than as an instrument for the continuation of high-speed mounted warfare and grand maneuver in the cavalry tradition in the way that the U.S. Army thinks of the tank. In fact, the Israeli attitude toward the tank is similar to that of the US Marine Corps, who rely on the tank as a mobile assault gun rather than as a successor to the horse in deep maneuver. As a result, the Merkava series of tanks are large, ponderous, and under-powered and slow moving.

There are certain theoretical principles in war that every good army follows.

One of them has to do with what are called "forms" of combat. "Form" here means the basic type of combat. There are two basic "forms of combat," the "Defense" and the "Offense." This is just like in football but in this case "Defense" generally means waiting for the other side to attack you. It was usually said by people like Napoleon and Clausewitz that "Defense is the stronger form" of the two, but that "Offense is the more decisive." What is meant by that is that a determined Offense can usually push its way through a Defense if it is strong enough and resolute enough although the Offense will lose a lot more people and equipment relative to the losses of the defenders. An attacker's war aims are usually located in the enemy's country and so it has come to be widely thought that to win a war it is necessary to fight your way through the enemy's forces on "Offense."

There is, however, a "school" of military thought that believes that the opposite is true. That theory holds that it is possible under favorable conditions to decisively and strategically defeat a strong opponent while defending well prepared ground with skilled troops.

At this point in a discussion of the Defensive as a decisive method of war, someone always brings up the subject of the Maginot Line. This was the massively hardened fortified belt that was constructed along the border between France and Germany in the inter-war period. The French built this maze of underground forts, pillboxes, tunnels, living quarters, and railways for much the same reason that influenced Israel in adopting the fighting methods that it uses. That reason was fear of casualties.

France bled "white" in World War I. The scale and demographic devastation of her losses was so severe that the psychological effects lingered on for generations. As a result, successive French governments in the inter-war period of the 20s and 30s sought desperately to find some way to defend against Germany without "throwing away" more millions of Frenchmen. To have an idea of the cumulative effects of such losses on a people, it is only necessary to know that the Napoleonic Wars diminished the average height of French men by about an inch, and the First World War by yet another inch. Why would that happen? Simple, the tallest and strongest men are the most desirable for military service.

In an attempt to prevent a similar butchery, the French built the famous Maginot Line. Germany's "easy" defeat of France in 1940 has caused many to think that this fortified belt was a useless and fanciful idea, but the truth is that the Germans never attacked the Maginot Line frontally, they simply went around it. Budgetary problems and inter-party bickering caused the French to build the Maginot Line only along their own border with Germany, leaving the Belgian border largely unfortified. Naturally, the Germans decided to invade France through Belgium.

In fact, the use of hardened, fortified positions in depth has often been a powerful tool in "whittling down" a stronger opponent. If we look to the history of our own Civil War, the First World War on the Western Front, and at Gallipoli, we can see that armies which "stood" on the defensive in individual battles were often able to "bleed" their enemies' physical strength and morale to the point that a "breakthrough" was simply beyond the strength of the attacker. It is hard to imagine what might have broken the stalemate of World War I if the tank had not been invented specifically for the purpose of getting through the defensive belts.

There is a natural "seesaw" process in the alternation of dominance by the "offensive" and the "defensive." After the tank restored mobility to warfare by "neutering" machine guns and barbed wire it was in the interest of the great and powerful nations of the world to have the tanks and aircraft continue to "rule" the battlefields. Only the rich could afford such "toys" in large numbers. For more than eighty years the tank was the true "emperor" of the battlefield. This was true even though experience continued to show that well dug in infantry equipped with cheap, light, anti-tank and antiaircraft weapons could halt an armored force, inflict horrendous losses on it, and through those losses deter further attacks.

That is what happened in Lebanon recently. A friend of mine was in

Israel during the war. He had dinner with an old IDF associate who said, when asked what was wrong with the campaign: "These are not Palestinians. They (Hizbullah) went to "school" on us for twenty years. They know how to make us stop. They kill the tanks and anyone outside the tanks." Hizbullah had truly 'gone to school" on the IDF. As a result, they amassed obsolescent anti-tank missiles and rockets, constructed a maze of underground shelters and pillboxes and in these shelters waited for the IDF to finish bombing and for the tanks to come. To the surprise of the IDF air force, their targeting of such facilities was poor and their ability to penetrate them with anything other than a direct hit was minimal.

When the tanks did come, they were channeled by selected terrain and obstacles into what the "tankers" call "kill boxes." Often these were situated on lower ground than the fighting positions from which the anti-tank weapons were fired. In other places, the anti-tank ambushes were laid in the streets of the towns which the Israelis sought to search. Ruined buildings actually make better fighting positions than whole ones. Attrition, in numbers and political and military spirit and resolve decided the issue after a month of bloodletting.

Israel essentially gave up on its attempt to emasculate Hizbullah. They gave up on this attempt even though Hizbullah continued to fire ever increasing numbers of rockets into Israeli towns. To add insult to injury, Hizbullah twice demonstrated during the war that its command-and-control system was intact and capable of turning its rocket fire on and off as though it had been a faucet. Hizbullah accomplished something of note. It survived a massive Israeli onslaught while fighting on the defensive the whole time. It is now re-building south Lebanon and its positions there with Iranian money. The next time the Israelis attack there they will find a newly re-designed fortified zone and effective anti-aircraft weapons.

Revisionist propaganda from Tel Aviv is already trying to soften the blow to Israel's strategic deterrent, but it will not "wash." The entire world saw what happened and has taken note. Syria has already declared that it no longer believes that negotiations are the only path to recovery of its territory from Israel. Across the "poor man's world," this lesson" is being studied for possible application.

Will the US armed forces learn from this little war? Certainly. Unfortunately, given the ponderous mechanisms of "lessons learned," doctrine formulation, approvals, and funding it will probably be ten years or so before any effect becomes visible in our armed forces.

Will it be possible to apply this methodology in other places and in other times? Certainly, but the "long pole in the tent" in using this set of techniques is the possession and organization of the ground **before** the assailant attacks you. This means that you must have undisputed control of the zone to be defended for quite a long time before the battle. Where would that be the case? Iran, or just about anywhere in "hostile" Sunni, or Shia Iraq, the eastern province of Saudi Arabia. The possibilities are abundant if you "own" the ground in advance and you have the determined fighters needed to fight the battle. How could it be that eastern Saudi Arabia might be vulnerable to this kind of war? Well, there are a lot of disaffected Shia in that province. There are many construction companies and Iran is nearby.

Taking all this into account, it just may be that "terrorism" is not going to be the predominant form of warfare in the 21st century after all.

Israel's Juvenile Ground Army
(April 30, 2018)

I worked with and conducted liaison with The Israel Defense Force (IDF) for many years. This activity occurred as part of my regular duties as a US Army officer and later as a civilian executive of the Defense Intelligence Agency (DIA). Since my retirement from US government service, I have had many business or religious occasions to visit Israel and to watch the IDF in action against various groups of Palestinians all over the West Bank. I have many friends who are retired or reserve members of the IDF. My observations concerning the IDF are based on that experience.

I write here of the ground force. The air force and navy are unknown to me from personal experience except that I know some of their officers from their service in joint (inter-service) assignments like general staff intelligence.

In my opinion, the IDF is an army built to very specifically suit Israel's circumstances, needs, and philosophy. It is in some ways, a singular force. It actually more closely resembles the Swiss military establishment than it does a large standing force backed by reserve units in the way that the US Army is built.

The IDF ground force is essentially a reserve or militia army that keeps most of its forces in inactive status while maintaining a handful of units on active duty as a training base and a force-in-being to meet short term contingencies.

In this essay I am writing of the "line" of the ground forces as represented by armor, infantry, paratroop and artillery units at brigade level and below, i.e., battalion and company.

The special operations forces are a small part of Israeli capabilities and are manned and maintained on a very different basis. In many ways they are more like a "SWAT" team than a military force.

To understand the IDF ground forces as an institution, there are certain things that must be understood to "see" clearly the actual capabilities of this army:

* Because of the heavy reliance on reserve units filled with older, part time soldiers, any mobilization of a large number of ground force units for considerable periods of time places a heavy burden on the Israeli national economy. Mobilized reservists are lost to their jobs. Israeli soldiers are among the strongest and most skilled members of their society. They are typically well employed in the civilian world. When they are gone in military service the economy suffers. This automatically limits the scale and duration of reserve mobilizations.

* Older reserve soldiers serve in units made up almost entirely of similar reservists. These units are hard to maintain at a high level of training and readiness. Only limited amounts of training time and money are available for this necessity. As a result, units are often unready for deployment into combat in an emergency. On a number of occasions this problem has caused IDF troops to be committed to combat in a less than "ready" status. In other words, troops have gone into combat with equipment not properly maintained and with insufficient unit training. It must be said that they have typically been lucky in their enemies and that if they had faced more serious enemies, they would have had a much different experience than the ones they had. In the Golan Heights, the Syrians gave them a very difficult time in 1973 and in the same war their victory against Egypt featured a renewal of offensive activity under the cover a cease fire which they had accepted.

* There are no career ground force sergeants except as technicians. Unless the system has changed very recently, the IDF ground forces typically do not have career NCOs in the LINE of the combat arms. This is a structural tradition that derives originally from the Russian tsar's army, which came to Palestine through Russian and Polish

Zionist immigrants. This tradition of organization passed through the Hagenah into the IDF. The IDF "line" conscripts are the yearly classes of recruits. More promising soldiers are selected from them and are given NCO level command responsibilities as infantry leaders, tank commanders, artillery gun captains, etc. The IDF does have career NCOs, and those that exist are typically found in jobs of a more technical nature, rather than junior combat command at the squad or platoon (section) level. As a result, junior officers (company grade) are required to perform duties that in more traditionally organized armies would be performed by sergeants. Leading a small combat or reconnaissance patrol would be an example. As a result, a non-reserve infantry or tank company in the field consists of people who are all about the same age (19-22) and commanded by a captain in his mid-20s. What is missing in this scene is the voice of grown-up counsel provided by sergeants in their 30s and 40s telling these young people what it is that would be wise to do based on real experience and mature judgment. In contrast a 22-year-old American platoon leader would have a mature platoon sergeant as his assistant and counselor.

*   As a result of this system of manning, the IDF's ground force is more unpredictable and volatile at the tactical (company) level than might be the case otherwise. The national government has a hard time knowing whether specific policies will be followed in the field. For example, the Israeli government's policy in the present action in the Gaza Strip has been to avoid fatal shootings whenever possible. Based on personal experience of the behavior of IDF conscripts toward Palestinian civilians, I would say that the Israeli government has little control over what individual groups of these young Israeli soldiers may do when given the chance to pick their own targets.

In the Christian Beit Sueur village outside Bethlehem, I have seen IDF troops shoot at Palestinian women hanging out laundry in their gardens. This was done with tank turret coaxial machine guns from within a dirt walled fort a couple of hundred yards away, and evidently just for the fun of it. In Bethlehem itself a lieutenant told me that he would have had his men shoot me in the street during a demonstration that I happened to get caught in, but that he had not because he thought I might not be a Palestinian, and that if I were not, the incident would have caused him some trouble. I have seen a lot of things like that.

One might say that in war, bad things happen, but is the Gaza massacre actually war by any standard? Such behavior is indicative of an army that is not well disciplined and not a completely reliably instrument of state policy. In my travels in the West Bank, it has been noticeable that the behavior towards Palestinian civilians of IDF troops at roadblocks is reminiscent of that of any group of post-adolescents given guns and allowed to bully the helpless, in order to look tough for each other. I think the IDF would be well advised to grow some real sergeants.

All in all, I think the IDF ground forces can best be described as a specialized tool that reflects 20th century Zionist socialist and nationalist ideals, and which have military traditions that are in no way reflective of those of the United States. They can also be justly said to have been fortunate in their enemies. The Jordanians gave them a run for their money in 1948-49. Hezbollah delivered a hint of the inherent limits in such a socio-military system in 2006 and now we are seeing whatever it is that we will see at Gaza.

Death of a Legend: A Loss of Deterrence
(August 1, 2006)

Deterrence is like a bank account. You build up a bank account by making deposits of money and then draw down the account by writing checks. In establishing deterrence, one makes "deposits" through actions or impressions and then over a period of time, the "account" is "drawn down" by using the fearful perceptions of adversaries as if they were money. Often the "money" in the "account" is just a legend.

The "legend" of the Israel Defense Force (IDF) ground army nearly died in the last couple of weeks. It remains to be seen if it can be revived in the coming weeks.

In the Middle East, perception is often as important as reality, and the perception of the IDF as a nearly invincible force has been a dominant factor of political life in that region for many decades.

The military value of armies to the states which maintain them is often a matter of a belief lodged in the hearts of enemies that an army cannot be beaten. The Muslim belief in the invincibility of the IDF has been absolute and that belief suffered massive damage in the last days.

The IDF has always had a great reputation, a reputation which it has not, itself, sought or promoted and which has been "grounded" in a number of wars against Arab armies, in Hollywood productions, and in popular novels.

The IDF was born of the "marriage" of the Haganah, the Palmach, and the British Jewish Brigade in the Israeli War of Independence. In that war, these three forces fought well but, not as well as legend indicates. Most of the Arab national armies simply fought worse and made more mistakes. The combat actions of the Lebanese, Syrians and Egyptians were a travesty. The Iraqis could not seem to make up their minds about anything for years on end. Only Jordan with its tiny Bedouin Arab Legion commanded by British WW2 veterans gave the new state a serious adversary. At Jerusalem and most particularly at the Latrun Police Fort on the road from Tel Aviv to Jerusalem, small Arab Legion forces fought well and held their ground. At Latrun, the Israeli forces lost more than a thousand men in attacks that lasted for months and never captured the fort. In that fight the odds were heavily in favor of the Israelis in both numbers of men and equipment.

What sort of army is the IDF? Most Americans will be surprised to learn that it is an army completely unlike their own in structure and tradition. The IDF is built on a model of military organization derived from the experience of the Russian Tsar's army that early Zionist settlers brought to Palestine in the late 19th and early 20th Centuries. Like the Imperial Russian Army, the IDF ground army is almost entirely recruited by conscription. It has no career sergeants in the ground combat forces except for technicians. There are no professional soldier leaders in the IDF below the middle officer grades. There are no tough, experienced old sergeants in the IDF. Instead, the draftee stream is screened for talent, and some are picked to become sergeants-major, corporals, etc. This pool of new sergeants is further screened, and a few are sent to officer training schools for a few months. The net result of this process is that the conscript "class" for one year provides the leadership for the following year's conscript class, and all these draftees are led by lieutenants who are only a year or so older than they. With the exception of a small number of specialists, none of the junior officers have any education beyond the Israeli version of high school. Some of the more promising lieutenants and captains are invited to stay in the army and are eventually sent to university by the IDF. Officers do not normally serve past age 50. After conscripted service soldiers finish their active duty, they go into the reserves where they receive periodic training. Most (70%) of the IDF ground force is made up of older men in reserve units who once did a couple of years of service.

What this means is that the level of experience and training in this force is questionable. One must ask just how good their proficiency in difficult skills like artillery and tank gunnery really is.

In addition, years of employment in occupation duty in the two intifadas cannot have made a great contribution to unit combat skills.

IDF ground operations in the Lebanon border over the last two weeks have been mediocre in the quality of their effort. The famous IDF sensitivity to friendly casualties has been on full display. Their enemy in this fighting has no such sensitivity.

Hizbullah still holds the ground that the IDF withdrew from after fighting the guerillas. The guerrillas are still firing rockets into Israel out of that ground.

The IDF's new plan to drive to the Litani River will either put deterrent credit in the bank "account" that protects Israel or make further "withdrawals." The IDF's soldiers understand that.

The Islamic world is watching.

Post-Iraq War Gaming in D.C.

(November 17, 2007)

In the last six months there has been a marked increase in the number of government and academic "war games" played in the policy, intelligence, and military communities in the Washington area. Many of these have the same theme; "What will be the shape of future history in the Middle East in the context of American partial or total withdrawal of its armed forces from the territory of Iraq?"

Universities, consultant "think-tanks," and government agencies themselves all have facilities for the conduct of what the Prussian General Staff first called the "Kriegsspiel." (The war game) Such "games" are played by two or more teams of highly qualified and experienced players who represent real world actors. The validity of the outcome of such "games" is dependent on the quality of the player teams. These must be able to anticipate the actions of those they embody in the action of the game. Such a game is played in "turns" and begins with a "control group" "feeding" the players the scenario of the game. The players are then asked to decide what the country or movement that they embody would do or seek to do in that situation. Once that is done, the player teams brief the control group about their conclusions and the control group decides how those briefings affect the reality depicted in the scenario. The next "turn" begins with the control group's announcement of the evolved scenario (affected both by the passage of "game time" and team game actions) and the teams are then left to consider how the people they represent would react to that. This is the cyclic pattern of game play. There can be any number of "turns" and such games can last for a long time if necessary. Such war games are often played in private settings and the resulting conclusions are also often distributed to the patrons of the game alone.

The results of this kind of simulation are not truly predictive of the future but the aggregated weight of the opinion of game players of the first rate is usually a good indication of how the future is likely to emerge. That indication provides opportunities for actions which may divert the path of events from that to which the game points.

With that *caveat* in mind it is useful to mention a number of prevalent common *player* opinions that have emerged from the spate of recent Iraq withdrawal centered games:

- The player teams for the countries of the Middle East all expect that the United States will withdraw the great bulk of its forces from Iraq over the next several years. There is some disagreement over the size and mission of US forces that will be left somewhere in the Middle East/Indian Ocean area but the players in recent games all believed that the American war in Iraq is ending. There is some thought that a residual force might stay in Iraq a few more years in a training and supply role.
- The player teams for countries of the Middle East are not particularly concerned with this coming American departure so long as it is not total and that American forces remain available "over the horizon" and in a continuing supply role. The economic benefits of a periodic presence and the stabilizing factor provided by alliance with the US make all the current governments want to see a continuing but smaller role for the United States in the region.
- The current "governments" are inclined to believe that the "freedom agenda" of the Bush Administration is a "dead issue." In other words, the "governments" believe that Iraq and Afghanistan have been "sobering experiences" for the United States and that there will not be more pressure from the American government for western style political and cultural changes in their countries.

- The depicted Middle Eastern countries do not wish to see Iran emerge as a nuclear armed power but if it does, they think that they can live with this new environment. The countries of the Middle East believe that the Iranian government is not controlled by the wilder people in the Iranian state. Rather, they think that Iran has matured greatly and that its' state interests now predominate in calculations of international relations and strategy. In other words, the Middle Eastern countries believe that a nuclear armed Iran would be subject to the deterrent calculus of MAD (mutual assured destruction) and that it would be deterred from a first use of nuclear weapons by the prospect of its own certain destruction by the United States and Israel.

- The Middle Eastern countries' player teams assume that Iraq will remain under Shia rule from Baghdad, that *de jure* Iraq will continue to have the same borders, but that the power of the central state will not be effective in Kurdistan or many of the Sunni Arab dominated parts of the country. The players believe that the central government will simply lack the military strength to make its will effective in those places. The Sunni Arab country players expect to play an increasing role in Iraq in defense and support of their co-religionists. It is expected that Al-Qa'ida in Iraq will cease to be a powerful force in Iraq and that this is the result of effective counter-insurgency methods used by the United States but most especially because of the Sunni and secular Arab revolt against Al-Qa'ida domination of their areas and lives.

- Iran is not expected by the expert players to attempt to annex or occupy any part of Iraq. Rather, it is expected to continue to play the four major Shia factions, parties, and militias in Iraq against each other to maximize its influence. It is thought that the Iranians are acutely aware that it is not in their interest to take the place of the United States in Iraq as an occupying power.

- Within these games the players for countries of the region consider Israeli fear of the possibility of future Iranian theater nuclear delivery capabilities and its lack of confidence in the American nuclear "umbrella" to be very dangerous. The "Middle Easterners" reason that Israel's stated unwillingness to rely on nuclear deterrence makes the possibility of a pre-emptive Israeli attack on Iran (possibly with nuclear weapons) a distinct possibility. The large number of Iranian nuclear system targets, their "hardness," their great distance, the limited Israeli aerial re-fueling capability, all incline player teams toward the possibility that Israel might use nuclear weapons in such an effort. Since such an attack would be profoundly de-stabilizing for the region. This Israeli option is deeply feared in these games

The conclusions of such war games are provided as opinion to the patrons of the gaming and because of the unusually high reputation of those invited to play in the games, it must be assumed that the opinions of the players carry considerable weight,

Lebanon Again on the Brink
(November 16, 2006)

Executive Summary/Analysis. Lebanon once again hesitates on the brink of massive political turmoil caused as always by the disunity and competition of the many ethno-religious factions and tribal groupings within the state of Lebanon. The country was "born" in 1943 as a compromise between mutually hostile interests and has never been able to overcome that burden. The distribution of political power existing in Lebanon from the time of independence has always given an exaggerated share of power to the minority Sunni Muslims and Christians. This was marginally acceptable until the Shia Muslims became by far the strongest and most numerous community in the country. Last Summer, the Shia Muslim Hizbullah Party and militia demonstrated to the world that it could stand up to one of the strongest military forces in the world in a "pitched battle" in which they persisted for a month and emerged from the fight with a "stalemate" as the result in their struggle with the Israelis. Understandably, the Shia people in Lebanon now believe that their sheer numbers and demonstrated military power enable them to demand a larger, perhaps decisive role in the Lebanese Government. Specifically, they insist that Hizbullah and Amal, the other Shia party, should hold more (and more important) portfolios in the Lebanese cabinet. The specific cause of the present crisis was the insistence of the United States and other interested parties that the Lebanese should create a special court to try the accused assassins of Rafiq Hariri. The circle of the implicated reaches the top in neighboring Syria, and the determination to press this issue insured that all those who incline toward Syria in Lebanon would resist the action. At the same time, Iran stands firmly behind its Shia allies in Lebanon, determined to demonstrate its own power.

Main Text. Lebanon remains a country that like many others in the Developing World continues to be more an idea than a political entity. The various peoples and sectarian groups that make up the actual population of the Lebanon persist in being an assemblage of fragments of the assortment of peoples who made up the supra-national population of the Ottoman Empire. That empire was ruled by a polyglot Islamic aristocracy, but it contained within its borders hundreds of varied Islamic, Christian, and Jewish communities who lived in uneasy quiet under the threat of Turkish retribution for disorder. The land now contained within the borders of the state of Lebanon was a microcosm of the larger empire. It was filled with tiny fiefdoms and city identities amounting almost to "city states." To this day Lebanese from Beirut look down on all others as not being cosmopolitan and irretrievably rural in their outlook. This was one of the things that was often said of the late Rafiq Hariri. "He is from Sidon" would be whispered from man to man around rickety wooden tables in the coffee shops, whispered through a bluish haze of "narghila" smoke.

The French acquired the League of Nations Mandate for Syria after World War I. An attempt to establish a Sherifian, Hashemite government had failed in the midst of the dissolution of the Ottoman Empire. Why the French wanted Syria is now difficult to say. Perhaps it was just a matter of imperial competitition. What is now Lebanon was then merely a geographical expression. The French "carved" modern Lebanon out of the "flank" of the region of Syria, more or less as a "reservation" for Christians in general but specifically for the Maronite Arabic speakers of Mount Lebanon. These folk had been allies of France since the Crusades, and the French, sometimes a remarkably sentimental people, had in mind to "protect" them from the Muslims. To that end, the state of Lebanon was "gerrymandered" into boundaries that might serve to maintain a Christian voting majority indefinitely so long as France remained on the scene to "referee."

World War II and the end of colonialism ruined that "scheme," and brought into being a Lebanese state apprehensively committed to Maronite Christian ascendance, an ascendance maintained with the acquiescence of the Sunni Muslim element in the population. Under the 1943 "National Pact," high office and parliamentary seats were distributed according to artificial ratios which, even then, did not represent reasonably the actual numbers of the various communities in the country but were thought necessary to maintain power and economic relationships. The Sunnis accepted Maronite supremacy on this basis for many decades because the acceptance insured their prosperity and security within the society. Time passed and both geopolitics and the "revenge of the cradle" intervened to make the refugee Palestinians and the Shia Muslims of South Lebanon larger and larger factors in the demography of the country. By the late 1950s and early 1960s it was clear that the overwhelmingly Muslim Palestinians and Shia Lebanese greatly outnumbered the Maronites and their Sunni allies. From that time on, political instability has plagued the country, an instability often expressed in armed violence and civil war. An anxious "truce" was settled on at Taif, Saudi Arabia for the purpose of ending the long, long civil war, but the intercommunal tensions remained, perhaps worsened because the underlying issues of representation and power sharing were unresolved. Syria's prolonged oppressive and heavy-handed military and police presence in Lebanon prevented a decision on these issues even as it served to temporarily stabilize the country. The Syrians were not doing the Lebanese a good turn in this. No. They did it because it served their own interests in the country.

Now the Syrians are more or less gone from Lebanon and the country is ruled by a coalition of the Christian establishments (mostly Maronite) and those Sunni Muslims who are determined to run the country themselves, rather than agree to a renewal of Syrian influence in the country. These Sunnis are led by Saad Hariri, the Saudi-raised son of the martyred Rafiq Hariri who is now remembered as a reformer and Lebanese nationalist. This grouping has the support of the American government because it understands the coalition to share the goals of President Bush's "Freedom Agenda."

Opposing them are the Shia political parties, Hizbullah and Amal. Between them they receive the loyalty of nearly all the 40% or more of Lebanese who are Shia Muslim. Allied with them is a faction of Maronite Christian who are led by General Michel Aoun, a former semi-dictator. These are devotees who would probably cling to the diminutive soldier in any eventuality, but who would almost certainly be more comfortable on the other side of the present political impasse if Aoun only had a bigger role in the country. The roles of Syria and Iran in the present Lebanese crisis continue to be relevant in that Syria allows re-supply and reinforcement of Hizbullah through its territory and Iran seeks the aggrandizement of its Hizbullah "protégé as a key feature of its own drive toward leadership in the Islamic World.

Likely Futures. It is hard to see how this dispute can be resolved peacefully since the basic interests of the groups that collectively make up Lebanon are seen as threatened by all concerned. At the same time, external players in Israel, Iran, Syria, France, Saudi Arabia, and the United States have all insisted on playing major and often mischievous parts in "stirring the pot" in the Levant. It is certain that they will continue to do so. The United States, in encouraging the Siniora government in Beirut to resist Shia pressures, has contributed to the crisis. Sources in Washington believe that street demonstrations in Beirut are the least that can be expected if Shia demands are not met. Commercial enterprises operating in Lebanon should exercise caution in the next weeks. Mob action against foreign companies or embassies of countries thought to be "meddling" in Lebanese affairs is possible.

Natural Allies?

(April 28, 2006)

I have long been a reader of the strategic thought of Professor Edward Luttwak. His *"Grand Strategy of the Roman Empire from the First Century AD to the Third,"* struck me at the time of its publication as a lively and creative expedition into the realm of the specialist historians. I have recommended the book to many, including my former students at West Point.

I am therefore surprised that I disagree with some of the arguments in his recent article on what might be wise American strategy vis a vis Iran and its nuclear program.

Early in the article, Luttwak makes the assertion that air or missile delivered "smart weapons" could inflict enough damage on the Iranian program so that in "a single night of bombing," and with minimal collateral damage the program could be "interrupted in lasting ways." This seems to reflect an unrealistic faith in the dependable accuracy of the weapons and the predictable accomplishment of missions undertaken with "smart weapons." It is true that the manufacturers of such weapons stoutly maintain at trade shows that their products are "wonder weapons" that have revolutionized warfare. Performance in recent wars does not support their claims. In fact, they have revolutionized little and the application of Chaos Theory to warfare remains appropriate. Murphy's Postulate holds that "whatever can go wrong, will go wrong." This is particularly true of warfare, a human endeavor involving countless variables and the interactions of people gripped by fear and uncertainty.

It is evident that the Iranian nuclear program could be set back for a considerable period by air attack, but it seems clear that the effort would involve a major campaign and at least a thousand strike sorties by aircraft and missiles. Some weapons will always miss their targets. Aircraft will fail to reach their targets. Re-strikes will be necessary, etc. Excessive cleverness in attempting to target any complex system inevitably leads to a reliance on too few resources to do the job well. Iraq should be a reminder of that phenomenon even if the system badly analyzed in that case was human rather than technical. The faith in the "perfectibility" of technology reflected in Luttwak's projection of an easy victory is reminiscent of recent and similar faith in the Department of Defense.

Professor Luttwak further asserts in this piece that Iran and the United States are "natural allies" because the Iranians need protection from Russia and the Americans need to keep Iran's Gulf coastline out of the reach of "troublemakers" who could threaten the "weak and corrupt desert dynasties" on the other side of the Gulf.

Luttwak writes that he believes it will not be much longer before the inherently progressive and pro-American Iranians shake off the bonds of the "mullocracy" which has been in power since the revolution, and put their collective foot on the path to "progress" in an ever upward and more modernizing pilgrimage toward a post-Islamic World and integration into Tom Friedman's "flatworld." Luttwak also seems to believe that, having been "oppressed' so long by theocracy, the Iranian "people" will reject traditional Islamic life and embrace behaviors and institutions alien to their ancestral ways, and all will be well.

That sounds remarkably like the vision of Iraqi society and the Iraqi "people" that was embraced by the neo-Jacobins and the Bush Administration before our intervention in that pain filled place. There, too, the expectation was that if the Iraqi "nation" were released from the bonds of tyranny and Oriental obscurantism, then all would be well, the civil servants would show up for work (unless they were Baathist), the country would embrace Western style government as an emblem of "globalization," and the awkward and backward tendency of a lot of Iraqis to think of themselves as members of ethno-religious communities would atrophy.

This concept of history and human nature has not worked well in Iraq and it will not work well in Iran. There is no more real evidence that Professor

Luttwak's Iran exists than there was that Paul Wolfowitz' Iraq existed. The evidence runs the other way. The "revolution" that Luttwak hopes for is invisible except through the lens of hopefulness. There are no revolutionary movements in Iran that can be discerned with the naked eye. The much-vaunted expectation of a youth revolution that was to be manifested in the last general election never materialized. Instead, a medieval fanatic, representative of the most extreme elements of the Pasdaran and Basiij, became president. He does not appear to be concerned about the stability of his position.

Visitors to cultures foreign to their own backgrounds often fall into the snare of believing that the people they talk to during their visits are representative of the masses and are unfailingly truthful about conditions and attitudes general in the country. There is nothing in present Iranian behavior that supports Professor Luttwak's contention that inside most Iranian breasts there are friends of America waiting to emerge. If there are Iranian voices opposed to the course of nuclear ambition being pursued by their country, where are they, in Los Angeles?

The Heat's Turned Up

(December 4, 2007)

Treacherous Alliance
The Secret Dealings of Israel, Iran, and the U.S.
By Trita Parsi
Yale Univ Press. 384p $28
ISBN 9780300120578

In large part, this book about U.S.-Iranian-Israeli international relations sets out to make a case for the progressive secularization of the post-revolutionary Iranian state. In *Treacherous Alliance* Trita Parsi, adjunct professor of international relations at Johns Hopkins University, argues cogently that the fires of Islamic zealotry as the main determinant in Iranian foreign policy were largely burned out in the holocaust of the six-year Iran-Iraq war. His command of the details of state relations in the period is impressive, but he does not quite convince me of the complete disappearance of Shia zealotry in Iranian external relations. Iran has continued to be the largest state sponsor of religiously inspired terrorist activity. That fact is hard to ignore.

Nevertheless, Parsi convinces that Iran has largely become a "rational actor" in the terminology of the international relations discipline. That is, she can be expected to make logical decisions based on considerations of national survival, power, and prosperity in the Middle Eastern region. If these considerations are congruent with the goals of Shia eschatological dreams, then so much the better from the point of view of the government in Teheran. In the same way, Iranian clandestine "meddling" in Iraq can be seen as serving state aspirations for regional dominance as well as help for Shia brethren.

The existence of an Iranian nuclear program (possibly a weapons program) makes the issue of whether or not Iran can be expected to act rationally in situations threatening national survival very important. To be blunt, the main question that must be asked is whether Iran can be deterred from first use of nuclear weapons out of fear of annihilation by the United States or Israel. If state interests prevail in Iran's calculus, the answer would be yes. If a search for martyrdom prevails, the answer would be no. Parsi believes that Iran will not commit national suicide and that therefore a Middle East stabilized through fear of Mutual Assured Destruction (MAD) is possible, indeed desirable if the Iranian program eventually produces deliverable weapons. The recently released "key judgments" of a US National Intelligence Estimate on Iran elevate doubt as to whether or not the Iranian program is about weapons at all, but neither Olmert nor Bush seem inclined to be governed by such doubt.

Neither the United States nor Israel accepts the idea as yet that Iran is a country like all other countries, subject to deterrent pressures.

Israel has made it clear that, with regard to nuclear weapons it does not accept deterrence as a principle in making decisions. The Israeli logic in this is quite simple. Strategic bombing targets (nuclear) come in two varieties: counter-force (these are bases, missiles, aircraft, etc.) and counter-value (these are population centers). Israel's own counter-force targets could conceivably be "hardened" and defended enough to ensure sufficient survival for a retaliatory strike. This "second strike" capability is the basis of any MAD deterrent solution.

On the other hand, Israel is largely an urban country and has a highly concentrated population. There are only a few major towns, and these contain most of the Jewish people of Israel. Tel Aviv, Haifa, Ashkelon, Beersheba--the list is short. A successful nuclear strike on these towns with just a few weapons would destroy Israel as a country. It might be possible that a retaliatory strike could be made, but what would be the point, revenge?

On the basis of this thinking Israel simply does not accept MAD as a basis for making decisions concerning whether or not to "wait and see" if countries like Iran prove to be rational actors. From the Israeli strategic point of view the risks involved in this gamble are simply too great. As a result, Israel is inclined toward pre-emptive attack against evolving nuclear threats. The Bush Administration speaks of the need to prevent the acquisition of the *knowledge* of making nuclear weapons by the Iranians. From that, it seems likely that Israeli strategic thinking in this matter has become American thinking as well.

Finally, Israel's reach, with regard to Iran's nuclear program and bomb delivery systems is not sufficient. There are a great many Iranian targets. They are scattered and "hardened." Distances to Iran's facilities are long. Israel has a limited number of tanker aircraft for re-fueling. Israel's strategic strike force is not large enough to deal decisively with these targets using conventional weapons. Civilians want to believe that the provision of "bunker buster" bombs by the United States would give Israel the needed capability. In fact, this would not be enough firepower to do the job. Would Israel decide that nuclear weapons must be used? Who knows?

Then there is the issue of routes to the targets. Iraq, Turkey, and Saudi Arabia would have to be over-flown, but none of these countries would give permission. What would the United States do? Surely, America would not shoot down Israeli aircraft in such a situation. In fact, the United States would be politically powerless to stop a first wave of attacks.

The United States would be blamed for the attacks across the world, prompting an asymmetrical Iranian response in Iraq, the Gulf and across the world. The truly frightening thing about this scenario is that the United States might have very little warning beforehand. There might be even less control over events as they developed.

Parsi's book provides a useful source of facts and background for contemplating this conundrum.

The Neocons are Selling Kool-Aid Again
(April 16, 2018)

In 2004 I published an article in the journal Middle East Policy that was entitled "Drinking the Kool-Aid." The article reviewed the process by which the neocon element in the Bush Administration seized control of the process of policy formation and drove the United States in the direction of invasion of Iraq and the destruction of the apparatus of the Iraqi state. They did this through manipulation of the collective mental image Americans had of Iraq and the supposed menace posed by Iraqi weapons of mass destruction. Not all the people who participated in this process were neocon in their allegiance but there were enough of them in the Bush Administration to dominate the process. Neoconism as it has evolved in American politics is a close approximation of the imperialist political faction that existed in the time of President William McKinley and the Spanish-American War. Barbara Tuchman described this faction well in "The Proud Tower."

Such people, then and now, fervently believe in the Manifest Destiny of the United States as mankind's best hope of a utopian future and concomitantly in the responsibility of the United States to lead mankind toward that future. Neocons believe that inside every Iraqi, Filipino or Syrian there is an American waiting to be freed from the bonds of tradition, local culture, and general backwardness. For people with this mindset the explanation for the continuance of old ways lies in the oppressive and exploitative nature of rulers who block the "progress" that is needed. The solution for the imperialists and neocons is simple. Local rulers must be removed as the principal obstacle to popular emulation of Western and especially American culture and political forms. In the run up to the invasion of Iraq I was often told by leading neocon figures that the Muslims and particularly the Iraqis had no culture worth keeping and that once we had created new facts, (a Karl Rove quote), these people would quickly abandon their old ways and beliefs as they sought to become something like Americans. This notion has one major flaw. It is not necessarily correct. Often the natives are willing to fight you long and hard to retain their own ways. In the aftermath of the Spanish-American War the US acquired the Philippine Islands and sought to make the islands American in all things. The result was a terrible war against Filipino nationalists who did not want to follow the example of the "shining city on a hill." No, the "poor fools" wanted to go their own way in their own way. The same thing happened in Iraq after 2003. The Iraqis rejected occupation and American "reform" of their country and a long and bloody war ensued.

The neocons believe so strongly that America must lead the world and mankind forward that they accept the idea that the achievement of human progress justifies any means needed to advance that goal. In the case of the Iraq invasion the American people were lectured endlessly about the bestialities of Saddam's government. The bestialities were impressive, but the constant media display of these horrors was not enough to persuade the American people to accept war. From the bestialities meme the neocons moved on to the WMD meme. The Iraqi government had a nuclear weapons program before the First Gulf War, but that program had been thoroughly destroyed in the inspection regime that followed Iraq's defeat and surrender. This was widely known in the US government because US intelligence agencies had cooperated fully with the international inspectors in Iraq and in fact had sent the inspectors to a long list of locations at which the inspectors destroyed the program. I was instrumental in that process.

After 9/11 the US government knew without any doubt that the Iraqi government did not have a nuclear weapons program, but that mattered not at all to the neocons. As Paul Wolfowitz infamously told the US Senate: "We chose to use the fear of nuclear weapons because we knew that would sell." Once that decision was made an endless parade of administration shills appeared on television hyping the supposed menace of Iraqi nuclear weapons. Vice President Cheney and Secretary of State Condoleezza Rice were merely the most elevated in position of the many vendors of the image of the "mushroom shaped cloud."

And now we have the case of Syria and its supposed chemical weapons and attacks. After the putative East Goutha chemical attack of 2013, an OPCW program removed all the chemical weapons to be found in Syria and stated its belief that there were no more in the country. In April of 2017 the US-Russian de-confliction process was used to reach agreement on a Syrian Air Force strike in the area of Khan Sheikoon in southern Idlib Province. This was a conventional weapons attack, and the USAF had an unarmed reconnaissance drone in the area to watch the strike go in against a storage area. The rebel run media in the area then claimed the government had attacked with the nerve gas Sarin, but no proof was ever offered except film clips broadcast on social media. Some of the film clips from the scene were ludicrous. Municipal public health people were filmed at the supposed scene standing around what was said to be a bomb crater from the "sarin attack." Two public health men were filmed sitting on the lip of the crater with their feet in the hole. If there had been sarin residue in the hole they would have quickly succumbed to the gas. No impartial inspection of the site was ever done, but the Khan Sheikoon "gas attack" has become through endless repetition a "given" in the lore of the "constant Syrian government gas attacks against their own civilians."

On the 4th of April it is claimed that the Syrian Government, then in the process of capturing the town of Douma, caused chlorine gas to be dropped on the town killing and wounding many. Chlorine is not much of a war gas. It is usually thought of as an industrial chemical, so evidently to make the story more potent it is now suggested that perhaps sarin was also used.

No proof that such an attack occurred has been made public. None! The Syrian and Russian governments state that they want the site inspected. On the 15th of April US Senator Angus King (I) of Maine told Jake Tapper on SOTU that as of that date the US Senate Select Committee on Intelligence had not been given any proof by the IC or Trump Administration that such an attack had occurred. "They have asserted that it did" he said.

The US, France and the UK struck Syria with over a hundred cruise missiles in retaliation for this supposed attack, but the Administration has not yet provided any proof that the Syrian attack took place.

I am told that the old neocon crew argued as hard as possible for a disabling massive air and missile campaign intended to destroy the Syrian government's ability to fight the mostly jihadi rebels. John Bolton, General (ret.) Jack Keane and many other neocons argued strongly for this campaign, as a way to reverse the outcome of the civil war. James Mattis managed to obtain President Trump's approval for a much more limited and largely symbolic strike, but Trump was clearly inclined to the neocon side of the argument. What will happen next time?

What did happen?
(April 22, 2018)

The US Government claims that 100% of the 100 plus cruise missiles launched by the coalition it heads reached their targets on Syrian government chemical warfare connected sites.

The Syrian and Russian governments state that 75% of these missiles did not reach their targets.

Who should we believe?

The extreme nature of the US claim should inspire caution. No system functions at 100% efficiency and effectiveness. None. A very senior civilian colleague in DIA once asked me why sophisticated weapons so often malfunction or are otherwise defeated. I told her that it was simply a fact of life that in actual warfare "whatever can go wrong, will go wrong." She resolutely stated that this should not be. "The manufacturers guarantee that they will work as advertised," she insisted. "They lie," I told her. "That's business." She was not happy with that answer, but it was the truth. There is no such thing as a perfectly functioning weapon system.

System malfunctions are only one of the many things that can and will go wrong in war.

Complex air defense systems like that in Syria should not be thought of as merely a collection of Surface to Air Missiles (SAM), air defense guns, radars and Electronic Counter Measures (ECM) jammers for use against the cruise missiles from ships or air launched missiles from aircraft.

These tools are not successfully used separately. In a well-designed system they are employed holistically as integrated parts of a whole linked together electronically with centralized air defense computers coordinating their effects. The radars detect their incoming targets, the jammers disrupt the navigation systems of the missiles and in many Russian systems then give the missiles a new and harmless target. The SAMS and Anti-Aircraft guns are tasked by the air defense computers and the hope on the defense side is that one does not run out of SAMS and ammunition before the attackers run out of missiles. In bygone years the Syrians were unable to integrate all these various systems to defeat their great enemy, Israel. That time has now passed, and the Russo-Syrian air defense has become one integrated whole functioning according to the standards and discipline brought by the Russians even though the best of the Russian equipment present in Syria has not yet been committed to the fight.

It has been noted that a lot of the SAM systems presently in the hands of the Syrians are old Soviet era materiel. This is largely irrelevant. Such weapons systems are subject to repeated product improvement projects that essentially make them into new and more modern instruments of war.

This takes place in the supply chain of every military equipment manufacturing country in the world. If they do not do that, their equipment will have a short service life and is not worth buying when others do better. Good examples of product improvements are the service cycle of warships. These are repeatedly programmed for a year or so in a shipyard being modernized. Another is the venerable US B-52 heavy bomber. Named for the year they first went into service (1952) they continue to "soldier on" having been repeatedly made into modern aircraft through re-fits. On that model of design the Russo-Syrian air defense force should not be thought of as backward at all.

Russia has dedicated a lot of its limited industrial resources to refining old Soviet systems and developing many new ones. These have a great export potential as we have seen in Iran, Turkey, and India so it is easy to justify the expenditure of so much in these projects,

The US has been committed to global war for seventeen years. This has been a special kind of war waged against Islamist guerrillas and terrorists worldwide. Such a war often demands equipment quite different from that used against states, especially a peer state. In that context relatively scarce funds have not been devoted to product improvement on things like TLAM (Tomahawk). Instead, the funds available have been devoted to UAVs (drones) and the incredible costs of large ground forces in the absence of conscription. The Obama Administration liked to use the armed forces but did not think of them with anything like the high priority it gave to its social programs. The resulting sequester of defense funding played a role in the decline of US equipment efficacy against that of the Russians. There will be a change in that funding.

So what happened?

I am told by several foreign sources with access to the information needed to make a valid judgment that the Russians are correct. These people are friendly to the United States as are their governments. Over two-thirds of the US coalition missiles failed to reach their targets. Why? All the reasons cited above must have played a role in this aerial defeat. Obsolescent weapons, a fully integrated air defense and skill brought to the fight.

There is an ongoing investigation to determine what is to be done to rectify the situation.

At the same time, it is clear that there was an understanding between the governments to insure that Russian red lines were not crossed. The evidence for the Douma gas attack is non-existent. The film evidence has now been thoroughly de-bunked as part of the information operations (propaganda) of the White Helmets scheme funded by the Saudis and largely conducted by the UK info warriors of 77 Regiment. It seems clear that US DoD was not privy to that IO project and for that Reason SECDEF Mattis was blind-sided by the deception. The struck targets (successful or not) have long been known to the US IC as facilities of the former Syrian Government chemical warfare programs. The Russians were told to stay out of those areas and so a reasonable compromise was made with a president easily fooled by social media and under heavy pressure by a population equally easy to deceive.

Nevertheless, most of the missiles failed and that failure must be dealt with.

PART VII

Strategic and Historical Studies

In this section, the author takes a broader look at some historical moments that
have shaped modern warfare and the evolution of the U.S. armed forces within
that process. In one of the essays, he shares a deeply personal insight into the
soldier's life.

"Dear Hearts Across the Seas"

(May 24, 2009)

"For 14 hours yesterday, I was at work-teaching Christ to lift his cross by the numbers, and how to adjust his crown; and not to imagine he thirsts until after the last halt. I attended his Supper to see that there were no complaints; and inspected his feet that they should be worthy of the nails. I see to it that he is dumb and stands mute before his accusers. With a piece of silver, I buy him every day, and with maps I make him familiar with the topography of Golgotha."

--Captain Wilfred Owen, The Manchesters
Killed in Action, 4 November, 1918

This famous quotation from the work of the soldier poet Wilfred Owen sums up both the awfulness and the beauty of a combat soldier's life. It is particularly meaningful to those who have been given the chance to train and lead men in war. I came to know Owen's work a few years back through the writing of Paul Fussell, whom I had the great privilege to meet recently. Professor Fussell was badly wounded in World War II and is still filled with the righteous outrage that fills most combat men. God Bless Him.

Many will recoil in horror from the idea that there can be beauty in the life led by combat soldiers, the immortal "grunts" and "Grognards" who live in historic memory. It is all too easy to see nothing but the pain and the misery of loss, wounds, and experience so horrible that it scars for life. Perhaps the worst is the memory of suffering necessarily inflicted on others whose motives are often no more base or lacking in what the Romans called "pietas" than our own.

Not political enough for you? Go talk to a soldier and see if he agrees with you. On the good side of the ledger there is the fact that there are no better friends than those with whom you have been deeply, and comprehensively afraid. "Go tell my mother," says Private Ryan in Spielberg's exquisite film. "Go tell her that I will stay here, with the only brothers I have left." This rings so true that it requires no explanation. Those ties bind unto death, until "the last jump" as I have heard World War II paratroopers express it.

The friendship and indeed love of comrades often long gone is, perhaps, the greatest "good" in war.

It is often said that war brings out the best and the worst in people. This is profoundly true. Men who, in civilian life, would not have crossed the street to help a stranger often fall in the effort to help near strangers. There are many good things to be remembered. All of them have to do with comrades. These days we are served by professionals and militia soldiers of the National Guard and reserve. These are men and women who bring to mind Lt. Colonel Arthur Fremantle's description of the infantry soldiers of Lee's army at Gettysburg. Fremantle was a Coldstream Guards officer who had come to America to observe.

He got a belly full of observing but said of "Les Misérables" that they were "simply beyond praise." Our people are like that now. A friend's son is now on his way back overseas for his fourth tour of duty in the Asian war against the Jihadis. Soon, his experience will not be unusual. Forty-five years ago, his father and I, looking down the barrel of another war, would never have believed that we would see this. We were short sighted, blinded by the myopia of youth. What is the old saw from Plato? "Only the dead have seen the end of war..." I sometimes receive letters from people who are filled with a great and high-minded attitude about war. "Well, that is why soldiers exist..." "Losses are worth their pain in a good cause..." "Our soldiers will prevail through their skill and the great weapons we buy them."

I would say to such people that the soldiers already know that. They do not need your boosterism to help them do their duty. They will do their duty to the last as so many of our soldiers have done. Just let them get on with it without suffering the indignity of your remarks.

Just after the war in Vietnam, Laos. and Cambodia, an Army chaplain said Mass one Memorial Day in the post chapel of the Presidio of Monterey. He was a member of the Society of Jesus as so many other Army chaplains have been. He had served in World War II, Korea, and Vietnam. He had served with a lot of infantry units. The infantry are the people who always do the serious, up-close, killing and dying. The Army reckons that over 90% of all combat deaths happen in the infantry. At his homily this priest looked out at his congregation which was overwhelmingly populated with combat men and their families. He said that he wanted the people of God to remember their brothers asleep in the Lord's embrace. He wanted them to remember how each man died alone, alone in fear, alone in misery, usually with no one to comfort him, often in the dark with his life running out through mutilations that left little doubt of the outcome. He asked them to pray for their brothers, for the brothers who had died for us all as Jesus died for us all. The congregation sang. "With the beauty of a lily, Christ died across the sea, with a glory in his bosom that transfigures you and me. As he died to make men holy, let us die to make men free. His truth is marching on."

Nothing has changed. The wounds inflicted by Improvised Explosive Devices are appalling. Go to Walter Reed or Bethesda and see for yourself. The troops are not complaining. They never complain, and so nobody has any right to be less committed to the eternal mission of the soldier than they are. This Memorial Day, remember that the cemeteries and physical therapy wards are full of men and women who gave their all for you, and who, in many cases ask nothing more than to be allowed to go back and do it again. Pray for them. Please.

"I have eaten your bread and salt. I have drunk your water and wine. The deaths ye died, I have watched beside. And the lives ye led were mine. Was there aught that I did not share."

Creighton Abrams' Army
(October 11, 2006)

By the end of the Vietnam War, the United States Army was largely destroyed as a fighting force, and the United States Marine Corps was not in much better shape. Neither of these previously undefeated military forces had lost a sizable battle in that decade long struggle, but a process of morale decline, leadership failures and home front political attrition had reduced discipline and effectiveness to such a low level that the major ground forces of the United States had to be rebuilt from the "ground up" when the war ended. The Marines were in somewhat better condition than the Army because they had been allowed to withdraw their major forces from Vietnam a year or so before the Army. The Army was a "shambles" and its reconstruction took decades and was a most difficult process. The man who designed that reconstruction was General Creighton Abrams.

We have all heard of the Abrams Tank. Since the First Gulf War it has dominated the battlefields of the "Greater" Middle East. Agile as a cat, fast, turbine powered, fitted with a murderous long-range gyro-stabilized gun, the Abrams Tank can hit targets miles away, in the dark, in a storm, without halting. It is the greatest tank ever designed or built. Unfortunately, few of us know much about the man for whom the vehicle is named.

He was Chief of Staff of the United States Army. That is, he was the *institutional head* of the Army in the period just after the Vietnam War. He is the man who re-built the Army, without the draft, from the "wreckage" created by that long hell. At the same time, he deliberately re-designed the structure of the three components of the Army to prevent the civilian government of the United States, any government, from any party from ever sending the Regular Army to fight alone as they had in Vietnam.

General Creighton Abrams graduated from West Point in 1936. He was the son of a working-class family from Massachusetts. He obtained admission to the military academy the hard way, that is, by being the smartest boy to apply for his congressman's nomination. After graduation, he began his commissioned Army service in the horse cavalry. I heard him say that he knew that kind of warfare had come to an end when the Panzers destroyed the Polish cavalry in a few days in 1939. He quickly joined the new Armored Force where he was one of the most brilliant frontline commanders of World War II. "Abe" was an unusual man. It was always very hard to find anyone who would say anything bad about him. A gruff, plain-spoken person, he naturally attracted loyalty.

I first met him while standing behind a rubber tree in the highlands of Vietnam. I was accompanying some US infantry on an operation for which I had provided the intelligence. The Americans had advanced into this grove of rubber trees and made "contact" about fifty yards inside. A firefight was underway, and I was carefully standing in the "fire shadow" provided by the smallish tree, listening. I was trying to judge progress in the fight while bullets "whizzed" by or "thunked" into trees. I heard a helicopter land somewhere behind me, and reckoned it was a "medevac." Unexpectedly, a hoarse voice behind me said, "What's up?" Turning, I discovered that Abrams was standing three feet away. The cigar, the wrinkled, square face, the four black stars on his cap, there was no doubt who it was. He had been flying around, listening to the radios while en route to somewhere and had decided that our little fight should be looked at. This was the commander of all US forces in Southeast Asia. He wore no armor, did not have a helmet, and was armed with the .32 caliber "pop-gun" automatic pistol that the Army used to give general officers. This was a toy, really, in that environment. He listened gravely, asked a couple of questions about what we were going to do next, nodded and said. "It looks like you fellahs have this under control." We shook hands and he walked back to his helicopter while bullets cut the grass around him. He never looked at that, just kept walking. He was always like that.

Years later, when he was Chief of Staff, and I was a student at the Armed Forces Staff College, he came to speak. He was already ill with the lung cancer that killed him. The audience revered him. They sat silently while he gathered his strength to speak. He had a hard time talking at first.

He told us that he had not understood how nearly the long war had destroyed the Army until he went back to the Pentagon to run the whole thing in 1973. There, he had discovered that of all the "line" troops in the Army only the paratroops were reliable enough to be used in any real crisis. He had the "Wounded Knee" rebellion in mind. It had recently occurred. He said that one of his office staff had recently told him that if he wanted to know how bad things were, he should go to the corridor where the official portraits of all the past military heads of the Army were hung. When he looked at them, he saw that these oil paintings had been covered with glass and all of them were coated with dried spittle. Soldiers were walking by and spitting on the pictures as they passed. He looked up at us and said that this was clearly the result of government mistakes and rotten leadership in the Army. He said that he was going to try to do enough good so that American soldiers would not spit on his picture when he had gone.

He told us that the Johnson Administration had made a number of very bad decisions with regard to the war, but that the worst from the Army's point of view as an institution was President Johnson's politically driven decision NOT to call to active service the National Guard and Army Reserve. That this decision was made in the context of the war's ever-increasing unpopularity made it worse.

This decision was clearly prompted by Lyndon Johnson's unwillingness to accept the disfavor of home town America. From Johnson's point of view it was easier to rely on the cadres of the Regular Army (now usually called the "active force"), increase draft calls (even if that required lowering admission standards), and to create new units using these sources of people (The Americal Division [My Lai] was one such unit formed) while hoping for an early end to the war that would make available the monies needed for Johnson's social programs.

One of the results of these decisions was to make the National Guard and units of the Army Reserve into havens for people who were seeking to avoid combat duty. At the same time, the Army had made similarly misguided decisions. First, a pronouncement was made that officers lucky enough to obtain command in Vietnam were limited to six months in that position before they were sent to staff jobs. This decision was intended to give as many officers as possible a chance to command but the concept deprived troops engaged in combat of seasoned leaders whom they know well. Second, the Army decided that a fear of having units who had arrived as one group in Vietnam leave all at the same time required that units be broken up as they arrived in Vietnam and repopulated with people from other units. This destroyed unit cohesion and the loyalty of man to man so necessary in combat. As a result, units in Vietnam remained there as organizations for the duration of the fighting while a continuous stream of individual replacements arrived in units where they knew nobody and where they served under leaders who would be gone in a few months.

The net result of these political and military mistakes was an Army that by the end of Vietnam was broken in spirit and internal cohesion. This effect "spilled over" into Europe and America itself where troops were undisciplined and on the edge of mutiny for several years.

The US Government's decision to abolish the draft set the stage for widespread change in the Amy. Volunteer soldiers are a much easier leadership task than are citizens conscripted against their will. This change set the stage for the "Abrams Reforms" that made possible the Army now fighting in Iraq, Afghanistan and across the world.

On that day in 1973, General Abrams told us what he intended to do:

- He would stabilize command tours of duty for officers, making them much longer and with commanders selected by Army-wide boards seeking the best people and not the most favored.
- Create a "Ranger Regiment" of selected elite light infantry troops to serve as a model for what enlisted soldiers should be in his new model Army.
- Re-emphasize unit identity for soldiers so that the Army would accept the idea that soldiers are social creatures and would not again send people to combat as individuals rather than units.
- Raise recruiting standards; educationally, physically, and with regard to proven character.
- **Most importantly, Abrams said that he was going to spread the skills and capabilities needed to fight big wars across; the "active force," National Guard, and Army Reserve in such a way**

that it would be impossible to send the "active force" overseas alone again as was done in Vietnam. In other words, much of the sustaining logistics base needed for large scale expeditions would be located in the National Guard and Army Reserve where the political cost of mobilization would be high.

The message was clear. There would be no more big wars fought by Regulars leading conscripts. Even in the absence of the draft any new war would force experience of the struggle in towns across America.

Abrams was dead a couple of years later, but the Army was re-built on that model. As a result, the National Guard and Army Reserve have been heavily engaged throughout. Secretary Rumsfeld does not like the political obstacles presented by that structure. It provides one of the few "brakes" on decisions for war that are left. He has expressed a desire to create balanced "active force" units that can be committed for long periods of time.

Thus far, he has not succeeded.

The President is not CinC of the US
(May 14, 2018)

"The Constitution explicitly assigned the president the power to sign or veto legislation, command the armed forces, ask for the written opinion of the Cabinet, convene or adjourn Congress, grant reprieves and pardons, and receive ambassadors. The president may make treaties which need to be ratified by two-thirds of the Senate. The president may also appoint Article III judges and some officers with the advice and consent of the U.S. Senate." Wiki on the US Presidency

US media figures are in the habit of referring to the president of the United States as the "Commander in Chief of the United States"

People who do that badly misunderstand the structure of US government as described in the Constitution of the United States. This misunderstanding may have been caused by the disappearance of "Civics" (government) from state mandated high school curricula over the last few decades.

In fact, the president "wears two hats," hats that are separate in function and scope of authority.

The constitution makes it clear that the president is commander in chief of the armed forces of the United States. As such the armed forces are subject to his orders. The only limits on his authority over the armed forces are those established by federal law. Some examples of acts beyond his power would be controls over methods of acquisition of materiel and the weak restrictions placed on his powers by the War Powers Act. Nevertheless, in general, the president orders the armed forces to act and they then act.

Wearing his other, civilian, "hat," the president is the head of the Executive Branch of the federal government. The other two branches are the Congress and the Federal Courts. The president, as president, cannot order the Federal Courts or the Congress to do anything. Rather than commanding them he or she must proceed by persuasion, cajoling and support for re-election efforts. This last is always a primary consideration for members of Congress.

In other words, the president's two roles are essentially unrelated and should not be conflated. To confuse these two roles is to imply the possibility of dictatorial rule. The United States has the government that exists because the learned men who drafted the constitution feared the re-creation over time of government that concentrated too much power in a small number of hands.

I have long been an originalist strict construction libertarian, believing as did Mr. Jefferson that "the best government is the least possible." The problem has always been to discern what the least possible might be.

Nevertheless, I find what is being widely said in the media advocating very narrow limits of presidential power to be disturbing. Among the various themes:

1. That the Attorney General and the Department of Justice are not really subordinates of the president and that they are somehow exempt from his control. This, although the AG is appointed by the president, is a "line" subordinate and serves "at his pleasure." That means that the president can fire an AG at any time, for any reason or for no reason although the political costs may be high.

2. It is said with a pious air of violated rectitude that Trump fired all the US Attorneys across the country. For those who do not know, these are the federal prosecutors in each federal court district. They are politically appointed employees of the Justice Department, not

of the federal courts, and it is a normal practice to replace them all in a new administration.

3. John Brennan, James Clapper and Admiral Rogers stage-managed a paper in January 2017 that asserted that the Intelligence Community believed various things about Russian government tinkering with the US election (much as the US does in other countries' elections). The paper was represented to be an IC wide opinion (like an NIE). In fact, the paper was the work product of two of Brennan's analysts. Clapper gave it his *imprimatur as* Director of National Intelligence, but Admiral Rogers at the National Security Agency could not get his people to express more than limited confidence in the document. DIA, State Department INR, the Army, Navy, Air Force, and other agencies were either not consulted or did not deign to "sign on." Donald J Trump thinks this is a "rum deal," a phony politically motivated procedure run by a group of "hacks". Why would he not think that? The reaction of the Left is to excoriate him for his lack of "respect", for the people who "cooked up" this document. We should remember that the people who "cooked" the document have no legal or constitutional existence outside the framework of the Executive Branch. Any president, in any circumstance could dismiss them all at will. No president is under any obligation at all to accept their opinion or that of anyone in the Executive Branch on anything. They are his advisers and subordinates, tools in his kit box, and that is all they are.

The US federal government is not a parliamentary government. The president of the United States is not "first among equals" as the Prime Minister in a parliamentary government often is.

The president's powers are limited by law and the constitution but not by custom, tradition, or opinions.

Trump's opponents in "the Resistance" should consider how much they will not want the idea of a shrinking presidency to be applied when next they win the White House. But then, they will have the media behind them.

Why Humiliate Russia?

(June 14, 2007)

There is no Iranian missile or nuclear threat to Europe. There is no possibility of such a threat for a decade. The problems of missile development, nuclear warhead development, miniaturization of warheads, engineering those warheads to "fit" a given missile, testing, and industrialization of this whole process all ensure that any Iranian nuclear missile threat to Europe will be nothing more than material for plots for cheap novels for a long time. The CIA and other parts of the government have been trying to tell the world that. Why has the Bush Administration not been listening? President Putin knows there is no such threat. Russia lost the "cold war," but still possesses a vast army of scientists and engineers who have told him that.

That being the case, the Russians asked themselves what the true purpose of the proposed anti-missile defenses in Poland and the Czech Republic might be. They have decided that the missile defenses are intended to consolidate American "control" of Eastern Europe and to demonstrate the supremacy of American power. Putin as much as said so recently. In a number of fora, he complained that although Russia understands that it is no longer a super-power, she is not willing to be reduced to a subordinate who must bow to whatever is dictated by Washington. He said that Russia accepts American primacy in the world, but that this primacy requires a prudent restraint and caution. He said that we Americans are in danger of becoming "bad actors" in the same way that his country has been in the past. He made reference to the United States' internal system of constitutional checks and balances. He said there must be some balancing force in the world, and that Russia would play that role.

Such a statement should be taken seriously. Russia remains an immensely powerful nuclear power, and now she is also a country swimming in oil money. Her capacity for mischief in the world is growing, not diminishing.

Poland and the Czech Republic were client states of the USSR for many years. Now they are members of NATO, the alliance that the Russians believe threatened them for fifty years. Putin "grew up" as a KGB officer, a man whose life was devoted to protecting the Soviet Union against that same NATO alliance. What are he, and the Russian people, to think of the emplacement on their doorstep of a missile defense system against a threat from Iran that does not exist?

Putin stated last week that the creation of what he thinks would be an anti-missile defense aimed at Russia would "require" a response in the form of target selection in Western Europe. The anger that causes decisions of this kind is dangerous to humanity. How many thousands of warheads does Russia still have? How many?

Russia and President Putin, as the Head of State of Russia, clearly believe themselves to be held in little regard by the United States. In Prague President Bush referred to Putin as "Vladimir." It is not likely that Putin wished to be referred to by his Christian name at a press conference in a country that is now an ally of the United States. Some consideration for the dignity of the head of state of a great country should have prevented that.

At Rostock, Putin has proposed that the site of the anti-missile defense should be located in Azerbaijan, and that Russia would want the program to be "transparent" to the world. On that basis, he said that Russia would cooperate in this matter. President Bush responded that this idea had merit and that America would carefully consider it.

These statements indicate a resumption of statesmanship on both sides. We must not forget that history did not, in fact, end with the fall of the USSR. Mankind is still "at risk" from far more dangerous weapons and vanities than those likely to be possessed by Islamic fanatics. The nuclear powers must treat each other with a prudent regard born both of self-interest, and common courtesy.

There is no reason to humiliate our former enemies and present friends. Let us be more careful!

Two Very Different Wars

(June 22, 2006)

In recent weeks the stories of investigations of alleged atrocities by American troops in Iraq have saturated the media. "Haditha" seem likely to become a name that we wish we had never heard. There are other such names, seemingly more each day. What the outcome will be of investigations and possible courts-martial is impossible to say at this moment in time. Many of the incidents under discussion involve Iraqi and Afghan civilians. Some involve people who clearly were combatants on the other side. The responsibility of our soldiers or anyone's soldiers to safeguard non-combatants is crystal clear in our law and in international law. The problem of how to deal with enemy fighters is another and more complicated issue. At the commencement of this war a decision was made within the Bush Administration that enemy fighters would not be considered "Prisoners of War," although they would be afforded comparable protections. This judgment has made possible the internment and interrogation facility at Guantanamo, "rendition" of prisoners to countries like Egypt and a general lowering of standards in the treatment of prisoners in places like the Abu Ghraib prison complex.

It will probably be a surprise to many to be told that in Vietnam enemy prisoners of war were treated in accordance with the Geneva Conventions and were accorded that designation. Many people have seen photographs of American or South Vietnamese soldiers with VC and North Vietnamese Army prisoners. The question that should arise from these pictures is – "What happened after that?" The answer is that these captured enemy soldiers were held by the MPs, interrogated by military intelligence, and then went to prisoner of war camps which were run by the South Vietnamese army under the tutelage of American MP Advisors.

There were exceptions to this destination. Captured underground political cadres were not thought of as prisoners of war. They were treated as criminals and traitors to the South Vietnamese state. Enemy intelligence personnel apprehended in civilian clothes were subject to the sanction traditionally reserved for spies. Many will remember the famous photograph of the chief of South Vietnam's police shooting a captured North Vietnamese intelligence officer in the street during the Tet 1968 offensive.

The great majority of captured enemy personnel, and by that I mean soldiers and guerillas captured on the battlefield went to prisoner of war camps. There were camps like that distributed around the country and they held a great many prisoners under conditions that met the standards of the International Red Cross. Although I was not an MP, I visited a number of these camps in 1972 and did not see anything very objectionable about them. When the war ended these soldiers were repatriated and the first thing they generally did was to take off the clothes they had been issued as prisoners. That was understandable enough.

During the war itself, thousands of these prisoners decided to change sides and take service either with the American Forces or those of the South Vietnamese. One of the most useful things the "turncoats" did was to serve as "Kit Carson Scouts." These were former enemy soldiers who became auxiliary members of American combat units and who accompanied our people in the field. Their knowledge of the enemy's methods and habits was invaluable. In the great majority of cases, they proved to be loyal to their new allegiance and some eventually arrived in the "States." A good many of them now live in various American cities. Many communist Vietnamese soldiers had similarly changed sides during the "French War."

I spent a lot of time talking to prisoners that year. I particularly remember the day I spent with a North Vietnamese lieutenant. I was "scouting" for someone suitable in the PW camps for a special project that my unit was "running." We were notified that there was someone in a facility near Saigon who might be interested. I drove out there to see him. We sat all day in a whitewashed room smoking "Gitanes," drinking tea and chatting. He had been a rifle company commander in the 325th NVA Division. He had been captured a month earlier by South Vietnamese Marines during a night trench raid at Hue. Like me, he had served a previous tour of duty in South Vietnam. At that time, he had been a sergeant. He was an Olympic competitor in marksmanship and was sent to the games in Europe after his first combat tour. When he returned home, he was made an officer and sent back to South Vietnam with the 325th, a very fine outfit. He had been unconscious when captured, knocked out with concussion grenades. We discovered that we had actually fought each other a couple of times in the Highlands. This was a kind of "bond." At the end of the day, he said that he wanted to get out of "this place," and that he had no one to go home to in the North. He asked if I thought he could live in California "afterwards." He left the camp with me. I hope he made it to the Golden State.

None of this sounds like Iraq. We don't seem to really grasp the variety of our enemies. We don't seem to know how to take advantage of that. I hope I am wrong.

Letter to the Editors, Washington Post
(June 16, 2007)

Dear Sirs,

I write concerning the feature article entitled "The Crusaders' Giant Footsteps" which appeared in the Style section on October 22nd. I believe the article portrays correctly the general "timeline" difficulties experienced by many Arabs (largely for linguistic reasons), and the unending sense of grievance which they nurture towards the West.

Unfortunately, in her exposition of the history of the Crusades and the general experience of Christian-Muslim relations, I believe that Professor Deeb has omitted a few salient facts.

First - she states that for the Muslims the Crusades "evoke an unprovoked war against their religion and their very way of life." She does not make it clear if she shares that view. I do not. Islam arose in the desert of the Hijaz in the 7th century A.D. in a process of bloody internal warfare in which the Prophet Muhammad crushed opponents to his rule among the animist peoples of the Arabian Peninsula. Having dealt with them, the armies of his successors or Caliphs (Khulifa' for sticklers) swept north into the Levant and Sassanian Persia in what is now Iraq. Luckily for them they arrived on the scene in those parts just at the end of a very long and debilitating war between the Eastern Romans and the Persians. In short order they "rolled up" Iraq, Egypt, Syria, Palestine and flowed westward along the coast of North Africa, essentially expanding into a vacuum. In the course of this march of conquest, they fought many battles. The surrender of Jerusalem was accepted by the Caliph Omar himself who was accompanying his armies in the field. The Muslims took all these lands by force of arms. There were no referenda or plebiscites in which the advocates of the new religion asked if the Eastern Romans (Byzantines) or the Persians wished to be incorporated into the Empire of Islam (The Umma'). Within a few decades, the Islamic Empire arrived by sea at Constantinople itself and besieged the city seeking the downfall of this strongest bastion of Christendom in the East. They failed in that siege, but the war between the various dynasties of Caliphs and successor regimes of Turks on the one hand and the Byzantines never ended with the Muslims more or less continuously on the attack and the Byzantines playing a very persistent "game" of defense with occasional counter-offensives. In 1071, the Seljuk Turks defeated the Byzantine army decisively in eastern Anatolia in the Battle of Manzikert. The defeat was total and crushing. As a result, the Turks advanced rapidly throughout nearly all of Anatolia (modern Turkey) overrunning in the process the ancient Greco-Roman civilization which existed everywhere there. The inhabitants were nearly all Christians or Jews who were also forcibly integrated into the World of Islam. This disaster left the Byzantine Empire in a truly perilous condition with the Turkish Sultan making his capital at Nicaea (Isnik to the Turks) just a few miles away. The further intentions of the Turks were clear. In this condition, in 1095, the Byzantine emperor appealed to the Pope for help, ignoring the protests of the Orthodox clergy to do so. News traveled slowly in those days. By the time the Pope, Urban the 2nd, got people together, to make an appeal to the nobles, some time had passed. At first, he intended to pass on the emperor's appeal in a straightforward way, but he knew with whom he was dealing. These men had no love of the Byzantines. Instead, he appealed to the semi-civilized Germanic warriors before him in terms he knew they would understand. He asked them to go and deliver Christ's Tomb from the unbeliever. He told them that the Church would relent in its attacks on their warlike way of life if only they would make this "armed pilgrimage" to the East. He probably thought that in the process, they would wreck the forces of Islam enough to give the Byzantines the "breathing space" they needed. If he thought that, he was right. At Nicaea, at Doryleum, at Antioch and many other place along the way, the army of the 1st Crusade mauled the Turks unmercifully and weakened them for decades. Did the army of the 1st Crusade behave like the barbarians they were when they took Jerusalem? Certainly, but the Bedouin and Sudanese soldiers of the Fatimid Egyptian garrison would have done well to refrain from bringing crosses and statues from the churches of the Holy City to the walls to urinate and spit on them in front of the Crusader army. They would have done well not to have expelled the native Christian population from the city just before the siege began. It might have been better. Unprovoked war? I think not.

Second - "The First Crusade touched off 400 years of warfare between Islam and the Western world." The Latin Kingdom of Jerusalem endured for something less than two hundred years. Of what does Professor Deeb write when she speaks of "400 years?" As we can see from the record in my first point, there had never been an absence of warfare between Islam and Christendom. From the beginning of Islam until the British victory over the Mahdi's army at Omdurman in the Sudan there was always warfare, war without end. Winston Churchill fought at Omdurman in the late 19th century. Now it has begun again.

Third - Professor Deeb says that "Islam, in its early centuries, was quite tolerant of Christians and Jews." That is true if you understand that "tolerance" means just that. It did not mean, does not mean that Muslims accept Christianity or Judaism on anything like an equal footing. Indeed, it does not mean the Christians or Jews are to be accorded an equal place in society. It does mean that they are not to be killed for clinging to their own beliefs. This injunction in Qur'an and Sunna (tradition) was most often observed but not always. In medieval times there were Muslims groups much like bin Laden's Al-Qa'ida. The dervish fanatics who repeatedly swept into Spain and who the Spanish and Portuguese call Mohavids (Muwahiddun) and Moravids (Murabittun) were such, killing all unbelievers who fell into their hands. In the lands of "orthodox" Islam Christians and Jews were suffered to live as such. A tax upon their heads was collected, they were not allowed to possess arms or serve in the military. They wore distinctive clothing. They were usually not allowed to build new churches. Their churches were not allowed to be taller than mosques and often were not allowed to have bells. They were expected to accept their status as less than second class. If they did that, then they were "tolerated." At the same time an unrelenting pressure toward conversion was exerted through the medium of a promise of acceptance into the dominant order. This worked and over the centuries the ancestors of the masses of Muslims whom we know today were converted from Christianity and Judaism. Fair enough, but the trial in Afghanistan of Christian charity workers for preaching Christianity to Afghans revives the memory.

I have worked among the Muslim peoples for nearly thirty years. I respect them deeply and the message of Islam as well. Nevertheless, it is necessary to know with whom we are dealing and not to distort the truth by selective memory.

W. Patrick Lang
Alexandria, Virginia

"You are not who they say you are."
(April 2, 2005)

John Paul II to his countrymen in Krakow under communist rule.

This was perhaps the most consequential political and moral speech of the last hundred years. With these words the late pope called on his fellow Poles and indeed us all to remember that we are human beings and not merely the objects of propaganda and media conditioning for whatever purpose. He called them to remember that as Poles they were heritors of a proud and noble tradition and people of real substance in their own right. He reminded them that they did not have to submit to

redefinition as clones of the creature that communism tried so hard to bring forth as "Soviet Man." He was clear in his own mind that we can be whatever we resolve to be.

It is clear that Poland heard him.

It is to be hoped that everyone will continue to hear him.

America Cannot and Will Not Succeed in Afghanistan/Pakistan

Intelligence Squared Event, New York University, New York City, 2009

The Obama Administration has implemented a significant change in policy toward Afghanistan and Pakistan, which they view as a single challenge, AfPak. More troops and a new commander have been sent to Afghanistan, and the US has increased its level of support and aid to Pakistan. To many, this means we are becoming further entrenched in an open-ended quagmire where any military solution will ultimately fail. Others question whether we should care if Afghanistan has a strong central government or a democratic one. While most agree it should not become a terrorist haven, opinions differ on how this should be accomplished: more troops, covert operations, diplomacy? And what to make of Pakistan? We cannot allow its nuclear arsenal to fall into the hands of radicals, but President Obama has ruled out putting US troops on the ground. The task of rooting out al Qaeda and Taliban militants falls to Pakistan's army, which has, until recently, supported these groups as a hedge against future conflict with India. How much tolerance does America have for the long road ahead with AfPak? Can we ever "win," and how would we even define a win in this region?

For: Steven Clemons
For: Patrick Lang
For: Ralph Peters

Against: James Shinn
Against: John Nagi
Against: Steve Coll

Col. Patrick Lang – Opening statement

This is a fascinating topic at this particular moment in American history, and I would have thought, maybe that people were tired of it by now, but I can see that that is obviously not the case. As the chairman said, in fact, I don't think you can decide that question other than in the context of what American policy is and what the stated foreign policy of the President of the US is in regard to this question.

I had the fortune, or misfortune, to go to a number of Army service schools; one of them was the Army War College where they taught me a lot about what the strategy ... the planning itself. You start with Mission, National Purpose, the Policy, and you devise a strategy from that, and you implement that strategy. That's how that works.

Now, last March, I listened carefully when President Obama announced that our policy in Afghanistan was to disrupt, destroy and disorganize our enemies, our specific enemies who were a danger to the United States. That's a nice, clear policy. It's not too hard to understand that

And to that end, Gen. Stanley McChrystal was put in command out there and was sent out to make what is called s Commander's estimate of the situation. Which he did – with the help of various people for several months and it is now, as you know, the object of great contention in the Washington world. And the problem with his estimate, I think, that is causing so much trouble, is that it is normal in an estimate of that kind, for a commander to propose several options to his superiors, among which the boss can choose.

Presumably one option, in this case, the option of a large-scale counterinsurgency campaign across all the really hostile parts of Afghanistan in the context of their ruined, if ever alive, economy, their obviously rather feeble political system, is a daunting task. Now, somehow it has now become, what we would call, an implied task for Gen. McChrystal that the pacification of large parts of Afghanistan in the most hostile premises are in fact a necessary thing. And for that reason, he has opted for counterinsurgency.

I am happy to see so many members of my generation in the audience. There are usually too many young people for my taste. I started in the counterinsurgency business, in the Church of the Counterinsurgents, really, in 1964 if you can believe that. When the Army sent me down to Fort Bragg to study this subject with intensity at the feet of the most learned French and British exponents of this theory of warfare, which had been created as a result of the experience of former colonial powers after WWII, in fighting against the wars of national liberation as they were called then.

And the Communists had gotten involved in all these wars, and we were against this as well. So, we studied up on this in a big way. And one of the most interesting of the guys who taught from the stage there was a great scholar named Bernard Fall. Some of you undoubtedly know who he is.

And I remember watching him. I really had no idea who he was at the time. But I remember watching him write on the blackboard on the stage, Counterinsurgency = Political Reform + Economic Development + Counter-guerilla operations. And that is really all – really all of it in a nutshell.

And it is in that context that when you look at Afghanistan, this huge place, the size of Texas with 35 million people of very disparate origins, many of them speaking languages that are not mutually intelligible, and who, a lot of them don't like each other very much, in fact, you can see that this is a very difficult thing to do.

We tried applying this theory of warfare, Counterinsurgency, across the world in the 1960s and 70s and 80s. I did it myself in South America, in East Africa, in Southwest Asia, and all kinds of places, and of course, Vietnam, how could I forget that. And we found that in places where the task wasn't too big – the country wasn't too big, the problems were manageable one way or another, or the people weren't thoroughly converted to some ideology that demanded revolution, that you could do this, with enough good works and suppression of guerrillas. You could turn this around, and I could name places, if we had time.

In places that were really big, where none of those conditions apply, you could struggle like the devil, but you wouldn't get very far. And this is the problem that I have with the idea of the application of counterinsurgency – those three things – to Afghanistan. In fact, I think it's too big a task for us. We have been fighting for eight years, Afghanistan is a huge place, it has terrible problems, economic ones, political ones, and the combat problem, from the point of view of a guy who fought in several wars like this, including Vietnam, is really very difficult.

And I would submit to you that, if what we're going to do, as Gen. McChrystal says, is that we're going to try to protect the people, which means essentially, control the population, because that's what Counterinsurgency is about. Just like Insurgency by controlling the population by positive means, or some that is not so positive sometimes, you're going to have to have a lot of troops to do this.

Gen. McChrystal evidently wants 40,000 more people; well, I would say to you that that's just the beginning. That's how we started in Vietnam too. This is a big problem we're facing in Afghanistan, and in fact, this slice of the pie, will be followed by further slices of the pie. And my objection to all this, and the reason that I don't think you can win with a counterinsurgency strategy is, in fact, because I think that three or four years down the pike, if we apply that strategy, all you good people and your fellow citizens across the country will ask, "Are the Taliban, or whatever it is that we're calling the Taliban, are they really our enemies? In the sense that Al Qaeda was? Is this really what we want to do?"

And when that happens, and I suspect that what's going to happen, is you're going to tell your members of Congress that you've had enough of this, and they will vote for the end of the war as they did in Vietnam.

So, I don't think we can do this. I don't think we can do Counterinsurgency in Afghanistan. There are other methods that could be applied that would be able to control the situation over a long period of time. I don't think we can withdraw altogether. But Counterinsurgency in Afghanistan, I find to be a very difficult idea.

Thank you very much.

Book Review of *the Atomic Bazaar:*
The Rise of the Nuclear Poor
By William Langewiesche (September 5, 2007)

This book has convinced me that just about any country on earth can have nuclear weapons if it wants them. My conclusion from reading the book is that it is still possible to stop or impede any particular program but the general process of nuclear proliferation is now so advanced that it is virtually certain that a great many under-developed countries will eventually build their own atomic bombs.

The author, William Langewiesche, believes that nuclear weapons are now an achievable ambition for most of the world's states. He reached that conclusion after researching and reporting nuclear proliferation stories for "The New Republic," and "Vanity Fair" for many years. In the course of that work, he met and interviewed engineers, government officials and other journalists specialized in that field across the world. The evidence of his eyes and ears and the words of potential and actual participants in the "atomic bazaar "drove his conclusions.

Langewiesche argues that it is unlikely that entire, functioning nuclear weapons will be sold to developing countries by those who possess them. He believes, correctly I think, that the nuclear powers have instituted sufficiently stringent controls on such weapons to prevent theft and sale.

He also believes that it is probable that a "poor" country seeking to construct its own nuclear weapons is likely to opt for building "gun type" weapons in which the fissile core would be made of enriched uranium (HEU). Another possibility would be to attempt to build bombs in which the fissile core is made of plutonium. North Korea followed the plutonium pathway toward nuclearization, but the relatively small amount of plutonium available has been a severely limiting factor in its program. The general opinion in the community of experts watching North Korea's efforts has been that North Korea must have also been pursuing an HEU based program if its nuclear ambitions were ever more than a negotiating tactic.

Langewiesche finds that the reasons for opting for HEU bombs are quite simple; 1- Weapons built of plutonium are of necessity much more complicated in design and fabrication, and 2- There is a great deal more HEU in the world than there is plutonium and a lot of it is very poorly safeguarded. (There is something close to 20,000 metric tons of HEU in existence at the present). Much of this material is located in the countries of the former Soviet Union in a wide variety of facilities in many of the former "closed cities." Laboratories, industrial sites, medical plants, storage sites possessing HEU are scattered across the Eurasian landmass by the thousands. In many of these places the custodians are members of the former Soviet academic and managerial elite whose standard of living has been severely stressed by the lengthy transition to a market economy. Langewiesche observes that in many places possessing HEU there are no longer explicable sources of the funds which continue to support standards of living far above the populations of the surrounding region. These are often the same places where the lowest standards of government safeguarding exist.

Langewiesche cites several specific examples of the creation of nuclear bomb programs by relatively poor countries. He describes the Pakistan case in the greatest detail. He describes the easy availability of technical education in Europe and the United States which produced such capable men as AQ Khan and his associates. He describes their practical workplace experience in such places as the Netherlands. He describes the sense of grievance against the "developed world" which caused Pakistan to seek atomic weapons and the huge "slice" of available funding that successive governments devoted to this program. He makes it very clear that for Pakistan (and probably for India as well) nuclear weapons are not thought of as merely a deterrent. They are thought of as the ultimate battlefield killer. From his chronology it is clear that Pakistan has probably been at the brink of nuclear weapons employment against India several times.

The manufacturing and research facilities for making the kind of bombs discussed here are not very advanced. The plans for such "gun type" bombs are widely accessible on the internet. The possession of such weapons holds an almost mystical significance for small countries. The ownership alone would make them major "players" in their own minds. Saddam Hussein would have had a fission weapon in the early '90s if he had not ruined his prospects by invading Kuwait.

The present nuclear powers have learned to live with the possession of such weapons. The new owners will not have been through the sobering experiences of the Cold War.

Someone should "get busy" explaining to them why these weapons have not been used since Nagasaki.

PART VIII

A Look into the Future

In this final work of fiction, the author branches out into futuristic science fiction, with the same insights into the human dilemma and the rules of combat that inform all the other writings contained in this volume.

Carolina in the Mornin'
(Undated)

No one really noticed at first that the end of the road had probably been reached for mankind.

The crisis began in the magic few days which lay between Christmas and New Year's, 2027. As historians later reconstructed events, the first sign that something unusual was happening was a "flash" precedence message from "Copernicus," the permanent orbiting laboratory of the International Space Commission.

"Meteor Activity - distribution heavy across northern hemisphere, impacts unmarked by sensor-predictable readouts. Kelleher sends." That was the message. NASA and the U.S. Air Force's Space Command listened and watched after they received the "flash," but there was nothing more to hear, nothing until "Copernicus" reported similar meteor activity in each of the following three days. Nevertheless, there was no follow up activity because no reports came in that anything had happened on the ground. Holiday cheer and a desire for peace and quiet in which to celebrate prevailed in the defense and scientific worlds and as a result the story, and interest in it died quickly.

It was only in February that someone noticed that machine driven data collection had generated astronomical observations of this meteor activity from mountaintop observatories and also from the Hubbell telescope in orbit. This data had not been considered significant and it was routinely routed on the Internet to consumers who had registered a demand for such information with the National Science Foundation in Washington.

In March, a Cal Tech mathematics graduate student named Taylor Harrison Walker III working late at the Jet Propulsion Laboratory in Pasadena found that the information available showed that the points of impact of all the meteor strikes had been grouped in several places on the earth's surface. The Ural Mountains in Russia, the massif central of France and three areas of the United States were all heavily bombarded by what was thought to be the remnants of an asteroid. Upstate New York in the Adirondacks had been a center of activity. The Blue Ridge Mountains west of Asheville, North Carolina were another as was the upper peninsula of Michigan.

The graduate student's supervisor showed little interest, but the student himself called his uncle, a captain in the North Carolina Civil Air Patrol, to discuss the meteors. The captain normally would not have paid much attention, but his squadron had been planning for some time to fly a practice search near the forested and nearly roadless quadrangle described by his nephew's data. Two days later an O-1 Bird Dog light observation plane lifted off the runway of its CAP base on the civilian airport at Raleigh. After an uneventful flight to the west, the aircraft refueled at Asheville and headed west into Haywood County. North Carolina CAP operations headquarters monitored the flight over the old Collins KWM2a single sideband radio in the Bird Dog's fuselage behind the back seat. The last thing operations heard from the plane was a frantic call from the Flight Observer that the Pilot was circling an area on the ground where the trees had all been knocked flat. The girl CAP Cadet flying as Observer then said, "There are survivors, there are ..."

Nothing after that.

Meteor showers do not normally have survivors or even passengers. This caused some curiosity, perhaps even a little humorous comment in the operations room. When the Bird-Dog became overdue past its fuel endurance, the CAP notified the North Carolina State Police that it might have an aircraft down in Haywood County and also asked the U.S. Air Force for assistance.

By the end of the following day only one thing was clear. That was that we were at war, all of us, against them. What they might be was not clear at first. What was known by the end of that first day was that the State Police, and the Air Force had lost every man and piece of equipment that they had sent into the area in question. Aircraft and ground search parties alike vanished without trace except for strangely interrupted radio messages which ended in midsentence. The recorded messages, when played back, babbled of circular areas with trees bulldozed flat, presumably to build obstacles and field fortifications.

The governor of North Carolina asked for federal assistance. It was granted and preliminary instructions issued from Washington. In response, the North Carolina Air and Ground National Guard mobilized behind a battalion of airborne infantry and a battery of field artillery of the 82nd Airborne Division brought in from Fort Bragg. In an earlier time, the task force might have been made up altogether of regular, active-duty forces, but thirty years of intermittent budget cutting and government shrinking followed by unsustainably high levels of military spending had made a difference. As a long-term trend military spending had shrunk slowly but steadily ever since the Bush Administration. Research and Development had been at a virtual standstill for two decades with almost all available money devoted to keeping the Regular forces at a high state of readiness for participation in the interventionist foreign policy which enjoyed the support of so many voters.

No one had seen a really new piece of military equipment in decades. As a result, the Federal Armed Forces now made up a fairly small portion of the country's armed might, and the regular units that still existed usually were committed to overseas operations. It was thought at this point that the Haywood County woods were infested with backwoodsmen from the Tar Heel Volunteer Militia, an anti-tax and federal government group that had sworn the year before to liberate the state. They had been active along the North Carolina-Tennessee border. People on the ground in western North Carolina did not know at that point that National Reconnaissance Office satellite photography showed a dozen areas stripped of tree cover along the interstate border and a new network of roads being built to connect the open spaces. The pictures also showed some dark markings that the photo interpreters believed to be the entrances to tunnels.

Three days after the loss of the CAP Bird Dog, the government's response, Task Force Westgard moved forward into the forest from a start line on a two-lane tar county road that ran east-west down a valley filled with small farms. It was just after dawn. The sun was shining with a few small clouds at middle altitudes. It was warm for a winter day and as they advanced, the men were of the opinion that this was shirt sleeve weather. The force was named (as was Army custom) for Brigadier General Phillip Westgard, a Regular Army man brought in from Fort Bragg to command in the emergency. In the force were the Army paratroops and artillery, a battalion of M-1E3 Abrams tanks from the National Guard as well as two battalions of National Guard infantry, altogether about two thousand soldiers and fifty odd tanks. For the first mile or so the only problem faced by General Westgard's Task Force were those to be expected in maintaining order in a scratch brigade that had never worked or trained together. The terrain was very rough, a series of mixed pine and hardwood-covered ridges perpendicular to the line of advance. Westgard had wisely grouped the armor on two logging roads that directly penetrated the zone of operation, and which led to two of the clearings that only he knew of from the satellite pictures. One road went into the hills almost in the center of the zone, the other was parallel to this and halfway from the center road to the grease pencil line that marked the southwestern edge of the area on the acetate covering of his map.

He led on the center road with the Regular paratroop battalion teamed with a ten-tank company. He followed that with his command group of several vehicles including a massive-armored force command track which was basically a room sized superstructure built on a tank chassis. On the southwestern road, the penetration force was made up of one of the 800-man National Guard infantry battalions (1st Bn., 26th N.C. Infantry Regiment) and another tank company. The rest of the Task Force waited in reserve where the two logging roads crossed the state tar road. The artillery was "in battery" in the reserve area and "registered" by map on likely targets. On call at Asheville were six Air National Guard A-10 "Wart Hog" fighter bombers and three Apache helicopter gunships from the Aviation Brigade of the 82nd Airborne Division.

Westgard was an interesting man, a civilian-baffling mixture of combat hardened light infantryman and intellectual. In the long, long Balkan Wars, he had earned a fearsome reputation as a man who relished combat for its own sake and for whom enlisted soldiers would generally go anywhere to do anything. At the same time, his four years as a professor of chemistry and then of applied mathematics at West Point puzzled many. When asked about his varied background by civilians who hoped that he would prove to be merely a misfit in the army, he would turn away with a shrug, unwilling to discuss the matter.

On this particular morning in the Smoky Mountains, he was doing what he liked best, leading soldiers into battle. His stooped frame stalked through the trees following the tanks and their whining clatter. Camouflage dress covered his bones. His helmet rode in the crook of his arm. Up ahead, he could see the last of the tanks grinding and slipping up the clay of the logging road as it climbed toward the top of the next little ridge. The smell of hardwood mold and rotting leaves filled his head along with the exhaust of the tanks. His head was wet with the mist and dew of dawn. The vehicles were shaking water off the leaves on the hickories and locusts of the forest. Behind him walked radio men. Their packboards carried full loads with antennae waving above. His aide de camp, 1st Lieutenant George Frederick Wilson followed the radiomen. Behind Wilson, lumbered the big command track with its communications to the air support and the ground reserve at the tar road. The track driver's head protruded from his hatch. Westgard noticed that the soldier wasn't wearing his helmet. A black armored force beret perched jauntily on one side of the black man's head. A good idea! "George, take this damned thing and stow it in the back," he told the aide. George Wilson accepted the general's helmet, and handed it up with his own to the driver who grinned down at him. "I he'ped you out, Lootenant," the man said with a grin. "You don' wan' to weah that thang." "What's your name, soldier?" the young officer asked. "Gaston Rutledge, Lootenant. Ah'm f"um Winston-Salem. How 'bout you, suh?" Wilson smiled back. "Virginia, Alexandria actually. Nice to meet you Gaston." He turned and walked up the muddy road to catch up with the general.

The last tanks were in sight again from the top of the little hill the command group had just climbed. General Westgard stood on the crest looking at the two tanks with his field glasses. "3/B/1/2NC" was marked on the last tank's stern. Below this was the cavalry's rectangle with a single diagonal slash through it. "Third Platoon, Company B, First Squadron, Second North Carolina Cavalry Regiment," he translated to himself. A real mouthful, he thought. Somehow, they have more flavor, the old names do. The National Guard had gone back to using the Civil War era names of their units ten years before. It had seemed strange at first, but now it was very natural. Westgard would have rejected the idea that the change was a symptom of the growing weakness of the national government. On either side and in front of the tanks just up the road, he could see paratroopers from the 82nd, pulled in close to protect the big, deadly, but somewhat helpless monsters from closein attack by men with courage and the right tools.

One of the radios spluttered. It was Lieutenant Colonel Peter Black, the Airborne battalion commander calling from up in front. Westgard took the handset while standing facing the radioman's back, tethered to him by the length of the armored cable. "This is Borderguard 6, over," he said. "Gliderman 6 here," Black answered. "We have visual contact with the open space. It starts at the bottom of this hill. GPS will tell you where I am. It looks about one to two clicks north to south and about the same on the other axis. There are several destroyed aircraft in view, and what looks like a uniformed body out in the open, probably one of the state troopers, over." "This is Borderguard 6. Any hostiles?" "Gliderman 6, negative on the hostiles right now. I don't like this. It's too quiet out there. I am going to get my lead two companies into a perimeter here on the west side of hill 765 with the tanks inside. Request TAC air orbit in vicinity. Request confirm they're loaded with Nape." Westgard looked at his map and nodded to himself.

Black was about 300 meters to the west on the road, just over the crest of Hill 765. "Borderguard 6. Nape and Hi-drags," the general answered. This meant that the Guard A-10s were armed with napalm and high drag, high explosive fragmentation bombs for low level attacks. They also had their 30-millimeter cannon. "Oldnorth 6, this is Borderguard 6," Westgard said to the radio, calling the commander of his other column of attack, Lieutenant Colonel Joseph Ashton McClung. There was silence for a moment while he imagined someone calling the Carolina Guard officer to the radio . . . There were birds in the trees. He heard the sharp little cry of a cardinal and looked around for the red bird. The deep throated idling of the tanks across the little valley made a reassuring backdrop. Black and the rest of his unit, 2nd Battalion, 325th Infantry Regiment (Airborne), would be just beyond the top of that next hill. He noticed that his little staff were staring at him anxiously and he made an effort to smile at them.

"This is Oldnorth 6, over," came the voice. "Status report, Oldnorth 6, over." "We just came out of the woods and are now 100 meters into a cleared area. It's roughly circular. The CAP plane wreck is right in front of us." "Oldnorth 6, that clearing must be closer to the Line of Departure than Gliderman's. You are ahead of him relative to the clearings. Stay where you are. Can you see anyone?" "This is Oldnorth 6. There are two bodies in the CAP plane. Nothing else . . . Wait a minute Borderguard 6 . . . There are a couple of holes in the ground near the wreck." Firing started to the southwest where Oldnorth was talking into the radio's handset. First there was small arms fire, both rifles and machine guns chattering with the staccato thump-crump of a grenade launcher mixing into the sounds.

Then a tank's main gun spoke with a roar across the forested hills. "Oh Shit!" Oldnorth 6 bellowed. "They're coming up out of the holes! There are hundreds! There are two, maybe three kinds!" The Carolinian stopped talking on the Task 6 Force command net. He still had the handset tightly gripped in one hand, keeping the transmit key depressed. Westgard could hear him talking to his own people. "Open fire damn it! Keep shootin', keep shootin' . . . Get C Company up here and put'em in the middle of the firin' line. Now!" To the immediate front, Westgard heard the paratroopers yelling at each other on the top of the hill in front of him. "Gawd Damn! Look at'em go! What the hell are they?" "Beat's me."

The two Abrams tanks on the reverse slope of the hill right in front of him changed gears and charged up and over the crest, disappearing in a shower of broken saplings and red mud thrown by the treads. "Borderguard 6, this is Gliderman 6, over!" "Borderguard 6, what's up?" He did his best to sound as cool as Black. A lot of people were listening. "There are several openings in the surface of the clearing. Things are coming up out of those holes by the hundreds. They are . . . not human. I don't know what they are. They are not coming at us. They are going away toward the southwest corner of the clearing. Uh! Uh! They're going around a corner of the trees there. Sweet Jesus! Does this clearing connect?" "Oldnorth 6, this is Borderguard 6!" Westgard demanded. "They are assaultin' my position," McClung answered. "We're in a wedge formation with A and B Companies and the tanks in the line. I'm bringin' up the rest of my battalion. Request priority of fire support!"

Westgard nodded to Lt. Wilson who walked back to talk to the Fire Support Coordinator, a woman captain, who was seated at a map board in the command track. "Oldnorth 6, you have priority of fires, talk to me," Westgard said. "There are a whole lot of things like furry Great Danes with big teeth and claws," McClung said. "They came right at us like they thought maybe we would just run. They're easy to kill once you get used to the idea of shootin' things that look like dogs before they bite you. They killed two of my men who froze at first. They seem to be animals of some kind. They're pullin' back now. I can see maybe a hundred bodies. They've stopped now and are just looking at us from a couple hundred meters off. We've pretty much stopped shootin'." "What else, over?""

There are some great big brown things that're draggin' machines out of the holes and carryin' them to different parts of the field. Some of the machines have wheels, three wheels. Excuse me, Borderguard. I want to talk to my Forward Observer." Westgard knew he must not interfere with the National Guard officer's ability to run his battle. "Come on boys!", he yelled over a shoulder as he ran toward the front line. Down the 7 hill he jogged, down into the mucky bottom. It had a little stream in it, flowing across the road. As he splashed through the mud, he heard the command track start to move behind him. Up the hill he went jumping from one relatively dry spot to the next. Now he was passing paratroopers standing in formation on either side in the wood. Black's reserve company.

"Airborne!, General," someone called to him. He waved without stopping. "Hoowa!" another laughed in the morning. He topped the rise to find a tank in the road. The tank commander, a sergeant was standing in the turret watching something below. He ran around the hull and stopped. Black was standing ahead in the road. His men and the armored vehicles were neatly spread out to bring maximum firepower to bear with as few blind spots as possible. Out in front of the troops in the flat, denuded clearing was the spectacle of the century. There were perhaps three hundred definitely alien beings. Two thirds of these were running toward the corner of the clearing that Black had mentioned. The rest were drawn up in a half circle facing the humans on the hillside. He trotted down the slope to reach the paratroop colonel. Black heard him coming and turned to salute as he came to a sliding stop in the red mud. A corporal burdened with one of Black's radios put out a hand and steadied him. "Hello, General. What do you think?" the paratroop officer asked with a sweep of his arm toward the scene below them. "Remarkable, Peter, remarkable..."

A couple of the soldiers laughed a little at that. Black looked at them. The laughter disappeared. "As you can see," Peter Black said. "There are the doggy ones that Colonel McClung mentioned. They are on leashes here. Then there are the variously brown or grey human looking ones, except they all seem to be about five feet tall. They hold the leashes or are gathered in those groups of twenty or so each behind the lines of "dogs" and handlers. I guess they are handlers for the dogs and not the other way around.

You notice that the 'humans' all have what look like shoulder weapons on slings." "And the big, brown ones that he talked about?" "Ah, yes, there were some out here a minute ago, just before you showed up. They were dragging those four, three-wheeled machines you see in the background." He looked at Westgard. "I am assuming they are crew served weapons of some sort." Westgard looked at the objects in question through his electronically boosted field glasses. There were three "humans" for each "gun." As he inspected them, he began to think of the "humans" as people. They were built like homo sapiens but smaller and without hair on the head. They wore harness of some kind and were truly carrying things that looked a lot like rifles. There were also tools that seemed very like pistols suspended from the belt portions of the harness. They were naked and had organs that looked both male and mammalian showing under the belts. The "field guns" had barrels with a three or four-inch aperture at the end of the tube. There did not seem to be a "breech" for loading but there was something else attached to the side which might be a battery pack. "Directed energy weapon?" Westgard asked.

The soldiers looked at each other until Colonel Black decided to reply. He was frowning at the thought. "Could be. Shall I open fire?" "No. Have your men start digging right here. Let's see what happens in the other clearing. Let's stand behind this tank." Commands were passed and soldiers unloaded entrenching tools from each other's rucksacks to begin the process of excavation which would make them disappear into the earth. Westgard looked at the "dogs." They were brown and grey like the "men" and strained at their leads while looking at the soldiers a few hundred yards away. He could see the teeth. They resembled boar's tusks more than canine teeth. The lower teeth protruded over the lip in several places. The eyes had an oval shape. He looked back at the "humans." They also had oval eyes. "Borderguard 6, Oldnorth 6." It was McClung. "Borderguard 6, over." "Sir, they are fillin' up this whole clearin' with the ones they brought from your location. I think they are goin' to open fire with those "cannons," and then try to overrun us." "This is Borderguard 6. Are you digging?" "Oldnorth 6. You bet!" In the background you could hear sergeants bellowing. "Borderguard 6. If they attack, hold your ground employing priority air and artillery fires. I am going to commit the maneuver reserve on this axis to capture their base." He looked up.

"Roger that, Oldnorth out." Black was grinning at him. The man turned away and called on the radio to brief his company commanders. "But first, I want to talk to Corps," Westgard said to no one in particular, referring to his own commander at Fort Bragg two hundred odd miles to the east. He was on way to the satellite communications rig in the command track when the war started up again in McClung's clearing.

The first sound was a tremendous CRACK!-WHSSH!-BANG!, then another, and another. The sky in that direction seemed to have changed color slightly to a more violet blue. This was followed by many similar sounds that were less distinct and which seemed to come from smaller weapons. The rifles, he thought "Dragon! This is Borderguard Six. Dragon This is." A familiar voice emerged from the small speaker mounted next to the radio. "This is Dragon Six, over."

It was Major General Marcia Grayson, acting commanding general of Eighteenth Airborne Corps. Westgard liked Marcia Grayson, but didn't think she was qualified for Army Corps command. This had to do with the indisputable fact that she was a Signal Corps Officer whose career had largely been spent in the White House Communications Agency. So far as Westgard knew she had never heard a shot fired in combat. Political influence had brought her to Fort Bragg as Deputy Corps Commander to "qualify" her for higher command. There were a few combat arms women officers, but not many, and she was not one of them. Her boss, the lieutenant general commanding, had suffered a heart attack the previous month and so Marcia was in charge. It was an old, old, army story. "Borderguard 6 here, I am engaged on both axes at the first clearings.""

Dragon 6, we have your positions on GPS readout and the hot satellites show massive electromagnetic activity in Oldnorth's clearing. I have been monitoring your traffic with him, over." Well, well, good for you, old girl. That will save time. "Request permission to attack as described, over." "Standby Borderguard while I talk to the Chairman."

My, my, the Chairman of the Joint Chiefs of Staff no less. He began to hum to himself while listening to the speaker of the radio that was on the Task Force command net. "Nuthin' could be finer than to be in Carolina in the mahnin. Nuthin'..." There was a little knot of radiomen standing in a circle around him and Peter Black. They were all intently watching him for cues. A couple started to smile at his humming. He began to account for the radiomen, Three were his and two were Black's. Then there was another radio carried by a soldier wearing the 18th Corps' Blue Dragon shoulder patch. Ah, Corps Artillery, he's on the fire support net. "Oldnorth, how are you doing?" he asked trying to keep the anxiety out of his voice. "Borderguard, I have all the tanks up online and firin'. You must hear them. I have lost one so far. One of the things on wheels burned a hole right through the turret and set off the main gun ammunition in the racks. You must have heard the bang. The tankers are knockin' the shit out of the wheeled things, now. They pretty much have driven them underground again."

Lieutenant Colonel Peter Black, a regular's regular frowned at the use of profanity on the radio. Westgard could imagine his thoughts. Ah, yes, the militia. "Roger that." Actually, he had not noticed anything different, but he was holding the handset away from his ear because the flat "Craack! Of the 120 mm. smoothbores on the tanks 10 threatened to deafen him. "And the sky is a funny color over you," he said to McClung. "Have you called for air and arty?" He looked at the man carrying the fire support net radio. The soldier nodded. "How about your infantry, Oldnorth?" "We've lost a few, mostly hit with the shoulder weapons, but some with the junk from the explodin' tank. Everybody with a shovel is diggin' like crazy, includin' me. Here comes the air, the A-10s."

Westgard looked in that direction and saw two big, ugly, fighter bombers circling like vultures high over McClung's clearing. The Carolinian's Forward Air Controller was talking now over the fire control net. "Tarheel Leader, what did you see, over?" Westgard saw the lead airplane in the three-ship flight as it came into sight over the trees. It was climbing away to the right, rising from a low-level run on the clearing. Westgard looked around for his Aide de Camp. Wilson was right behind him. "George, call Colonel Parasiliti, give him a warning order to move up the track to close on us with the 2nd of the 26th, and the rest of the tanks. Why do you look like that?"

The lieutenant was smiling at him. "I did that ten minutes ago. They are on the Line of Departure on the tar road. I also warned the Snakes" By this he meant the helicopter gunships. "Well good for you, George, I do believe I'll keep you." An explosion behind him spun Westgard around to see what had happened. The A-10 that only a few seconds ago had been soaring away from the ground was now falling from the sky. A wing had been neatly stripped off near the fuselage. The canopy came off. The ejection seat rode outward on its rails, kicked out of the cockpit by two blank cannon shells. The seat flew parallel to the ground, then the drogue parachute appeared, dragging the main parachute canopy out of its packing. Seat and pilot separated, the pilot swinging free under a white canopy while the seat plummeted to the earth. A blue-white lightening bolt appeared for a second, connecting the ground with the parachute. It burned a six-foot hole in the nylon of the canopy just before the pilot disappeared behind the tree tops.

"Borderguard Six, this is Dragon Six." Marcia. What now, Marci? Would they like me to negotiate with them? "Borderguard Six, over." "Dragon Six. The Chiefs want to know if you feel certain they are hostile." How ever did I know? "They just shot down an A-10 that had finished a dry run on the clearing. Then they shot the pilot while he was still in the air. I think they are hostile, over."

The radio link from Dragon went silent. Come on Marci, give us a break! "Borderguard, this is Oldnorth, over." "Go ahead Oldnorth."

"That was the same thing they have been shootin' at the tanks whenever they get a chance. I have one tank immobilized with a tread burned off by the way. They hopped out of the holes and dragged the pilot down a tunnel right after she hit the ground. They have her underground. She was alive. We couldn't see her at first, because of the smoke from the burnin' A-10, but then we saw the struggle as they dragged her away."

"This is Dragon Six." For an old lady, you really are kind of a fox, Marci. "This is Borderguard Six." "Your attack plan is approved, Borderguard. Out." "Well, thank you ma'm!" he said to no one in particular. "George, get Parasiliti's people up here!" "Yes, General." "Oldnorth six?" "Oldnorth here." "Get the artillery working on all the wheeled weapons positions, then the tanks, then the two A-10s with Nape." "What about the pilot?" "I think we have to assume she's dead, Oldnorth." "Wilco, out."

The woman artillery captain in the command track began repeating for him the traffic she was hearing. "Remaining three A-10s inbound to orbit. Snakes lifting off now. 155's firing for effect." He nodded to her, and started to walk away, looking for Peter Black. "Sir," she said. Something in her voice made him turn. "There is something wrong with General Grayson. I could hear it in her voice," she said. He had not really looked at her before.

She was a remarkably pretty brunette. "You know her that well?" "Yes." He felt sad, in a way inappropriate to the moment. Oh, Marci, I didn't think you were yet another ... Then he saw the resemblance. "What's your name, Captain?" he asked. She looked at him suspiciously, guessing what he might be thinking. "Grayson, she's my father's sister, my aunt." "Thanks, Captain. Thanks very much, get this thing back over the crest before they start shooting here as well."

The aliens opened fire just as the big vehicle cleared the top of the hill and disappeared behind it. Evidently, they had been startled by the suddenness of its movement and the lightning bolt was high. It cut a pine tree in half dropping the top across a squad of Black's paratroopers. The armor company commander then made a quick decision and backed all his vehicles up and over the hill leaving their turrets and guns exposed in the classic "hull down" position that would give them the most protection. The aliens then switched their fire to the paratroopers. Most of the men were down in the four-foot-deep holes they had already excavated, and were safe, but the squad struggling to get out from under the pine top were caught in the open. Three died, burned to crisp, unthinkable objects only remotely human in remembrance.

The tanks and infantry returned fire with a roar that must have been heard in Asheville. The fight in McClung's clearing raged on for the hour it took for the rest of the Task Force to reach Westgard's position. The artillery pounded and pounded McClung's opponents, trying to keep them underground. In this situation, the aircraft proved surprisingly ineffective. The reason was simple. Every time an A-10 or attack helicopter came too close, it was destroyed. The loss of two more aircraft made that clear. It was up to the soldiers.

The Second Battalion, Twenty Sixth North Carolina Infantry Regiment under the command of Lieutenant Colonel T. J. Jackson Parasiliti arrived behind Hill 765 with the men heaving and steaming from the exertion of the long run across the ridges. Along with them came ten more Abrams tanks of the 2nd North Carolina Cavalry. General Westgard's plan was simple. He would have the 2/26 N.C. Infantry form in line with their armor support behind Hill 765 to the right of Black's paratroopers, but behind the ridge line and out of harm's way. At the last minute, he would switch the artillery fires from support of McClung to bombardment of Black's clearing with a mixture of high explosive and smoke shells.

At the same time, he would order the air support to do all they could against the same target. Parasiliti would come over the crest of Hill 765 and down the forward slope headed for the clearing. Peter Black and his 2/325 Airborne Infantry would climb out of their holes and move forward on the left as Parasiliti came abreast. Westgard made sure that Black's attached tanks would come forward to join the assault. The two battalion teams would assault across the clearing to capture the entrances to the tunnels. After that, they would play it by ear.

Westgard suspected that it would be necessary to go underground to dig the aliens out. It was not a thought he really wanted to face just yet. In the midst of his preparations, General Grayson called him again. "Borderguard, how long till LD time," she asked? Now, why are you pushing, Marci? he asked himself. What was it your niece said? "Five minutes, Dragon Six, why?" "Just get on with it, Borderguard. Everyone doesn't see this as clearly as we do." Ah. The Chiefs, and God knows who else. Westgard could picture the faces of the Joint Chiefs of Staff. The two women members, the heads of the Air Force and Navy, were known to hold the view that the proper role of the armed forces in the "modern" world was in U.N. 13 sponsored Peace Keeping and Nation Building projects. No one knew what the Army chief of staff thought. He was the ultimate uniformed Washington politician. The Chairman was not much better, a product of the new Science Corps. "Wilco, Dragon Six," he said. "Standby, we will have this underway in a minute, out."

He was sitting in a hole in the middle of Black's position during this conversation. George Wilson, his aide, sat next to him, and somehow the black National Guard driver of the command track had installed himself there as well. He had a radio on his back. He saw the general looking at him. "Back-up Task Force net, suh," he offered by way of explanation. Christ, if we have any more radio operators, there won't be anyone left to shoot!

He reached for the handset from the man's radio. "Net call, Task Force Borderguard, over," he said into the microphone. Gliderman (the 2nd/ 325th Airborne Infantry) Oldnorth (the 1st /26th N.C. Infantry) Saber (the 1st/2nd N.C. Cavalry tanks) Burgwyn (the 2nd /26 N.C. Infantry) Redleg (the 155mm. artillery battery) and Amelia (the air and artillery coordinator) checked in and went silent waiting for him. "Execute attack order," he said over the secure voice radio net. "Good luck to you all." They acknowledged in turn as he heard the tank engines start behind the crest. The crash and bang of 155 mm. projectiles landing in the other clearing stopped abruptly as the artillery gun crews back at the at the road responded to new instructions from their Fire Direction Center. After a few seconds, Westgard heard the Bang! Bang! Bang! Bang! Bang! Bang! of the six howitzers, then the whistling, rushing sounds of the shells passing overhead, clearing the top of Hill 765 by a few hundred feet, then the bang! bang! bang! bang! bang! bang! of the strike of the shells as white smoke billowed from them in a band across the near end of the cleared space below him.

The tanks rolled up and over the top of the ridge line. There were twenty in a neat line about forty yards apart with the tank commanders standing in their cupola hatches facing forward while anti-aircraft machine gunners stood in separate hatches facing aft behind their weapons. On the right, between each pair of tanks and a little behind, the 800 soldiers of the 2/26th N.C. Infantry crossed the topographic crest of the hill mass and started down the slope. Their mottled green and brown field uniforms blended in nicely with the colors of the hillside. Their formations and spacing looked like a demonstration at Fort Benning, the Infantry School. Very nice! Westgard thought. I hope the thingies don't have some kind of heat detection gear. He looked at Peter Black, the Airborne battalion boss in the next hole. The professional was watching the National Guard tanks and infantry advance down the hill. Black turned to him and held up a thumb in approval. Bang! Bang! Bang! Bang! Bang! Bang! The guns hammered. The white smoke drifted in 14 dense clouds across the valley. Whump! Whump! Whump! Whump! Whump! Whump!

A new sound as the artillery shifted to alternating salvos of smoke and high explosive. The advancing line came abreast of Black's position as the paratroopers climbed out of their holes. "Let's show these Legs how to do this," a sergeant yelled over the deafening, whining noise of the tanks, artillery, and mortar fire. "Remember Vladimirov!" yelled another paratrooper in the kind of non-sequitur so dear to veteran soldiers' hearts. It was a reference to one of the battalion's most memorable fights in the Third Balkan War. "Let's give these Romanian bastards what they came here for!" cried another. "Airborne! Airborne, all the way!" chanted the paratroopers as they started forward with the advancing Carolinians.

General Westgard found himself exactly between the two battalions going down the hill. He walked around the back of an Abrams to place himself in the midst of a moving Carolina rifle squad. They were in a diamond formation just to the right of the tank. They were big and bulky in Nemourlon body armor. There were four more such squads in the gap between the two tanks. Whump! Whump! Whump! Whump! Whump! Whump!

The high explosive shells crashed into the valley floor. bang! bang! bang! bang! bang! bang! White smoke drifted in protective clouds across the direction of advance of the force. In the squad to his right, Westgard saw a soldier reach into his shirt front to pull out a folded piece of colored cloth. The man hooked the metal grommet at one corner over the point of his bayonet, then fastened another corner of the cloth to the trigger guard of his rifle. He shook out the flag and held it over his head for the men to see. It was three feet square, and red with the blue Saint Andrew's cross and white stars. Embroidered in white across the blue "X" was "26th North Carolina Volunteer Infantry," and below that the word "Gettysburg."

Westgard remembered then. He remembered the simple marker at Gettysburg that showed the limit of advance of the 26th in Pickett's Charge. That day they had followed their leaders and red flags to within ten yards of the flaming Union lines. Today you're going all the way, Bubbas, all the way.

He heard laughter to his left and looked up at the black face and O.D. tanker's helmet of the .50 caliber machine gunner in the rear hatch of the tank. The man's head disappeared for a moment. When he reappeared, he had a brass trumpet in his hands, a band instrument. They were almost to the bottom now. There was still no fire from inside the smoke. Maybe a walkover? Nah! He heard the artillery shift to aiming points farther away. The impact sounds were distant. They had almost reached the smoke. He looked right and left. It was remarkable. The attack rolling downhill looked like one of the illustrations in the manual on how to do this. The three Comanche helicopter gunships rose from behind Hill 765 and the attacking force. From fifty feet above the ridge, they fired their Gatling guns and full loads of H.E. rockets 15 into the smoke ahead. In response, a lightning beam skewered the center Comanche neatly through the middle of the pilot's windscreen. The helicopter rolled over on its side and dropped like a stone to the hilltop where it exploded in a ball of fire.

Westgard could feel the heat from the burning Comanche three hundred feet away. Aw Shit! They can see through the smoke. He jumped a fallen tree trunk, and heard the tank smash the same log as it rolled over the piece of wood, reducing it to splinters in passing. The Abrams crewman began to play the old Hoagie Carmichael tune about Carolina in the morning. This was the tank we were standing behind. He looked up at the black face.

The soldier wasn't playing now. He was staring at something else. It was the red, square flag carried high above the infantryman's head. They had come to the wall of smoke. The lines were moving steadily forward. The tanks howled and whined in their mechanical fury. The gunner started to play again. It was "Dixie." Oh, I wish I was in the land of cotton. Old times there are not forgotten. Look away, look away, look away, Dixieland. There was a sob in the last notes. Maybe old times are forgotten, Westgard thought, or maybe not.

The infantry picked up the pace to a trot. One of them began to scream with a bone chilling, ululating, high-pitched sound. Suddenly the screaming war cry was everywhere, filling the secret places of men's souls. The tanks accelerated to keep pace, and then they all crossed the line into the hidden world inside the smoke. From her position on the ridge, it seemed to Captain Alison Grayson, the fire support coordinator, that they vanished from the sight of mankind, swallowed up by the whiteness. Only occasionally could she catch glimpses of them through thin places in the barrage. In obedience to Westgard's plan, she stopped the artillery fire since she could no longer see to adjust it. It's up to them, now, she thought, just them.

General Westgard later wrote that the first few yards in the smoke were almost disappointing. The ground was grey, soft, and flaky. The men's boots kicked up clouds of what looked like ash. The steel treads of the tanks spun faster as they felt for traction. The Carolinians were still screaming, and the bugler was still playing as they trotted forward. "Slow 16 motion, it was like we were in slow motion," he told people later, "and it stayed that way for a while." I wonder what the Airborne think of all this noise, he thought. They hate to be upstaged. It was right then, when they had penetrated about twenty yards into the smoke that they learned that they would have to fight for every square foot of the valley and that many of them would die that morning, for while they watched, something strange happened, but something in keeping with the morning's events.

Holes abruptly appeared in the ash to their front The holes opened everywhere as far as you could see in the smoke. Suddenly, there were hundreds of the holes. Out of them popped a type of alien no one had seen yet. These were over six feet tall, covered with fur of various colors and perfectly bipedal. They wore black harness hung with what could only be the tools of a warrior's trade. In their hands they carried the "rifle" seen before, but these weapons had a two-foot-long blade on the end that would have been called a bayonet in any army on Earth. Some of the aliens had blades hanging at their sides that were three or four feet long. There were hundreds and hundreds of these creatures within Westgard's field of view.

They came up out of the ground covered with ash, and they charged without a sound straight at the assault line. The shock of their appearance might have been expected to slow or even halt the momentum of Westgard's attack, but it did not. Black's paratroopers were the creme de la creme of the Regular Army. They were men who had no home but the Army and no destiny except their profession. They had come from nowhere, and to nowhere they would return when their service was done. "The scum of the earth, enlisted for drink," Wellington had called similar men. Their collective identity resided in their regiment. To them, the big, furry things with guns were just another in a long succession of opponents who had dared to challenge them. Like the others, these would pay for the privilege. The Carolina infantry and cavalry were lost in a different dream, a dream filled with tribal fury. This enemy was on their soil, and they would kill them all if they could. They would kill them together.

The tanks' coaxial machine guns opened fire cutting down the ranks of the aliens like a scythe cutting wheat. The staccato chatter of these guns rattled on and on. In the turrets, loaders pulled high explosive ammunition from the big guns and replaced it with anti-personnel ammunition. In these shells, each shot would deliver several hundred flexible, finned, steel darts. With the completion of the hurried process of reloading, the 120 mm. smoothbore cannon in the turrets roared, spewing their load of finned death as though they were giant shotguns, cutting swathes of annihilation through the charging enemy.

The aliens never flinched even though they dropped by the dozens, nailed in place by the darts. On they came, the big, furry creatures closing rapidly with Westgard's infantry. They fired their weapons as they came. Each shot from the "rifles" was accompanied by a SNAP! CRAACK! and a bluish streak of light that "connected the dots" between the targeted soldier and the weapon. The Carolinians returned the fire.

The steel jacketed bullets from their assault rifles and squad machine guns dropped aliens by the dozens. The alien charge swept in between the advancing tanks, forcing the cavalry to cease fire to avoid hitting American soldiers. The smoke began to clear, blown away by a light breeze from the southwest. A ray of light pierced the thinning whiteness, illuminating for Westgard a scene that might have appeared on the cover of the most lurid of science fiction novels. John Carter, Warlord of Barsoom, was the first title to flash through Westgard's mind. Or maybe, The Red Princess, he mused, or was it The Red Planet.

Out in front a bigger hole opened in the ground. A muzzle rose to appear in this opening, appearing in much the same way that antique coast defense guns could be seen in films to rise into "battery" on some sort of mechanical lift. A monster FLASH! WHZZ! burned the air as the "gun's" thunderbolt impaled the tank that Westgard had followed into the valley. This lightning was aimed low and missed the turret magazine. Instead, it ignited the tank's fuel with a roar, killing the driver and most of the turret crew. The anti-aircraft gunner scrambled out of his hatch and rolled over the edge of the burning hull, falling eight feet to the ground where he lay with his clothes smoking.

The trumpet was still gripped in one black fist. Lieutenant George Wilson ran to his side and beat on the smouldering clothing. Half a dozen "furries," as they came to be called, smashed their way into the middle of the squad around Westgard, killing two riflemen on their way in. Westgard was astonished to see that one of these men was done to death with a "furry's" bayonet which was wielded in a kind of stylized dance that was familiar but very unlike the technique taught at Fort Benning. He had his old 9 mm. Beretta automatic pistol in his right hand. He had been carrying it and wishing he had a rifle throughout the attack. Now, he shot the nearest alien twice in the head and watched the thing topple over in a kind of slow-motion collapse that didn't seem right for the amount of damage which his bullets should have caused.

Most of the "furries" near him went down in a torrent of bullets but two of them survived long enough to grapple with the Carolinians hand to hand. One of the aliens killed his opponent in a display of the strangely familiar bayonet technique before being dispatched with a 40 mm. rifle grenade fired into his chest by a corporal standing next to Westgard. The grenade traveled just far enough from the muzzle of the corporal's weapon to arm itself at a point about three inches inside the "furry's" chest. There it detonated, throwing black bone, silvery organ tissue, grey cartilaginous material, and orange "blood" in all directions. The second enemy warrior was clubbed in the head by the Carolina squad leader after it shot a rifleman and was attempting to bayonet the man's prostrate body.

Westgard yelled "No!" to keep the downed enemy soldier alive. It was a near thing, but he and George Wilson, managed to keep the enraged National Guardsmen from finishing the thing off.

Twenty minute later, Westgard raised his head to look around. The "furries" had countered-attacked three more times. The smoke was gone. The sun shone down on a landscape from the Inferno. The blue sky and puffy clouds overhead seemed utterly out of place. His troops had killed every alien who had emerged from the holes. Their bodies lay scattered thickly across the ash covered plain. The Task Force advance had finally stopped about halfway across the ash field, brought to a halt by emotional exhaustion and shock at American losses. He could see that his men had killed many, many enemy, but he had lost half his force. The tanks had wrecked the alien lightning machine but had nearly been destroyed themselves in the process. Their carcasses marked the path of the attack across the sooty valley. Some still burned with hatches billowing smoke from internal fires. Some stood silent with their shattered turrets lying upside down beside them, beheaded by magazine explosions.

He realized now that his assault had crossed only part of the valley floor, but there were no live aliens in sight except for his prisoner. This thing thrashed around on the ground trying to break out of its bonds. From the corner of his eye Westgard saw a Carolinian "butt-stroke" the monster in the side of the head with his rifle. It lay quiet. Westgard hoped it was not dead, but decided it was not worth discussing at the moment. Christ, let there not be more of these things! he thought. Please God! Please.

In the stalled assault force men were giving each other first aid, re-loading weapons and staring ahead grimly, waiting for the "furries'" next move. In every combat action there is a point at which the growing negative factors of lost materiel, murdered human potential, and expended will power begin to outweigh the positive factors in the situation. Carl von Clausewitz, the German philosopher of war, called this the "culminating point" of a battle. If the goal of the operation is reached before this point is reached, then victory is won. Somewhere in time and space, the god of soldiers rolled the iron dice of war to know Task Force Westgard's fate.

"Borderguard Six this is Oldnorth Six, over." The sound of the radio "squawk box" startled everyone near Westgard. "This is Borderguard, over," he responded. "Oldnorth Six here," McClung said. "I am maneuverin' to your," then nothing more. Behind Westgard on the ridge, Captain Grayson stared in horror at the carnage below. She could see that Westgard's force had nearly destroyed itself in wrecking the alien attacks. The paratroops had suffered even heavier losses than the Carolina Guardsmen. She thought the worst must be passed, but even as she watched several more large holes opened in the ash out in front of the survivors of Westgard's assault.

From the openings rolled two armored vehicles. They were not tanks. Tanks have treads and these things had four wheels on each side, but they did have a turret from which protruded the snout of the same "lightning" gun that had done so much damage. Grayson was a student of military history, an unusual thing in a woman officer. She recognized the silhouette of the wheeled armored vehicles. Except for the "lightning gun," these weapons were close copies of German armored cars of World War II. Down in the valley, General Westgard saw the armored vehicles rise from the earth and tried to prepare himself for the end. At least, I will die with the men, he thought and then was surprised at himself for thinking that. Around him, he could feel them sucking in breath, reaching inside themselves for whatever might be left. My God, the sun is bright, he thought.

In that shining light, under the blue Carolina sky, a strange machine climbed into the air from a third opening in the ground. A helicopter, not a helicopter! It can't be a helicopter, he thought, but there it was, hovering shakily in the air twenty-five feet above the ash, kicking up a blinding cloud of dust. Its rotors whirred and beat at the air. Beneath its chin hung one of the ubiquitous "lightning guns." It swung slowly on its vertical axis, turning toward a target on the left of Westgard's line. As its profile came into view, he saw that it was a "Cobra", a helicopter gun ship of the Vietnam war era. That can't be, he thought. That can't be. As he looked at it, he began to see that it was not really a "Cobra." It was an entirely new machine, rather crudely built, but resembling a "Cobra" and flown by someone or something that had no real skill in flying such a machine. Through the windscreen, he could see the "furry" pilot.

The "Cobra" fired. There was a massive explosion from the invisible target on the left. Another tank gone, he thought. "How many left, how many?" The nose of the helicopter began to swing back toward him as the two "armored cars" started forward in front of it. "Get ready!" young George Wilson yelled. Our Father who art in heaven, Westgard prayed, hoping that he would be forgiven for all this, for these men's deaths. With a rushing WHSSH! a shoulder-fired Surface to Air Missile rose from the far side of the valley, behind the aliens. The missile struck the helicopter squarely, just behind the crew compartment. The warhead did not arm because the range had been too short, and the body of the missile punched right through the "Cobra" opening a two- foot hole through which Westgard could see the blue sky. The ugly machine nosed down and crashed on top of one of the "armored cars." One of Westgard's remaining Abrams killed the other "furry" armored car with a discarding-sabot depleted uranium slug. The explosions were most satisfying, but Westgard could not see through the wreckage and burning fuel to know what had happened.

From her post up on the hill, Grayson could see what had happened. Lieutenant Colonel McClung had brought his battalion and its attached tanks around from the other clearing using the path opened by the aliens.

The mouth of this path was two hundred yards wide on the far side of the valley. Oldnorth's men and armor stood elbow to elbow in the opening, waiting. "Borderguard Six, this is Amelia Two Niner, over," she said into her radio handset. Westgard's voice came back to her over the speaker. "This is... WHHHSSHH..." White noise filled the speaker. She looked closely at the radio and saw smoke slowly begin to leak from seams and openings in the set. "EMP," she muttered. "The bastards have cooked our radios." Not having the time to contemplate the ability of the aliens to generate a communications-killing ElectroMagnetic Pulse, she instead searched hurriedly through the pockets of her combat jacket, increasingly frustrated at what she did not find. Then she began to rummage through the storage bins in the command vehicle. "What'r you lookin' fur ma'm?" a Carolinian from the crew asked. "A white star cluster, I'm sure I had one here, somewhere." The soldier pulled an aluminum-colored cylinder about eight inches long from a cargo pocket on his trouser leg. "You dropped this when we came over the top," he said, handing it to her.

She turned away to face the valley and pulled the covering metal sleeve off the signaling rocket. She slid the open end of the outer sleeve over the inner cylinder, making the explosive cap on the inner cylinder's end available to the firing pin inside the sleeve. She pointed the business end of the little pyrotechnic up and over the fighting below and slapped the end of the sleeve with the palm of her free hand. It fired with a bang as the payload flew out the end of the tube and soared up and over the valley trailing a plume of grey smoke behind it. At its apogee, over the burning "furry" equipment, it burst into a bright cluster of white stars. In the Task Force Standing Signal Instructions, a white star cluster pyrotechnic meant only one thing. It was "Continue the Attack." Westgard saw the stars and looked about him. The tank gunner sat on the ground nearby, his dented trumpet beside him on the white ash. "Soldier, do you know the Charge?" he asked. The man looked up, nodded, and struggled to his feet with Wilson's help. "Blow it now," Westgard said. "Sound the Charge!"

The first notes of the old bugle call were shrill and hesitant, but the soldier drew strength from his own music, and the summons of the trumpet for the last, irreversible, hopeless call to arms rang ardent and true across the valley. The ruined battalions watched Westgard, his aide de camp, and Gaston Rutledge, the radio man, trudge forward toward certain death and they followed. From the multitude of holes more "furries" poured forth, this time followed by a group of the smaller creatures that had been the first seen, as well as the huge aliens who had moved the "guns" around. From the far side of the valley, beyond the fire and smoke, cheering was heard, then the roar and chatter of the guns. The sounds grew and grew in volume. Westgard stopped to listen, and his men stopped with him. The aliens stopped too. They seemed uncertain, unsure of what to do next. They looked at each other, and then most of them broke, running in panic for the sides of the valley. Westgard's men began to cheer, and peering through the smoke he saw the advancing tanks and infantry.

Now he understood. Thank God for the militia, he thought. A Regular would never have moved from where I put him. A white flag appeared at the entrance to one of the bigger holes as the jaws of the attack closed on the center of the valley. A slender figure in an olive drab flight suit waved the flag. It was the A-10 pilot. Behind her emerged a bedraggled group of yet another type of alien being. "Don't shoot anymore! Cease fire! These were prisoners! Don't shoot.!" she screamed. "Cease fire!" Westgard ordered almost unnecessarily. His men were finished. Shooting was not in their minds anymore, and McClung's people were afraid of hitting Westgard's force, so it ended quickly, there in the middle of the valley of death.

The remaining alien soldiers, seeing that the pilot's group were not killed, lay down their arms and stood with their hands in the air. The pilot led her crowd of aliens to him. There were about twenty. They were man sized and looked human, remarkably human until you remembered that humans did not have blond fur covering their faces. "They're all dead, the leaders," the pilot told him. "They killed themselves when they knew you were going to win. These people were brought here from far away to work for them, they."

He was not listening anymore. Exhaustion had set in. He held up a hand to stop her. "Later, Captain, glad to see you made it. George, get the medivac working to get our wounded out of here. Get a count. Find McClung, I want to thank him." The armored command track roared down the hill and out into the center of the clearing. It stopped suddenly, rocking for a few seconds on its suspension. Alison Grayson jumped down from a side hatch and brought him a radio handset on a long lead. "Dragon Six," she said looking around at the destruction in awe. "What's your status, Borderguard?" Marci asked. He explained what had happened. "Estimate of losses?" she asked. "I'm getting a count now, but I would guess that Gliderman, Burgwyn and Saber all lost over fifty per cent on my axis. Oldnorth's losses are much less."

There was a pause while she absorbed that. "And the aliens?" she asked. "Over a thousand killed. We will have to count them." "No," she said. "I am relieved as corps commander, at least for the moment. You are directed to withdraw from the objective area ASAP on receipt of this order. You will then hand over command to Gliderman Six and report here to accompany me to Washington for debriefing, over."

"Gliderman Six is dead, he was killed in the first counterattack." "I am sorry, Phillip," she said. "I know you were close friends." "Borderguard Six, this is the Chairman," interrupted a voice. "Yes, sir." "Were they really hostile?" God Damn you! "Without a doubt, over." "Bring your prisoners to Washington, as well as a few of your officers, over." "Yes, sir." "Borderguard?" "Sir?" "The Russians now tell us they lost twenty thousand men in the Urals yesterday." "Sir." "Good work, Borderguard. Out."

Three weeks later, a meeting of the powerful took place in Washington. In the group were the President of the United States, her Vice President, the Secretary of Defense, The Joint Chiefs of Staff, the Director of Central Intelligence, and the leaders of the Congress. They met to consider the reports rendered by the survivors of Task Force Westgard, the news from other areas of confrontation with the Furries, and the information that had been obtained from Furry prisoners of war as well as the aliens who had been freed by T.F. Westgard.

At the beginning of the meeting, the Secretary of Defense announced Westgard's promotion to Major General and the award of a Presidential Unit Citation for Valor to Task Force Westgard. He also mentioned almost casually that General Grayson would be staying on at 18th Airborne Corps for a while. There were grim looks among the Joint Chiefs. The truth was that she had grown weary of their indecision and had allowed Westgard to attack on her own authority.

The head of the CIA was asked to summarize the data for the group. "According to the First Ones, as the freed aliens wish to be known, the Furries are descended from them, are actually the descendants of colonists sent to other star systems distant from the home world of the First Ones. They returned to First One Prime, the home world, two centuries ago, not as returning kinsmen, but rather as conquerors, adherents of a new religion which tells them that they must rule the worlds, all the worlds. The base Furry type is the five foot ones. The dogs are an indigenous Home World Prime animal, but the huge browns and the warriors are genetically engineered variants of the basic Furry stock."

"Where is this home world you speak of?" the president asked. "Arcturus, the planet circles Arcturus Three, Madame President." The CIA chief answered.

"You can see it here on the star chart." He pointed to the incomprehensible map of the heavens mounted on a tripod at his side. "There is an M-Class star here that was unknown until now. It is called Arcturus Three."

"How far is this from here?" the president asked. He told her. It was beyond belief that alien beings had crossed this distance to interfere with the ordered lives so favored by most of the people in the room, but there was the undeniable fact of the presence of two of the First Ones at the meeting. They sat across from the government officials next to Westgard, McClung, General Grayson, and her niece Alison. "And why is it that you speak English, and various other languages?" the president asked the older of the two aliens.

This being, who had announced at her first "debriefing" immediately after the battle that she wanted to be known as Eleanor Roosevelt replied in the mellifluous accent characteristic of her people's speech that all aboard the earthbound spacecraft had watched and listened to recordings of decades of broadcast human television and radio programming during the journey to Earth.

"And you are the leader?" the president asked. The two aliens conferred and then answered in the negative. They said that she was a respected elder. They had no real leaders. "And who are you?" The president asked the second alien, a male of great dignity. "I am the science officer, Captain." the alien replied holding up one hand with the fingers splayed. This was hard to do since the number of fingers did not exactly match those of Terran anatomy.

The president had to think for a minute, but she found the reference in a dimly lit corner of her memory. "Ah, yes. Are you really the 'science officer?'" "He is our most prominent savant," Eleanor replied gravely. "He would make an admirable colleague for Doctor Teller. Perhaps, we could." "Is this why the Furries had tanks and a helicopter?" the president asked, returning to her earlier line of thought. "You saw them on television?" The answer was yes.

They had built them for the Furries in imitation of machines they had seen on television. In the same way, they had adopted human methods of fighting. These were all things from television and films, which the "Furries" admired intensely. "So, they learned violence from us?" the Chief of Naval Operations asked. In a way, that was true "Eleanor" replied. The Furries usually exterminated all sentient life on a world before colonizing it. They did this instinctively and with weapons that simply destroyed everything they did not want, but they had been so taken with the unusual forms of warfare that they saw on human television that their High Council had decided to preserve the population of earth as a recreational resource. Earth had been made a place of exercise and leadership development for the Furry ruling class. They were not original thinkers, but the idea had come to them from watching a film called "The Predator" in which an alien hunter came to Earth to do similar things.

"What does that mean?" asked the Air Force Chief of Staff. "It means," said Westgard that we are a "training aid" for them. They will sharpen their skills here, and then use them on other planets, but they won't finish us off, because they want us around to play with." "But their leaders all died in your battle!" the Army Chief of Staff objected. "They killed themselves."

"That is so," Eleanor Roosevelt answered. "Failure is not tolerated. They would have been disgraced, and shamed..."

"How long will they stay?" the president asked. "Until they are bored with you, or until you no longer are a challenge. Then they will kill you all, as they killed our people, their ancestors."

"All, they killed all of you?" the Chairman demanded. "All, but the few they needed as workers and, teachers. They are not good at what you call science."

"How good is their genetic engineering?" the scientist Chairman of the Joint Chiefs asked. "Not good, which is why they have us. We designed the warriors. We built the toy machines for their game with you."

"Game?" the president asked horrified. "Yes," Eleanor Roosevelt said." "There will be many games now. You should prepare. You must play well. It is a form of social security. You have nothing to fear but fear itself." "Yes," intoned Doctor Spock, holding up his strange hand again. "Live long and prosper!"

The End of the Beginning.

Printed in the United States
by Baker & Taylor Publisher Services